Financial Futures and Investment Strategy

**Arthur L. Rebell
and Gail Gordon**
with Kenneth B. Platnick

DOW JONES-IRWIN   Homewood, Illinois   60430

ISBN 0-87094-491-6
Library of Congress Catalog Card No. 83-73719

Printed in the United States of America

1 2 3 4 5 6 7 8 9 0 B 1 0 9 8 7 6 5 4

DEDICATION

To my father Harry and the memory of my mother Sylvia:

She enriches our lives
and
Left beautiful memories.

Arthur L. Rebell

PREFACE

Professional money managers are just becoming aware of how large a role risk-management tools can play in their businesses. It is for these professionals—as well as the lawyers, accountants, and regulators who work with them—that this book was written. We have not attempted to present an exhaustive theoretical treatment of interest rates or futures markets. Rather, based on our own experiences, we have set out to guide the professional through setting up and evaluating hedge strategies using financial futures in their own spheres of activity—banking, insurance, pension funds, corporate treasuries, investment management, etc.

Hedging with financial futures is an art as well as a science. Such futures are not an answer to all investment management problems, but they do provide the money manager with new means to act upon market decisions. An understanding of the futures contracts and how the futures markets operate is critical to designing a successful hedge strategy. As with any innovative technique, potential hedgers need to take the time to study the markets and determine the risk/reward potential for each application.

The transition from viewing futures as pure speculation to recognizing them as a necessary tool is gaining momentum. We continue to be impressed by the advantages accruing to companies adapting to these new markets and using them to gain a competitive edge in money management and financial-product design.

With a subject such as futures, it is easy to be either too technical or too superficial. For someone beginning to look at futures markets, a general reading will be useful in determining where futures can be of benefit. A more complete understanding of hedging applications can be accomplished only by a full analysis of each contract and its effects on meeting hedge goals.

This book provides the professional money manager with a format for analyzing contract markets and hedge strategies. It is divided into three parts, which discuss the basics of the futures markets, individual contracts, and particular hedging strategies.

Part I deals generally with the world of financial futures, from the evolution of the market to the fundamentals of trading and begins to develop a basic format for setting up a hedge.

Part II examines each of the various contracts: Treasury bonds, Treasury notes, Ginnie Maes, Treasury bills, CDs, Eurodollars, stock indexes, and options. The financial futures market is growing and changing; and new contracts will undoubtedly be brought out from time to time. The basic material covered here will, however, be as pertinent to the use of these new contracts as it is for contracts currently traded.

Part III focuses on hedge strategy design for specific types of problems faced by financial intermediaries and managers. These applications are not all-inclusive; they are meant to suggest, instead, ways of making financial futures work for the individual money manager. The strategies presented are based on actual situations and are included to illustrate specific points and problems of concern to hedgers.

ACKNOWLEDGMENTS

We would like to express our appreciation to the many people with whom we worked to develop our approach to these markets and ultimately this book:

Joel E. Miller, David C. Fischer, and their colleagues at Arthur Andersen & Co., with whom we have worked closely, devoted much time and effort to the sections on accounting and taxation. Stephen Selig of Baer Marks & Upham has been a constant source of information and advice, and graciously contributed his legal expertise on regulatory matters. Our thanks also to Jane D'Amico for her research and editorial assistance.

We are also in debt to our colleagues at Wertheim for providing the environment and time for us to write this book. We especially appreciate the effort made by the Financial Instruments Department, particularly Alexandra Engel for her invaluable assistance and the many hours spent working on the text to ensure a high standard of accuracy, Sharon Stucker who helped coordinate this project, Stanley Rowen who developed the computer programs, and Susan DeRosa.

We each want to thank our friends and family members for their constant encouragement, support, and patience over the course of this project—especially Rita and Hy Gordon and Adele Rebell.

CONTENTS

PART ONE

Basics of financial instruments

1

Introduction

Commodity futures have been used to protect against price risk for many years. In industries such as agricultural production and processing, they permit economic business decisions to be protected from unpredictable factors which can radically affect pricing and upset economic planning. Money is the most widely used commodity—with its price defined as an interest rate.

Until recently, sharp price fluctuations over short periods of time had not been a consistent problem in the financial markets. However, increasing volatility of interest rates has created uncertainty about the cost of money, an uncertainty similar to that traditionally associated with other commodities. The heightened volatility of both long-term and short-term interest rates relative to the stock market are shown in Charts 1 and 2. Professional money managers must now face this uncertainty. Thus, the financial professional is left in a position resembling that of traditional users of a physical commodity. As a response to this changing economic environment, a futures market based on financial assets is a natural development.

The need to manage interest-rate exposure had been recognized prior to the 1970s by mortgage originators. These financial intermediaries commit themselves to providing fixed-rate mortgages for construction projects, although actual mortgages are not issued until

CHART 1-1   S&P 500 and Moody's AAA bond yield

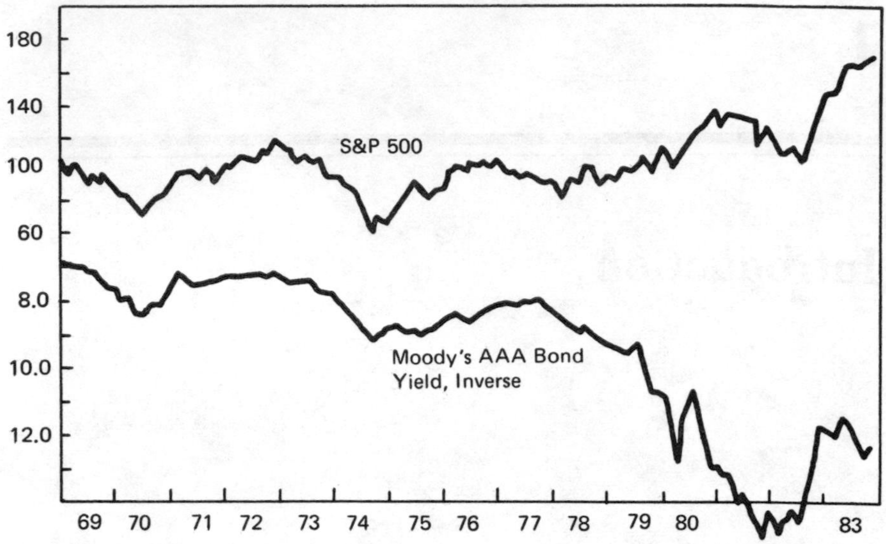

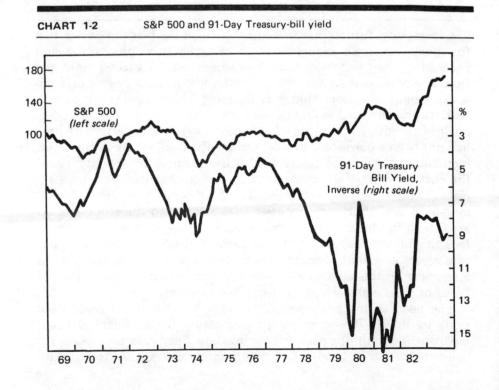

CHART 1-2   S&P 500 and 91-Day Treasury-bill yield

the project is completed. Originators whose business is packaging mortgages cannot prudently risk interest-rate changes between the time their commitment is made and the actual mortgage issuance. Therefore, they presell mortgages to investors at a price reflecting commitments at the current market rate, but for payment when the mortgage is delivered.

These **forward contracts** are agreements between two specific parties for delivery of a mortgage investment at a specified yield. The forward market helps originators transfer their interest-rate risk. Some problems exist with this arrangement; among them a lack of general credit guarantees and lack of contract-term standardization, leading to restricted liquidity and limited ability to revise commitments.

However, the growing economic rationale for a financially based commodity contract interested the Chicago Board of Trade (CBT), one of the largest organized commodity exchanges. The board recognized that members of the financial community had often been exposed only to the speculative aspects of commodity trading without focusing on the economic benefits of hedging to offset existing risk. Therefore, the board turned its attention towards those who had been active in mortgage forward contracts. In 1975, it introduced the first financial commodity contract. The contract was based on government-backed mortgage pools—"Ginnie Maes" or GNMAs.

The CBT sought to improve upon the forward contract in several ways:

Standardization and centralization. By bringing market participants together in one place and establishing contract terms for size, quality, and delivery, prices could be set competitively and trading efficiency enhanced. Participants could also easily offset contracts, buying one and selling another to eliminate a position.

Market oversight. Standards and safeguards were established and rules defined—resulting in an orderly market where disputes could be settled by agreement.

Creditworthiness. By standing as the intermediary on every trade, the exchange sought to expedite trading and minimize the default risk faced by any individual participant.

FUTURES AS MORE THAN A
DELIVERY MECHANISM

Because commodity values can fluctuate widely and often unpredictably, commodity users and producers rely on the futures market to protect their costs or returns. In effect, a futures transaction is a purchase or sale of the commodity for delivery at some later date. Thus, futures provide the ability to take advantage of changing values without owning the underlying commodity.

As an example, Eastman Kodak might want to maintain its prices for silver-based photographic products for six months, but may be concerned that silver prices could rise, increasing the firm's production cost. To hedge against the potential cost increase, Eastman Kodak can buy silver contracts. If silver prices increased by $5 per ounce, the silver future will appreciate by a like amount. Kodak can sell (offset) its contract position and use the gain to counter the higher cost of silver. Likewise, should prices decline, the loss the firm would incur in selling its commodity contract would be recovered by a lower cost of physical acquisition. Regardless of the change in silver prices, the company's cost for silver will approximate the cost of silver at the time the transaction was initiated. While Kodak could take delivery of silver from its contract, it wouldn't have to.

Thus, because hedgers, dealing in futures to minimize risk, can control their costs by buying and selling futures, there is a minimum need for using the contract to take delivery; the major use of futures is to offset volatility.

Trading in futures for this purpose offers several benefits:

Homogeneity and liquidity. The standardization of contracts creates interchangeable instruments. This brings about a level of participation that gives the markets their liquidity; trading can be undertaken with ease and with little impact on the market as a whole.

Low cost. Futures are a low-cost alternative. Trading in this market is often less complicated than trading in the market for the underlying commodity because there is no physical transfer of assets.

Investor anonymity. The position of an investor trading in the futures market is not obvious to other traders; nor need his purposes be known. Thus, trading in this market can be done with a degree of anonymity not possible in the cash market.

MONEY AS A "COMMODITY"

Many investors have begun to consider hedging with financial futures as a means of offsetting some of the risk inherent in money management. Once money is thought of as a commodity, hedging its price is much easier to conceptualize. However, given the traditional view of commodity markets as speculative—a view held by many professional money managers, as well as those accountants, attorneys, and regulators who participate in the financial decision-making process—some definition of hedging versus speculation is warranted. The breakdown between hedgers looking to offset risk, and speculators looking to assume risk, is not unique to futures.

Hedging versus speculating: Defining risk

In the spring of 1983, the National Hockey League play-offs were in progress. The New York Islanders had taken the lead in the best-of-seven series, three games to two. In the event that the Rangers won the sixth game, as an Islanders season ticket holder, Mike August could buy two tickets for game seven—the final and deciding game.

Then Al Strand made August an offer. He would pay $200 apiece for the two tickets if the seventh game were played. Strand refused August's counter offer to sell the tickets for a total of $200 before game six was played.

That put August on the spot. Depending on the outcome of the sixth game, his tickets were worth either nothing or $400. He bore all the risk of game seven not being played. His risk was not unlike the kind of hedging problem that investors face: how to transfer risk and protect one's investment.

August had an alternative: find a third party willing to take on a risk of the same magnitude. This could be done by finding someone willing to risk $200 that the Rangers would win game six. For all intents and purposes, this would have been the same as selling the game seven tickets for $200—an attractive, unconditional price to August.

| | Ticket value if Rangers | |
	Win	Lose
Ticket holder (August):		
Does nothing (alternative I)	$400	$0
Hedges (alternative II)	$200	$200

By transferring risk to a willing third party, August can assure himself of $200. If the Rangers win game six, he loses $200, but he sells his game seven tickets for $400. If the Rangers lose and game seven is not played, his tickets are worthless, but he makes $200 on the outcome of game six.

August can thus transform a high-risk situation into a virtually risk-free situation. He can **hedge** not speculate.

There is a **speculator** in this scenario, but it is not Mike August. It is the person who takes the other side of the hedger's "position," deciding that the chance of a Ranger win in game six was worth the risk. And, obviously, the role of the speculator is an important one, inasmuch as his or her willingness to accept risk makes hedging possible. In futures, as here, speculators (risk takers) and hedgers (risk reducers) are often on different sides of the same transaction. Both make use of the same vehicle to achieve very different goals. The speculator's willingness to assume risk is often the most economically efficient way for risk to be borne. Futures then serve the purpose of transferring risk.

There is an important distinction here—one that is often not made, perhaps because it is not well understood. *The simplest way to determine whether an activity is speculative or not, is to determine whether it increases or reduces existing risk.*

Obviously, though, August had another "alternative"—doing nothing. Hoping the market will go one's way in high-risk environments is a form of speculation—inertia speculation—and it is marked by a lack of action in managing risk. Recognizing inertia speculation for what it is makes the emphasis on risk-management tools easier to understand and accept. The ability to reduce risk through the use of futures and options on futures is the focal point of this book.

2

Financial futures

Since the introduction of the GNMA contract in 1975, there has been substantial growth in financial futures,[1] both in terms of new products and of trading volume. Shortly after the GNMA financial contract began trading, markets were developed in Treasury bills by the International Monetary Market (IMM) division of the Chicago Mercantile Exchange and in Treasury bonds by the Chicago Board of Trade (CBT). These contracts grew to be highly successful products for their respective exchanges, drawing participants from the short-term money markets as well as from the longer-term bond market.

By 1978, a variety of other contracts were proposed; and for those who were still unsure of what all this activity signaled, when the New York Stock Exchange announced in 1979 that it proposed to deal in financial futures, the financial community clearly perceived that there was a place for these instruments.

EXISTING MAJOR CONTRACTS

After a flurry of proposals and attempts to develop other contracts, six contracts have come to constitute the debt-instrument segment of

---

[1] For the purpose of this book, "financial futures" refers to interest-rate futures and stock-index futures. Currency futures are not included in our analysis.

the market. They are, in order of greatest activity: long-term Treasury bonds (CBT), 90-day Treasury bills (IMM), GNMA-CDRs (CBT), Eurodollar time deposits (IMM), domestic certificates of deposit (CDs) (IMM), and 10-year Treasury notes (CBT). (The designations *CBT* and *IMM* refer to the Chicago Board of Trade and International Monetary Market, respectively.)

Another trading advance was marked when stock-index contracts were approved for trading in 1982. The Index and Options Market (IOM) of the Chicago Mercantile Exchange, the New York Futures Exchange (NYFE, an offspring of the New York Stock Exchange), and the Kansas City Board of Trade (KCBT) each brought out a contract of this type—based on the S&P 500, the NYSE index, and the Value Line index, respectively.

These products were the first contracts directly based on indexes as opposed to a specific group of cash commodities. Like other commodity futures, they are vehicles reflecting the volatility of the underlying index—but without the complications of delivery. They were designed as cash settlement contracts, with no physical asset changing hands.[2]

The most recent innovation in the futures area is the futures option. Like a stock option, it involves the right to purchase a futures contract at a specified price within a designated time. Unlike a futures position proper, the option buyer has limited downside risk, but pays a premium for upside potential. However, the option seller who receives a premium risks an adverse market move and can only benefit to the extent of the premium received. Delivery is satisfied by assignment of a futures contract position, rather than by the underlying cash instrument. Potential applications of these options on futures are already being recognized.

Successful contracts are those that both meet a basic economic need in the marketplace and provide liquidity. Established liquidity has proved to be a major factor. Improved contract design, as exemplified by the NYFE's unsuccessful Treasury-bond contract, or a more specific contract designed to meet a perceived need, such as the CBT's unsuccessful commercial paper contract, cannot overcome the advantage of dealing in a more liquid contract market.

DEFINITION OF FUTURES

A futures contract is an obligation to make or take delivery of a set amount of the underlying commodity, whether that commodity is a Treasury bond, silver bar, or bushel of corn. Contract positions

---

[2] The Eurodollar contract was the first to use cash settlement. Delivery of a physical asset for this contract or for stock contracts would be cumbersome.

must be closed out either by an offsetting transaction or by delivery, although, in fact, a very small percentage of contracts are actually closed out by delivery. Delivery is at an established point and time. Because a contract position, if not offset, can result in a long (purchase) or short (sale) position in an actual commodity, the contract price reflects any price changes in the spot market.[3] Generally, by being long or short a futures contract, a trader stands to gain or lose to the extent that the market price of the underlying commodity changes from the price level at which the contract position was established.

TRADING AND MARGIN

An important aspect of the futures markets is the daily cash settlement procedure which is integral in maintaining the trading system. Each transaction calls for a good-faith deposit known as **initial margin**, to be posted with a broker. The minimum amount of initial margin required is set by the exchange based on the price volatility of the underlying commodity. The value of a contract position is assessed, **marked to market**, daily, and these changes are settled in cash on a daily basis. For example, if contract prices increase, the longs—who have purchased the contract—would receive cash equal to the value of gains, while the shorts—who have sold contracts—would have to pay in funds equal to the value of losses. This procedure, known as *variation margin*, keeps the value of each market participant's position current and contributes to the credit of the futures market. Initial margin ensures that participants will pay variation-margin deficits. How the system works is illustrated in the following table.

Trading and margin system

	Participant	
A	B	C
Buys contract at 70	Sells contract at 70	
Market moves up to 71, value of move $1,000		
Receives $1,000	Pays $1,000	
	Buys contract at 71	Sells contract at 71
Market moves up to 72, value of move $1,000		
Receives $1,000		Pays $1,000

---

[3] The market for the actual commodity on which a futures contract is based is called the commodity's "spot" or "cash" market. This is a source of some confusion when applied to financial instruments where the term "cash" also denotes short-term investments, such as Treasury bills. For the purpose of this book, the phrase "cash market" applies to the market for the commodity on which a future contract is written.

Because each contract is standard, and each position's value is adjusted to its market value each day, contracts are easily traded between any long and any short, regardless of their original price. As shown in the table, the positions of A and C can offset each other regardless of the price at entry because the contracts now have comparable value. This contributes to the highly liquid nature of the market.

The economic purpose of the futures market is to provide a tool for hedgers to transfer price risk. Ease of trading and a high degree of leverage lend speculative appeal to the markets, allowing for the transfer of risk from hedgers to speculators. Because of the method of trading and the ability of speculators to easily enter financial markets, volume in a contract will often be greater than the volume of trading among investors in the underlying instrument.

The **liquidity** of the financial futures markets can influence the pricing and efficiency of related cash markets. Corporate bond traders might use Treasury-bond futures to protect their bond position, avoiding some of the downside pressure a large sell program would put on the price of an individual bond. Futures prices are consistently available on all stock quote machines. Financial futures markets therefore have become closely watched indicators of general activity in both the debt and equity markets.

3

The auction market

Traders and investors, accustomed to the conventions of the more traditional financial markets, are often surprised by the style of financial futures trading. The basic method of trading financial contracts was established in the late 1800s for commodity trading. The financial futures market is an **auction market**; each futures contract is traded in a set location of its exchange called a pit. This octagonal structure, anywhere from 30 to 60 feet in diameter, is populated by as many as several hundred exchange members with an interest in trading the contract involved. Contracts are traded by "open outcry" and every bid and offer for a contract passes through the traders in the pit. The atmosphere appears chaotic, but the result is a highly organized and efficient market.

No one is obligated to make an orderly market as they are in the specialist system for stock trading. The concept is that with enough people and orders, the market itself will be the specialist, obviating the need for those exclusively handling certain instruments. There is no priority given to any order in the pit; a bid for one contract will be filled at the market price along with a large commercial order. There is no secondary market for futures; thus, no one trader can accumulate a position for resale at a dealer's markup away from the trading floor. Overall, an equality exists in the futures market that generally is not present in other markets.

TRADING IN FUTURES

Futures are traded by open outcry in an auction-style market. Traders constantly announce their bids and offers for contracts. In the heavily traded markets for bonds or stock-index contracts, traders can't necessarily be heard. Thus, hand signals become a very important trading language. A buyer would motion with his palms towards him, while a seller pushes his palms away from him. Fingers held vertically indicate the price, while quantity is signaled with the fingers held horizontal. Each pit, or contract market, has its own variations on these hand signals.

Only exchange members are permitted to trade on the floor. The vast majority of traders are known as **locals** who trade for their own account. **Pit brokers** (floor brokers) are also present to execute customer orders which come in through **futures commission merchants** (FCMs).[1] There is no direct way of identifying someone who is doing customer orders and someone who is trading only for his own account.

Locals are individuals who buy or lease their own exchange seats. Though trading solely for their own accounts, they are backed by member firms to clear transactions with the exchange. Through their trading activities, locals act as market makers and expect that over time they can profit on the bid offer spread, as would a cash-market dealer. The seat privileges of the local will determine in which pits on the floor of the exchange he may trade. For example, membership might entitle a local to trade any of the financial-instrument contracts on the floor of the CBT. Depending on the day's activity, the local might be found trading bonds or GNMAs.

Local trading tends to be technically oriented, concentrating on historic price patterns to project current price activity and charting daily activity to gauge the momentum of the market over short periods of time. Locals are physically located in the middle of a pit and take advantage of this proximity to trade over the course of a day in line with the order flow that comes into the pit from the **commission houses,** those member firms that handle orders from outside customers.

For example, suppose the Federal Reserve begins to buy bills for the system and cash-market bond traders take this action as a positive indicator. Suddenly, there may be a flood of orders coming in to

---

[1] An FCM is any organization or individual engaged in soliciting or accepting orders for commodity futures; the FCM may be an exchange member present on the trading floor or may conduct trading and clearing through a member firm.

buy futures. The locals watch the order flow. They may initially sell into the flood of orders, but if the orders continue, they will then turn and buy to at least offset the earlier sales. The only fundamentals they have is the order flow.

Locals, with the advantage of a low cost of doing business, may try to trade within a narrow price range, scalping the market for small profits and avoiding major losses. Locals may also trade over a day's session, looking for "resting" (unfilled) customer orders to buy or sell relatively large numbers of contracts, thus planning their trading strategy. They might choose to join commission houses on the bid or offered side of a market, but maintain the flexibility and discipline to reverse themselves quickly. These **day traders** seek out the most active pit and focus on events which may change market price levels in a given day. Some highly capitalized locals may also act as **position traders**, holding contract positions to take advantage of price movement due to longer-term directional changes in the market.

Individually, no one local controls a market. As a group, they represent a large amount of capital and can move markets within small price ranges. For example, locals in the bond pit may buy contracts, knowing that a customer order to buy 200 contracts at a level slightly below the market is being held by a pit broker. They will go long and make their market somewhat above the buy order's price level, in effect "leaning" on the existing order. The market might then drift up to the level of sell orders. The locals will watch closely to see whether the buy order below the market remains as support as the market begins to decline, while deciding whether they should sell out their previously acquired long positions. This might happen over an 8/32nd price range. Essentially, the local traders are moving the futures market in line with the price spread in the Treasury-bond market, maintaining an orderly market flow in response to the price movement in the contract's underlying asset.

ORDER EXECUTION

The population in a pit is dominated by locals, but the order flow is determined by the outside orders that come in from the commission houses. These orders are sent to the trading floor and transmitted to a **pit broker** for execution. Pit brokers are generally independent and not employed by a member firm. The broker will work the order in the pit and once it is filled at the market price or a particular level, will write down the name of the other party to the trade and the firm through which the other party clears (completes its transactions). The pit broker endorses the trade, which is then returned to the firm giving the order. The order fill is then reported back to the customer. Meanwhile, a copy of the trade is transmitted to an exchange official on the floor to be listed on the floor's electronic board and entered on the "time and sales" record.

The big risk for a pit broker is **out trades**. If an order to buy at 70-12/32 was filled, the broker wrote down who made the purchase and endorsed the order. The broker on the other side, in this case the seller, should have done the same thing. An out trade exists if the buy does not match the sale. However, the broker owes the commission house and the commission house owes its customer a fill on the order as reported. The pit broker must fill the order at the current price and bear the risk of any interim price change.

The auction nature of the futures market makes it very different from the over-the-counter-style dealer market. In futures, reports on market conditions might be given to customers, reflecting market level and size. A bid or offer is only good for the instant it was given, and the market marker is not obligated to do business for more than one contract. In futures markets, knowledge is available to all and changes are instantaneous. In this type of trading market everyone has access to the bid or offer price. This is where a commission-house broker's judgement can be very useful in determining how to place an order. The broker needs to gauge whether locals are positioned as longs or shorts and whether they will attempt to hit bids instead of taking offers. To some degree, a commission-house broker's success is a function of his market information and the speed with which he can enter or change an order. Information is relayed either by runners or by hand signals. Thus, a broker's position relative to the pit can be important.

Another important aspect of commodity markets is that there is no such thing as the "market subject" that exists in the cash market when trading is suspended to allow certain new facts to be disseminated. During trading hours, the market will not stop if new information, such as Federal Reserve activity, becomes available. If you placed an order to buy at a level below the current market and adverse news comes out, that order might be filled before you have an opportunity to change it.

When news is released that can fundamentally affect cash-market values, conditions in the futures pit can become chaotic. An exchange official will declare a fast market, and the word "fast" will appear on the pricing tape. The brokers obligation under such conditions is to fill market orders as well as possible.

THE CLEARING FUNCTION OF THE EXCHANGES

The settlement of all transactions made on the floor of an exchange is done through the exchange's clearing division. Moreover, through this separate legal entity, the exchange's guarantee of all contracts is generated. The clearing organization guards the financial integrity of the market by standing as the opposite side of every trade, becoming the seller for every buyer and the buyer for each seller, and ensuring that gains due to price changes will be realized.

When a trade is made, two exchange members are involved at the outset. The clearing house takes the side opposite each member. From the investor's point of view, this is highly advantageous, as the credit backing a contract is that of the clearing corporation and not that of another investor. In fact, no buyer or seller of futures has ever suffered a loss by virtue of default on a transaction cleared through any of the exchange's clearing divisions.

When this system is tied in with the variation-margin vehicle through which daily marks to market occur, an individual gains the ability to offset a position at any time without regard to who was initially on the other side of the transaction. This is a key to ease of trading and confidence in the futures markets.

The establishment of a clearing function evolved out of the goals that the exchanges had set for themselves. A contract was still only as good as the other party to the trade unless delivery or offset could be assured. By establishing clearing corporations (the Chicago Board of Trade's was formed in 1925—more than 75 years into the board's existence), delivery was guaranteed by exchanges. This made contracts more liquid and marketable than before. The clearing function of the exchanges has since allowed these markets to successfully meet their goals of providing an organized, equitable, and efficient means of trading futures.

4

Trading in futures markets

As futures become an increasingly important adjunct to financial market activity, professional money managers and traders are entering these markets as accounts of a futures commission merchant (FCM) or by becoming a presence directly on the exchange floor. Local trading helps create the market environment for handling the pit brokers' order flow. The customer orders handled by these brokers can be broken down into various categories, with each group trading for different reasons.

Speculators operate in the futures market for two primary reasons—volatility-related profit potential and the relatively small initial margin needed to control a contract position (i.e., leverage). The same volatility that exists in the cash market will move the futures market. The volatility that creates the need for a hedge vehicle also attracts speculative activity. For the speculator, an opportunity exists when there is the potential for consequential price moves over short periods of time. For a professional trader, the futures market tends to be a cheaper, more efficient way of trading than is the cash market. The leverage and inherent credit guarantee of a futures contract allows a degree of speculative trading on the part of individuals that is not available in the cash market. Structurally, it is easier for individuals to take short positions in futures because no securities need be borrowed, financing is not required and, as is not true in trading stocks, no uptick rule exists. Speculative activity is useful to the market's viability, because it helps to provide the liquidity needed to make the market work efficiently.

Hedgers represent the conservative side of the market. Unlike speculators, they are seeking to reduce risk. Managers of large portfolios who want to reduce some portion of the price risk inherent in their investments—whether money-market instruments, stocks, or bonds—can do so in the futures market. Professional traders and financial intermediaries can use these markets to offset the risk faced in their normal course of business. The hedger's goals can often be attained regardless of market direction, whereas the speculator always seeks to benefit from anticipating market direction.

Arbitrageurs are professional traders who seek to profit from price dislocations within the market or between futures and markets in the underlying commodity. This activity maintains the price relationship between a contract and its cash-market instrument over time. Profitable arbitrage activity depends on the ability to get the lowest available cost of funds, the fastest execution, and the best transaction price on cash instruments. Arbitrageurs constantly monitor the relationship between the contract price and cash-market value to trade their positions prior to contract delivery. Several large dealers, therefore, dominate this area of activity.

Arbitrage techniques are discussed in greater detail in Part II. The important point here is that such activity provides liquidity and tends to discipline the market to economic price levels. This makes the market more efficient—to the advantage of the hedger.

Commercials are a group of market professionals who take advantage of the ease of transacting business in futures. They include bond desks, government bond dealers, and stock trading operations trading for their own accounts and using the futures market to protect their inventory position as well as a means for acting on market projections. The futures market is a tool that allows commercials to put on and take off (acquire and divest) positions as needed, without disturbing the underlying markets and without substantial cost or complication.

TYPES OF ORDERS

There are various order specifications that give the floor broker different degrees of latitude in filling a given order. The simplest and easiest to fill is the *market order*. This specifies that some number of contracts should be bought or sold at the best price currently available. A floor broker will complete the order upon receipt. Because no single transaction can be identified as the first or last trade, of the day, contracts open and close within a range and a broker's obligation is to fill *market on the open or close* orders within this price range. A *market not held* order gives the broker some discretion to work the order around the current level.

Other types of orders place a variety of restrictions or qualifications on a trade. *Limit* orders specify price constraints. A *buy limit* order, for example, may specify that the purchase must not exceed some maximum price. A *sell limit* order would set a minimum price for the floor broker. In most instances, the exceptions being fast markets or on the open or close, the order is considered filled if the market trades through the specified level. For example, a standing order to purchase 10 March S&P contracts at 166.00 must be filled before the market can trade at 165.95. If, for some reason, the order is not filled and the market trades through the specified level, the broker is considered "held" and owes the customer the execution of the order.

All orders are understood to be good for the day unless otherwise designated. If it is not executed during that day's trading session, the order is assumed to be canceled. Suppose an investor has a buy limit order in for a Treasury-bond contract at 68-04 (68-4/32) and the market closes at 68-08, having not traded down to 68-04. The broker will inform the investor that the trade was "unable." The investor can then decide whether or not to leave the order in for the next day.

An *open* order, also known as a *good 'til canceled (GTC)*, may be placed instead. This would also specify the price constraints of the investor but would remain in effect as an active order until executed or canceled. Periodic confirmation of open orders is often required.

Stop orders serve to protect a position at specified market levels for the purpose of limiting losses or protecting gains. Suppose an investor bought a bond contract at 68-04. Over the next few days, the market rises to 70-00. The investor can place a sell stop at 69-15. This order specifies that, if the market touches the 69-15 level, the order should be executed as a market order, and the contract sold at the best price then available (which will not necessarily be 69-15). They are also used, often by technical traders, to initiate contract positions. Professional traders and locals are aware that specific price levels are considered meaningful based upon projecting past pricing patterns to the current market, and that when these levels are hit a rush of buy or sell orders may enter the pit. This will influence the course of trading.

More complicated variations of these orders that place other constraints on the trade include *stop limit* orders, and *fill or kill* orders. Each exchange has rules on what types of orders may be accepted. Understanding the primary orders described above, however, should prove sufficient. A capable broker will be able to provide the appropriate nomenclature for any given trade.

THE ROLE OF THE COMMISSION-HOUSE BROKER

The commission house performs a central and pivotal role in futures trading. Good performance requires a knowledge of the trading floor, expertise in the market, and ability to execute trades well. As far as execution of a trade is concerned, there is no advantage in size for a member firm. As one broker summed it up, "The nature of the auction market on the floor makes futures the 'great equalizer.' Each trader has equal access to the market and succeeds or fails on the basis of his own skills."

However, the capital of a member firm may be a consideration. All accounts are subject to a daily *mark to market*, requiring that cash be deposited with or allowing it to be withdrawn from the broker depending on the market value of the contracts traded. The exchanges guarantee that the member firm will receive such variation margin, *but on a net basis*. Thus, if a broker holds 100 long positions (contracts purchased) and an equal number of short positions (contracts sold), and the market is up by $1,000 per contract, the $100,000 credit on the long side would be offset by the $100,000 debit on the short side, resulting in a net funds transfer of zero.

The long investor, however, would be able to withdraw the accumulated funds the next day. If some unusual financial situation arose in which the broker was unable to secure the required funds from the short investor (or from the liquidated short positions), the member's capital must be sufficient to make good on any shortfall. Therefore, how well a broker manages its own credit and knows its customers is important.

The investor looking for a good futures broker may wish to consider the following items:

How good is execution capability?

How efficient is the accounting system?

What costs and charges can be expected?

How is a firm's credit policy managed?

What kind of support does the broker offer?

Quality of execution can give the investor an idea of what kind of setup a particular broker has and how good his response time is. Speed of execution is obviously important, although more so for the arbitrageur than for the hedger. The hedger needs a broker who knows the market.

Confusion in the accounting area may signal confusion elsewhere. Likewise, credit policy can shed light on a firm's ability to work within the market to the best advantage of each investor.

Costs are, in general, lower in the futures market than they are in the cash market—and relatively insignificant for the hedger. Commissions are usually paid once, when a position is offset or delivered against (i.e., on the round trip).[1] They range from $100 per contract at the retail level to substantially lower figures for large institutions. Initial margin must be deposited. Whereas the exchanges designate minimum initial margins, the brokerage firm may impose higher levels if it chooses to do so. There is a safety incentive for the firm to do this but no monetary incentive, because interest earned on Treasury bills deposited as initial margin belongs to the client.

Finally, broker support is particularly important in hedging applications. A broker should be conversant with the hedging needs of each investor as well as with the relationship of such needs to market dynamics. To the extent that the particular emphasis differs with an insurance company, or a bank, or a pension fund, the broker must be familiar with a variety of money management needs. In sum, a good broker knows the financial needs of his customer and has the market savvy to meet those needs.

---

[1] This is true for futures. For options, some brokers charge for both opening and closing transactions.

5

Contract fundamentals

The obvious link between financial futures and financial instruments is that various financial instruments are deliverable to satisfy the terms of financial futures contracts. A financial futures price will move in line with its underlying instrument, creating an important tool for the money manager. However, in concept and design, financial futures are closer to commodity futures than to their respective cash instruments. For the money manager used to dealing with cash instruments, some adjustment to the characteristics and procedures of the contract market is necessary.

All financial futures contracts have certain features in common, among them the contract cycles. These futures trade on a March quarterly cycle, which means that contracts mature in the months of March, June, September, and December—referred to as contract expiration months. At some point during each month, trading in the relevant contract stops; a price is determined for settlement of the contract; and, for those traders holding positions, delivery of a cash instrument or cash settlement (in the case of Eurodollars and stock-index contracts) is made.[1]

---

[1] Some contracts, such as those for Treasury bonds, can be delivered into throughout the delivery month.

FIGURE 5-1

Futures Prices

Wednesday, December 14, 1983
Open Interest Reflects Previous Trading Day.

EURODOLLAR (IMM) – $1 million; pts of 100%

	Open	High	Low	Settle	Chg	Yield Settle	Chg	Open Interest
Dec	89.55	89.57	89.51	89.52	– .09	10.48	+ .09	6,826
Mar84	89.11	89.14	89.08	89.08	– .03	10.92	+ .03	22,585
June	88.80	88.84	88.77	88.77	– .01	11.23	+ .01	11,737
Sept	88.57	88.61	88.55	88.56	+ .02	11.44	– .02	3,742
Dec	88.33	88.38	88.33	88.34	+ .02	11.66	– .02	1,623
Mar85	88.11	88.15	88.11	88.12	+ .02	11.88	– .02	428

Est vol 5,834; vol Tues 9,163; open int 46,939, – 256.

GNMA 8% (CBT) – $100,000 prncpl; pts. 32nds. of 100%

	Open	High	Low	Settle	Chg	Settle	Chg	Interest
Dec	69-16	69-19	69-05	69-05	– 11	13.336	+ .078	7,209
Mar84	68-08	68-13	67-31	68-00	– 9	13.603	+ .058	23,841
June	67-08	67-12	67-00	67-00	– 9	13.839	+ .060	7,101
Sept	66-13	66-17	66-05	66-05	– 8	14.042	+ .061	2,640
Dec	65-22	65-26	65-14	65-14	– 8	14.218	+ .062	2,160
Mar85	65-03	65-07	64-27	64-27	– 8	14.365	+ .062	330
June	64-23	64-23	64-11	64-11	– 8	14.491	+ .063	220
Sept	64-03	64-03	63-30	63-30	– 8	14.595	+ .064	135
Dec	...	...		63-19	– 18	14.683	+ .064	255
Mar	...	...		63-10	– 18	14.756	+ .065	30

Est vol 9,500; vol Tues 8,632; open int 43,921, +1,077.

TREASURY BONDS (CBT) – $100,000; pts. 32nds of 100%

	Open	High	Low	Settle	Chg	Settle	Chg	Interest
Dec	69-22	69-30	69-17	69-19	– 3	12.056	+ .017	14,487
Mar84	69-01	69-08	68-25	68-28	– 3	12.186	+ .023	106,976
June	68-14	68-20	68-06	68-09	– 4	12.295	+ .023	27,534
Sept	67-30	68-03	67-20	67-24	– 5	12.394	+ .030	13,575
Dec	67-17	67-20	67-08	67-09	– 4	12.482	+ .036	11,803
Mar85	67-04	67-07	66-25	66-27	– 9	12.565	+ .042	6,953
June	66-25	66-28	66-14	66-15	– 8	12.637	+ .048	3,197
Sept	66-16	66-20	66-02	66-05	– 9	12.698	+ .055	1,345
Dec	66-11	66-11	65-28	65-28	– 10	12.753	+ .063	354
Mar86	66-04	66-04	65-21	65-21	– 10	12.796	+ .068	1,141
June	65-29	66-00	65-15	65-15	– 12	12.823	+ .074	1,084

Est vol 95,000; vol Tues 89,715; open int 188,449, +1,475.

TREASURY NOTES (CBT) – $100,000; pts. 32nds of 100%

	Open	High	Low	Settle	Chg	Settle	Chg	Interest
Dec	79-03	79-07	78-28	78-28	– 4	11.628	+ .025	2,703
Mar84	78-12	78-15	78-05	78-05	– 4	11.774	+ .025	11,606
June	77-23	77-25	77-16	77-16	– 4	11.909	+ .026	89
Sept	77-05	77-06	76-30	76-30	– 4	12.026	+ .026	40
Dec	76-22	76-22	76-16	76-16	– 4	12.117	+ .026	1

Est vol 5,500; vol Tues 4,324; open int 14,439, +13.

TREASURY BILLS (IMM) – $1 mil.; pts. of 100%

	Open	High	Low	Settle	Chg	Discount Settle	Chg	Open Interest
Dec	90.95	90.99	90.93	90.94	– .03	9.06	+ .03	10,960
Mar84	90.41	90.45	90.34	90.36	– .06	9.64	+ .06	26,687
June	90.10	90.14	90.06	90.06	– .05	9.94	+ .05	6,124
Sept	89.87	89.90	89.84	89.85	– .03	10.15	+ .03	2,166
Dec	89.70	89.70	89.65	89.65	– .04	10.35	+ .04	731
Mar85	89.47	89.50	89.45	89.45	– .05	10.55	+ .05	310
June	89.31	89.31	89.25	89.25	– .06	10.75	+ .06	218
Sept	...	...	89.08	89.08	– .05	10.92	+ .05	58

Est vol 12,662; vol Tues 16,304; open int 47,154, –256.

BANK CDs (IMM) – $1 million; pts. of 100%

	Open	High	Low	Settle	Chg	Settle	Chg	Interest
Dec	90.19	90.20	90.07	90.07	– .12	9.93	+ .12	2,569
Mar84	89.53	89.56	89.50	89.51	– .02	10.49	+ .02	15,418
June	89.16	89.22	89.15	89.16	– .01	10.84	+ .01	4,546
Sept	88.91	88.96	88.91	88.91	+ .01	11.09	– .01	2,309
Dec	88.64	88.72	88.64	88.68	+ .01	11.32	– .01	1,402
Mar85	88.45	88.49	88.45	88.47	+ .02	11.53	– .02	11

Est vol 5,692; vol Tues 7,862; open int 26,275, +932.

S&P 500 FUTURES INDEX (CME) 500 Times Index

	Open	High	Low	Settle	Chg	Settle	Chg	Interest
Dec	165.10	165.40	163.40	163.50	– 1.50	175.05	138.00	9,511
Mar84	167.25	167.60	165.45	165.70	– 1.45	176.10	152.50	18,390
June	169.25	169.50	167.50	167.75	– 1.35	177.10	163.40	330
Sept	170.30	171.00	169.30	169.45	– 1.35	178.15	164.80	72
Dec	173.25	173.25	171.15	171.15	– 1.35	179.20	166.20	74
Mar85	174.30	174.30	172.85	172.85	– 1.35	180.25	172.00	9

Est vol 41,485; vol Tues 38,141; open int 28,386, –410.

S&P 500 STOCK INDEX (Prelim)
164.88 164.93 163.25 163.33 – 1.60 ...

NYSE COMPOSITE FUTURES (NYFE) 500 Times Index

Dec	95.50	95.65	94.40	94.55	–	.85	101.45	60.88	4,097
Mar84	96.50	96.75	95.50	95.65	–	.80	101.65	79.25	3,677
June	97.50	97.75	96.60	96.80	–	.70	103.00	82.30	841
Sept	98.75	98.75	97.90	97.95	–	.60	103.10	89.25	437
Dec	99.75	99.75	99.10	99.10	–	.50	103.55	96.70	72
Mar85	100.75	100.75	100.75	100.25	–	.40	103.25	99.25	11

Est vol 13,233; vol Tues 12,759; open int 9,135, +540.

NYSE COMPOSITE STOCK INDEX
95.28 95.28 94.39 94.41 – .87 ...

KC VALUE LINE FUTURES (KC) 500 Times Index

Dec	195.50	195.95	193.60	193.70	–	1.70	213.35	111.40	1,718
Mar84	197.40	198.05	195.20	195.25	–	2.15	214.80	161.65	1,475
June	...	...	196.75	–	2 20	212 00	193.30		11
Sept	...	...	198.25	–	2.20	213 50	194.50		9

Est vol 2,831; vol Tues 2,536. open int 3,213, 76.

KC VALUE LINE COMPOSITE STOCK INDEX
195.35 195.36 193.78 193.83 – 1.52 ...

Futures Options

Wednesday, December 14, 1983

Chicago Board of Trade

TREASURY BONDS – $100,000; points and 64ths of 100%

Strike Price	Calls – Last			Puts – Last		
	Mar	June	Sept	Mar	June	Sept
64					0-26	0-57
66	3-04	3-08		0-16	0-59	1-41
68	1-38	2-00	2-24	0-52	1-48	2-43
70	0-44	1-10	1-38	1-53	2-53	3-50
72	0-16	0-40	1-06	3-20	4-16	5-13
74	0-04	0-19	0-43	5-09	5-61	....
76	0-01	0-09		7-06	..	...
78	0-01	..	0-16	9-06	. .	...
80	0-01		0-08			...
82						

Est total vol. 12,000
Calls Tues vol 9,217, open int 43,106
Puts Tues vol 6,700 open int 22,609

Most financial futures have at least four traded contracts outstanding, covering a period of one year. Some have as many as 11 contracts trading, representing commitments deferred for as long as three years. The liquidity of the various markets and the ability to create arbitrage positions influences the number of "contract months" traded.

Open interest, which is the number of contracts outstanding for each contract month (and not satisfied by prior delivery of the cash instrument or by an offsetting purchase or sale), is reported in the right-hand column for each market, as shown in Figure 5-1. Changes in total open interest, along with daily volume, are used by technical traders to gauge the direction of a market.

Back-month contracts, those with more time to expiration, tend to trade less than front-month contracts. The exception is a contract trading in its expiration month; traders not willing to stand for delivery trade out of their positions prior to the expiration period, and volume consequently diminishes.

For each traded month, a series of prices is reported: open, high, low, and settle, as shown in Figure 5-1. The *high* and *low* prices each day are just what they would seem to be—the highest and lowest prices at which a contract sold for the day. The *open* price is an indication of the *opening range*, determined by those transactions which take place in the first few seconds of each trading session.

The *settlement price* ("settle") is set by the exchange based upon the closing range for the front contract for a given future. A precise level is required to calculate the daily cash adjustments. Most exchanges establish the settlement price for back-month contracts based on the closing price of the front contract and the prevailing price spread between the first or second contract and the more distant contract months. The change between today's and yesterday's settlement price is also reported.

CONTRACT PRICE AND SIZE

Treasury-bond, Treasury-note, and GNMA contracts are each based on $100,000 principal value instruments with a specified coupon of 8 percent. These contracts trade in minimum increments of 1/32 of a point, valued at $31.25. A price of 69-19 is equivalent to 69-19/32 or $69,593.75. Contract prices reflect an assumed delivery of an 8 percent coupon, although delivery of any coupon of an eligible maturity is allowed.

Treasury bond and note contract prices are adjusted to be comparable to any potential deliverable instrument by multiplying the contract price by a published pricing factor. The factor, which is different for each contract month, equates any potential deliverable bond or note, given its coupon, to an 8 percent instrument of comparable maturity valued at par. The **cash equivalent value**—the principal value a deliverer would receive—of the bond contract priced at 69-19/32, relative to a particular bond with a factor of 1.2505, equals 87.027 (69-19/32 × 1.2505). For GNMAs, the principal value for each coupon delivered is adjusted by a similar factor.

The Treasury-bill, CD, and Eurodollar contracts are written on instruments with $1 million par value. The contract price for these markets is actually an index that incorporates rates. Subtracting the price of the contract from 100 results in the yield (or discount, in the case of bills) for the underlying instrument upon delivery. A price of 90.94 on the Treasury-bill contract implies a 9.06 discount for the deliverable bill. Similarly, a 90.07 price on the bank CD contract reflects a 9.93 yield for the CD expected to be delivered. These contracts trade in basis-point increments, with each "01" equal to $25.

The size of the three stock-index contracts is determined by multiplying the index value by a constant $500. Thus, the S&P 500 December contract priced at 163.50 represents $81,750 of the stocks included in the S&P 500 index. These contracts are traded in minimum increments of .05, valued at $25. Each contract's final settlement value is set to the closing level of its cash index on the contract's last trading day.

Options on futures prices are related to the underlying futures contract and each option represents a right to a long or short position in one futures contract. Thus, an option on a Treasury-bond future with a **strike price** of 70 represents the right to buy or sell the underlying Treasury bond futures at a price of 70. Options on Treasury bonds are traded in increments of 1/64, valued at $15.625. If the Treasury-bond future is trading at 69, the right to sell at 70 would have a value of at least 1 point.

DELIVERY REQUIREMENTS

The greatest distinction between the various futures contracts arises in their respective delivery processes. What is deliverable and when influences price relationships between cash and futures and between different contract months. The implications of the varying delivery processes are discussed further in the individual chapters describing each of these markets in Part II. The following is a market-by-market summary of delivery features:

Treasury bonds. Any bond with a first call (redemption) or maturity date at least 15 years subsequent to the first contract delivery date can be delivered. The delivery period is any time during the expiration month for a given contract at the discretion of the short.

Treasury notes. Issues ranging in maturity from 6½ to 10 years are deliverable. Delivery can take place any time during the expiration month at the discretion of the short.

GNMAs. A collateralized depository receipt (CDR) representing $100,000 principal value of GNMA certified mortgages (adjusted by the appropriate factor) is deliverable. Delivery may take place at any time during the expiration month at the discretion of the short.

Treasury bills. A Treasury bill with three months left to maturity is the deliverable instrument. Delivery is on a specific day during the contract month. This day will vary for each contract month to accommodate the delivery of the last three-month segment of a Treasury bill originally issued for maturity in one year.

CDs. The contract calls for delivery of a top-tier bank's domestic CD, with the acceptable banks selected by an exchange committee. Delivery may be made any time in the latter half of the delivery month at the short's discretion. Given contract specifications for the CD's issuance date and the range of possible delivery dates, the maturity of the CD may be between two-and-one-half and three-and-one-half months.

Eurodollars. This is a cash-settlement contract. The contract expires on the last trading day of the expiration month, at which time the exchange adjusts the contract value to the three-month cash Eurodollar rate based on a survey of dealer's markets. Normal margin settlement adjusts the cash accounts of longs and shorts for the last day's trading.

Stock-index contracts. These are also cash-settlement contracts. On the last trading day, the futures value is settled in accordance with the closing value of the underlying stock index. Normal daily margin transfers settle accounts between longs and shorts.

Options on futures. An option, exercised at the discretion of the long, leads to the creation and assignment of a long and a short futures position at the strike price. Cash is then transferred to adjust for the difference between the current futures price and the strike price. Options with no intrinsic value are left to expire. Options on bond futures expire prior to the futures contract delivery month. Thus, a December option expires in late November.

Despite the fact that only a small number of contracts (perhaps 1 percent) are settled by delivery, the sophisticated investor must understand these processes because arbitrage activity and the potential for delivery maintains futures prices relative to those of underlying markets.

MARGIN RULES

The margin account is the vehicle through which the daily mark-to-market occurs. When a position is established, an investor is required to post *initial margin*, which is essentially a good-faith deposit to ensure that daily cash requirements are met. Minimum initial margin often runs less than 5 percent of the face value of the contract. Stock-index contracts require an initial margin deposit of 5 percent to 10 percent of face value—a fraction of that required for common stock transactions. Short-term Treasury instruments can be deposited to cover initial margin; an investor need not tie up nonproductive cash. The actual amount of initial margin required will vary with market volatility and customer credit. The exchanges occasionally revise their margin requirements to reflect current trading conditions.

The daily mark-to-market occurs through the addition or subtraction of variation margin to or from the margin account. *Variation margin*, which must be posted in cash, is the dollar value gained or lost on a daily basis.

As an example, suppose an investor has purchased a Treasury-bond contract at a price of 70-16/32 and the next day its market value declines to 69-16/32. The investor would receive a margin call from his broker requiring him to deposit $1,000 in his margin account. Posting variation margin ensures that adverse market moves will be covered by the purchaser in this case.[2]

Gains or losses are effectively realized on a day-to-day basis. An actual transfer of funds between accounts occurs; this is why cash is required for variation margin calls. The procedure also sharply limits credit risk, because any differential between the market value and the transaction price has been paid.[3]

The system expedites accounting for an exchange. After the first full day a contract has been outstanding, the price at which the contract was established is no longer a concern. The change in the market from day to day determines how much cash must change hands between shorts and longs. The exchange simply calculates the net short or net long position established and credits or charges accordingly. Brokers, in turn, effect the transfer of funds among their individual accounts.

If an investor cannot meet a margin call, the broker can liquidate that investor's contract position and apply the initial margin to any losses incurred. This system helps ensure the solvency of market participants.

Initial margin rates vary from user to user. Retail rates are typically the highest, followed by lower rates for institutional users. Investors trading in contracts for hedging applications generally post less

---

[2] For accounts meeting initial margin requirements in cash, some brokers permit adverse market moves to a lower level, called a *maintenance margin level*, before requiring a variation margin payment.

[3] See Appendix II for a description of brokerage statements for futures transactions.

than those undertaking speculative trades, and traders in spreads (see below) often have reduced margin requirements, because gains in one contract should largely offset any losses in the other.

The term "margin" is really a misnomer as applied to the futures market. For stocks and bonds, margin is a loan representing part of the value required to buy an instrument. Because it is a loan, it involves interest and other costs. In futures, initial margin is no more than a deposit of collateral, the purpose of which is to ensure that price changes in an underlying contract can be met. Variation margin is a daily accounting and settlement of gains or losses. In neither case is there any borrowing; there is no "buying on margin" and for a hedger, for whom the value of the cash position is matched by the value of the instruments underlying the futures contract position, there is no leverage.

SPREADS

Traders who participate in spread trades (long one contract month and short another) do so to take advantage of changes in intramarket (December versus March Treasury bonds) and intermarket (December CDs versus December Treasury bills) price relationships.

Spreads also play a role for the hedger, as they allow for flexibility in rolling along a hedge and aid in the purchase of back contracts with limited liquidity.

Rolling along a hedge. Suppose you anticipate a general market decline over the next few months, but want to hold a specific bond. Front-month contracts can be sold to reduce the risk of holding the bond position. Three months later, the contract is about to expire, but you, the bond holder, still nervous about the market, want to maintain the hedge. The front contract is bought and another contract should be sold to cover an additional time period.

Spreading allows you to buy in the contract while simultaneously selling a subsequent month's contract. The advantages to such a strategy, as opposed to treating the two trades independently, is that you can avoid the risk of being out of the market. You don't have to be concerned with filling orders at specific market levels, but can simply specify the price difference, or spread, between the two contracts. As long as the price difference between the buy and the sell creates a spread no greater than that specified, the transaction can be undertaken without regard to market level.

Assume that the December Treasury-bond contract is priced at 70 and the March contract at 69-25, a differential of 7/32. An investor who is short December and wants to roll into March may place an order for a spread trade at 7, which means that if a December contract can be bought (offsetting the existing December position) and a March contract sold simultaneously at prices no farther apart than 7/32, this roll will be done.

Two things should be noted. First, the price levels of the December and March contracts are not usually a concern as long as the spread can be achieved. Second, a position can, for all intents and purposes, be maintained forever, with the investor rolling on a quarterly basis.

Aiding in the purchase of limited-liquidity back contracts. It may be desirable to establish a hedge in a contract two years out, but contract liquidity may prevent an investor from buying or selling those contracts quickly. By utilizing the front contract, the hedger can be in the market almost instantly and protected against level changes; by then placing a spread order, the investor can roll back his position as soon as it becomes feasible. Locals utilize spreads, often to facilitate back-month trading.

Spreads provide a tool which makes hedging mechanics easier and more flexible. They can be set up independent of market levels, they can create liquidity, and they can facilitate accurate and timely hedge decisions.

6

Basic principles of hedging

The basic reason for hedging is to avoid suffering the whims of a volatile market. Professional money managers can look to the financial-futures market as a means of protecting principal, effecting ownership of relatively illiquid securities, or trading in specific securities with reduced exposure to the general market. Financial futures also provide a vehicle for creating synthetic money-market instruments and separating the timing of a rate decision from its implementation. Futures markets provide flexibility in managing existing risk and create the ability to act on rate decisions quickly. In a dynamic environment, such flexibility may be essential. This chapter is designed to provide an introduction to the principles of hedging which will be developed in detail in subsequent chapters.

Rate volatility not only creates the need to manage market risk, it also attracts speculative activity. And, like all commodity futures, financial futures benefit from this speculative activity to the extent that speculation creates liquidity and arbitrage opportunities, which lead to the efficient contract pricing required by the hedger. A return to a stable interest-rate environment would ease the speculative incentive in these markets as well as the incentive to hedge—in turn, diminishing liquidity and reducing the need for financial futures as a hedging tool.

Different participants in these markets have different objectives. Arbitrageurs have one frame of reference, speculators another, and hedgers yet another. Among hedgers, there are a number of objectives; the unique needs of individual hedgers often provoke variations on the basic applications of hedge strategies and call for the development of new techniques. A major corporation, for example, can sell bond futures to effectively "call" a bond prior to its call date. A manufacturer can sell CD futures to manage the cost of seasonal inventory borrowings.

DEFINING HEDGE GOALS

The first step in hedging with financial futures involves defining one's goals and putting together a program to meet those goals.

The function of a business will define goals in terms of managing interest-rate exposure. A savings bank may be interested in asset/liability matching, whereas an equipment lessor may be more concerned with maintaining an economical cost of funds. While each may find it has few alternatives available for managing such risk, accepting this volatility introduces unwanted uncertainty. *Interest rates are intrinsic to their business activities and must be actively evaluated and managed to reduce undesired speculation.*

Some professional money managers have other risk-management tools at their disposal, including cash-market techniques and risk-transference vehicles such as options. A program utilizing financial futures must be weighed against these other alternatives to determine what best fits one's needs at a particular time.

Once financial futures have been chosen as a tool, the hedger must identify whether his application requires going long or short contracts. In going long, a trader purchases the obligation to take delivery of a financial instrument[1] at a set price at a future time. In going short, an obligation is established to make delivery in a similar manner. The effect of going long is much like lengthening the maturity of a portfolio or increasing general market exposure. It is done to benefit from (or avoid being hurt by) a rise in market price.

Alternatively, going short is similar to shortening maturity or selling assets held in a portfolio. It is done to benefit from (or avoid being hurt by) a decline in market price.

There are, of course, many instances in which an investor would choose to be long futures: a lender with a fixed cost of funds might

---

[1] This obligation is satisfied through actual physical delivery or cash-difference transfer in the case of cash-settlement contracts (stock indexes and Eurodollars).

make a variable-rate loan to its client but use futures to secure current rate levels on this loan, a money manager would like to extend the maturities of a short-term portfolio, a pension fund manager knows he will have pension money in a number of months but the bond market looks attractive to him now, a bond-portfolio manager would like to own a particular issue today but a lack of liquidity in that issue means the purchase will have to be deferred, a stock-portfolio manager would like to own the market today without deciding on a particular issue or group of issues to buy. The common denominator in these situations is that the manager is acting on the expectations of an increase in prices of financial assets.

Conversely, the possibility of higher interest rates or lower market prices describe those instances in which investors might want to be short futures contracts: a pension account, comfortable with its investments, seeks protection against a general market decline without the need to sell securities, a company funding a capital project over several years would like to protect against rate-level exposure on its borrowing, a lender with funds available some months from now wishes to accommodate a client with a rate set today although he sees the potential for increases in interest-rate levels and funding costs, a retailer with inventory commitments in several months wants to secure today's financing levels, an equipment lessor wants to protect against his variable cost of funds affecting the profitability of his fixed payment leases.

Understanding the existing risks associated with rate volatility and then doing nothing about them is speculation—inertia speculation—which should be recognized by the money manager as a potentially costly way of doing business. To the extent that futures can help to manage risk and avoid inertia speculation, they will prove valuable.

The hedger can choose the extent volatility is reduced. By adding or subtracting contract positions, he can either adjust his exposure as his changing expectations dictate or put a hedge in place over a period of time.

When trying to control for volatility, one must ask to what degree precision can be achieved with alternative hedge strategies. Investors often expect futures to be a perfect solution to a problematic situation. All that should be required of futures is that they serve a need in the best possible way. Above all, futures should be considered an important tool available to the money manager. However, futures may not always be used, and the advantages of a futures hedge must always be contrasted with the available cash-market or internal alternatives. One purpose of this book is to explore futures' limitations and potential costs to help the money manager better evaluate strategic alternatives.

PROTECTION OF PRINCIPAL

Because futures have neither a yield not a unique credit risk, the main feature captured by the contracts is the volatility of the instrument on which the contracts are written. For this reason, futures can be used effectively as a principal management tool to offset general market volatility.

If a money manager owns what is the deliverable cash Treasury bill and chooses to short Treasury-bill contracts against it (see Chapter 10), delivering into those contracts, the price change of the futures contract position will track that of the cash asset. The principal volatility of both is the same.

If the hedged item in this case is anything other than the cash Treasury bill, the manager must be concerned with matching the price change on his asset—or, more specifically, with the risk that the price of the asset may move differently from the princpal value of the futures contracts with which he chooses to hedge.

Consider, for example, a borrower who has a variable-rate loan tied to the prime rate and who would like to short contracts to protect himself against a rate rise. To set up this cross hedge, he must choose the contract he expects to match the anticipated volatility in the prime rate.

Because there is no prime-rate contract, the borrower may choose to sell CD futures. What must then be accounted for is the current relationship of the prime rate to CD rates and the way in which that relationship is likely to change. Do both move in the same direction? Does one significantly lead the other? How can they be expected to move relative to each other for the period of the hedge?

The prime rate and the CD rates tend to move in the same direction, with CD rates moving first and more rapidly, influencing the spread to the prime. One must determine how much of a move in CDs can be expected, based on a move of 100 basis points in the prime from today's level. CD rates may have already moved up as the prime rate increased, and may subsequently increase by only 90 basis points. Thus, if the borrower shorts 10 contracts ($1 million principal value each) to hedge a $10-million loan (1:1 ratio) and this judgment is correct, the investor will be hedged for 90 percent of a prime-rate increase. By shorting one contract against each $1 million of loan, he has implicitly accepted a known divergence from a theoretically perfect hedge. To eliminate the basis risk implied in this analysis, the borrower will short one contract for each $900,000 pegged to the prime rate, or 11.1 contracts for a $10 million loan.[2]

Principal management, which involves assessing the match of a hedged asset to a futures contract and quantifying the associated

---

[2] This example is somewhat simplified (see Chapters 10 and 17).

risk, leads to the creation of a **hedge ratio**. This is the number of contracts necessary to offset changes in principal value between the hedged asset and futures contract.

Risk exists in any cross hedge where the cash-market instrument differs from the instrument on which the contract is written. Changes in the relationship on which this ratio is based create **basis risk**, (which becomes apparent in hedge-ratio imprecision), with the basis defined as the price relationship between the cash item and the instrument underlying the future.[3]

Using financial futures for the purpose of principal management requires an analysis of cash-market relationships. (How do CD rates relate to the prime? How do Treasury bonds move relative to corporate bonds?) This information is then applied to calculate a hedge ratio and offset price risk using futures. One of the benefits of using financial futures is that such activity forces an analysis of credit risks and supply-and-demand situations that would contribute to basis risk. The hedge analysis provides a framework for quantifying these variables. As a result, futures hedgers tend to become more precise in their cash market analysis.

A common assumption is that any misjudgment concerning basis risk will hurt the hedger. Often, the opposite is true because the presence of basis risk also creates an opportunity for the hedger to benefit from changing sector relationships. Hedgers can manage their positions to protect against general market risk and still receive the profit and relative performance advantage of a stock or bond portfolio that was structured to outperform the market.

In addition to protecting principal values, analyzing a hedge strategy requires understanding cash-future relationships, contract characteristics, and variation-margin financing.

THE CASH-FUTURES RELATIONSHIP

The spread between cash and futures—the price difference between a contract and its deliverable value—is basically due to the relative advantage or disadvantage of *delayed delivery* in a contract market. **Convergence** is the process by which the value of a futures contract at expiration comes to equal the value of the underlying cash instrument. It always occurs regardless of market moves. Convergence can create a cost or benefit for the hedger that depends on the relationship between short-term and long-term interest rates—the yield curve—when the hedge is initiated.

---

[3] The term *basis* is used generally in the commodities markets to describe cash-futures relationships as in the arbitrage described in Chapter 7. However, hedgers often isolate the convergence aspect of basis, discussed later, from the relationship between cash-market instruments and the futures equivalent value. For our purpose, basis refers to the difference in equivalent principal value.

Futures contracts trade at a premium or discount to cash and to each other. In some contracts, the relationship of futures to cash is very precise. In others it is less precise, but the movement of futures reflects that of cash. Stock-index contracts, for example, are cash-settlement contracts. The absence of a deliverable instrument makes arbitrage more difficult and pricing less precise than with bond contracts.[4] Even so, they remain within a fairly predictable price range near the level of the cash index.

Interest-rate futures will trade at a premium to cash (and back contracts at a premium to front contracts) when the yield curve is inverted. That's because, with short-term financing costs above long-term rates of return (an inverted curve), an investor would be willing to pay more to delay the purchase of a cash bond at a set price. He is better off investing in short-term instruments and buying the bond later (see Chapter 7).

The premium at which futures trade will generally disappear at contract expiration, when the holder of a short position can deliver against the futures contract. During its life, the contract will decline in value relative to cash, to the benefit of shorts and the detriment of longs. This price movement represents the amortization of the yield-curve premium rather than changing principal value. The relationship between the yield curve and convergence is illustrated in Charts 6-1 and 6-2.

Conversely, when the yield curve is positive, interest-rate futures will trade at a discount to cash. In the absence of a market move, a contract appreciates toward the value of the cash instrument at expiration. In this case, convergence will benefit the long and hurt the short.

An investor can usually determine the convergence effect and the level at which a contract will settle at expiration relative to cash. The amortization of the yield-curve spread will not necessarily be a linear process, however. The cash-futures spread will change during the life of the contract, depending on interim market conditions.

Convergence is important to all hedgers. Assessing the relationship between the contract price and the price of the deliverable instrument can help in determining whether or not a contract is trading rich or cheap relative to cash. Relative richness or cheapness is especially important when analyzing a hedge for a short period of time because arbitrage activity can cause a quick price adjustment. Convergence will also take on greater importance for hedgers concerned with applications oriented purely toward rate of return.

---

[4] For stock indexes, the exchange sets the price at expiration equal to the prevailing value of the underlying "cash" stock index.

CHART 6-1   Yield curve

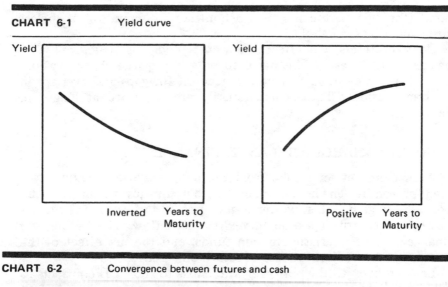

CHART 6-2   Convergence between futures and cash

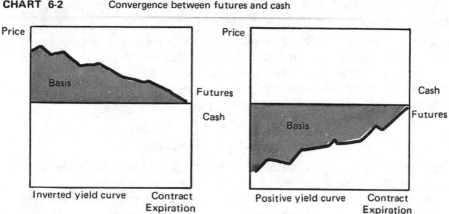

CONTRACT CHARACTERISTICS

Hedgers need to know the specifications of each contract they use so that they can evaluate any unique risks. These risks usually derive from a contract's delivery procedure and will affect the contract's price. Such contract technicalities are often the reason that a contract will trade rich or cheap, after the yield-curve effect is considered. Hedgers will have to evaluate the effect this pricing inefficiency could have on their results. When using bond or note contracts, for example, the extent of contract price adjustment for after-hours risk (caused by the fact that the futures market stops trading two hours before the cash bond market) or a change in the cheapest-to-deliver bond (the one that can satisfy a contract at expiration at lowest cost) might be evaluated.

Contract terms will affect the way a hedge is structured. The hedger using Treasury bills needs to be aware of the change in contract delivery dates so that he can account for gaps and overlaps in contract periods. These characteristics are described at length in Part II.

VARIATION-MARGIN BALANCE FINANCING

A financing effect results from the daily variation-margin-settlement procedure. The hedger is faced with a cash-flow timing problem, because the gain or loss on the original position offset by the futures position does not create an immediate cash flow. The hedger will finance or invest variation-margin funds, and the net effect of the financing might adjust the rate of return on a hedge.

Let's go back to the borrower who chose to short CD contracts to protect against a prime rate rise. He sold 11.1 contracts, based on an anticipated move of 100 basis points in the prime and a subsequent move of 90 basis points in the CD rate. If this rate forecast is wrong, and the prime rate declines rather than rises, the CD contract will appreciate in value; consequently, he will have to post variation margin. If the contract appreciates by 90 basis points:

$$90 \text{ basis points} \times \$25 = \$2,250$$
$$\$2,250 \times 11.1 = \$24,975$$

Thus, the dollar value required for margin would be $2,250 per contract. For 11.1 contracts, $24,975 would have to be posted.

Of course, this amount should be recaptured with lower interest payments on the variable-rate loan.

The length of time—and the rate at which a borrower must finance this variation margin—will determine the financing cost. If $24,975 is the average variation margin over a period of three months, and this amount is financed at 16 percent, the cost would be $1,000 for the period. This would add $4,000 (four basis points) to current annual borrowing costs.

In general, variation margin is unlikely to have a major impact on hedge results. Because variation-margin balance is a function of market direction and timing, the financing effect cannot be known in advance. But the financing effect can be estimated for the set of market conditions the hedger expects. It is useful to look at different cases and anticipate the potential financing impact. Relative importance of this variable will differ from one hedge application to another.

There are sophisticated techniques for managing variation-margin financing. However, these methods can compound the risk or cost of the overall strategy. For most hedgers, it is sufficient to have funds set aside for margin calls and to understand the associated financing cost or benefit.

Although a theoretical discussion of hedging is helpful, the more concrete examples to follow may clarify a few points.

BASIC HEDGE EXAMPLES

A long bond hedge

The All-Purpose Insurance Company has a continuous inflow of funds that it uses to make corporate loans. When interest rates are expected to decline, the company would like to undertake long-term lending at current rate levels, say 16 percent. However, a corporate borrower with an anticipated need for funds one year from today may be reluctant to enter into a loan agreement at these rates; if the borrower's own economists forecast the same rate decline, the borrower would prefer to delay arrangement of funding until the rates come down. How can All-Purpose avoid the trap of inertia speculation—doing nothing—while accommodating a client?

There is a solution.

With a rate decline anticipated, the borrower corporation might be willing to commit to a loan a year from today if it could provide the corporation with funding based on rates available at that time. The insurance company can make this sort of arrangement and still secure today's rate levels by using the futures market. Futures provide a mechanism for separating the rate decision from the writing of a loan, thereby improving All-Purpose's ability to conduct its business.

By going long the bond futures—that is, agreeing to purchase a cash instrument at an established price at some time in the future— the insurance company can protect itself against the potential of a decline in interest rates.

Here's how it works.

Assume rates have fallen to 13 percent. The borrower corporation now can secure its loan at 13 percent, as compared with 16 percent a year ago. The insurance company can write a loan at 13 percent and be no worse off; by purchasing futures, it has hedged against such a rate decline. As interest rates have come down, the value of the futures it holds has gone up. If the hedge was calculated correctly, this gain will offset the loss of writing the loan at a lower rate. The insurance company has effectively established a loan at about 16 percent, and the borrower has secured a long-term rate based on 13 percent.

In this situation, the use of futures has several advantages. Where a forward commitment might otherwise be used, futures provide an alternative with substantial flexibility. This derives from the very nature of the futures market. The "other party" to the contract—i.e., the party to whom the short or long has an obligation—is always the exchange rather than a private party. Then too, when a forward commitment cannot be agreed upon (if, for example, both parties believe interest rates will decline), futures can provide the means for separating the timing of a transaction from interest-rate decisions. In other words, the agreement to make the loan can be reached despite the complication of a changing interest-rate environment. This provides substantial flexibility to both the lender and the borrower.

A short bond hedge

You're the manager of General Hospital's pension fund, and you're basically comfortable with the long-term bonds you hold. The specific issues included in that portfolio are weighted as you wish among the component groups—utility, corporate, and telephone bonds—to provide both a given yield and an acceptable distribution of market risk. The composition of that segment of your portfolio is perfectly satisfactory.

In other words, the investment program you have constructed does meet your long-range needs with regard to income stream, maturity, and safety.

The trouble is, there's always the short term. Like it or not, you must certainly contend with the vicissitudes of the marketplace during the intervening months and years. Suppose, for example, you anticipate a sharp increase in interest rates (which may or may not persist) that will make your bond portfolio especially vulnerable. What choices do you have in dealing with such a prospect?

1. Do nothing. You may decide the benefits of owning your specific issues outweigh the short-term risk. To be sure, there are certain advantages to this strategy. The move in interest rates may be temporary, in which case you avoid interim transactions that would upset the portfolio balance—and probably affect duration and income as well. You also avoid the costs of those transactions, which can be substantial. However, if your concern with regard to rates turns out to be correct, you face the distinct disadvantage of suffering a loss of principal.

2. Sell all or some of the bonds.   This is the most direct—and perhaps the most obvious—means of eliminating the perceived capital risk. One disadvantage of this strategy is that the program you put in place has now been upset. The weighting of the portfolio components has been altered, and average yield and duration, more likely than not, are no longer at your target levels. In addition, you face the prospect of moving out of issues you will want to buy back into when things settle down. This implies not only significant time and and effort but also the potential for substantial transaction costs, which can be measured against the alternative of using futures.

In effect, the market decisions you need to make over the short term often come directly into conflict with long-term decisions related to portfolio composition.

3. Sell the risk.   This alternative avoids most of the disadvantages of the foregoing choices. To begin with, you protect yourself against principal loss. By selling the risk associated with an adverse market, you effectively offset the potential for decline with a matching potential for gain. By limiting your activity to the risk component of your holdings, you also avoid the need to change the makeup of your portfolio. You can keep your investment program intact.

Going short bond futures allows you to sell the risk. By being short a bond contract—which essentially means you agree to sell the underlying cash instrument at a later date for a price agreed upon earlier—you create a hedge that will appreciate in value as bond prices decline. A perfect hedge will thus offset, dollar for dollar, the anticipated decline in the value of your portfolio.

Risk considerations

As portfolio manager for General Hospital's pension fund, in the second example, you had the option of selling off risk by selling futures. In the first example, the All-Purpose Insurance Company can purchase futures to manage a risk inherent in its capacity as a lender. The futures market provides the means for handling the volatility, or risk, associated with the long-term interest-rate environment.

All this is not to say that every investor ought in every case to hedge his investment through the use of financial futures. Using the bond futures market as an alternative risk-management tool involves some important, basic considerations. In the first place, while principal value can be protected, potential yield effects do exist. These must be factored into the decision-making process. Sometimes they will prove important, at other times, of no consequence—depending on the objectives of the hedger. Second, a poorly structured hedge can leave the investor vulnerable to basis risk. The number of futures contracts purchased or sold may hot compensate exactly for price variations in the hedged instrument. And, finally, depending on the market environment, other investment opportunities—including doing nothing—may actually be more desirable.

What the foregoing does suggest is that every investor ought to consider the use of financial futures to determine whether or not they will serve his investment purposes. In many cases, futures will prove to be of enormous value.

PART TWO

Contract analysis

7

Treasury bonds

The long-term Treasury bond contract began trading on the Chicago Board of Trade in 1976. Since then, it has grown to become the most heavily traded futures contract on any exchange. In 1982, 16.7 million bond contracts were traded on the board, roughly one third of the total 48.2 million agricultural and financial contracts traded there. While stock-index futures can lay claim to being the fastest-growing instrument available, Treasury bond futures have already established their importance as a legitimate investment vehicle.

CONTRACT CHARACTERISTICS

The contract is written on a bond with $100,000 principal value, a nominal 8 percent coupon, and 15 years or more to first call. It is an agreement to make (in the case of the short) or take (in the case of the long) delivery of such an instrument at a specified price within a specified period of time. Whereas many bonds qualify as deliverable, only a limited number are likely to be delivered. Under almost all conditions, bonds with longer maturities—27 to 30 years—are delivered. Contracts terminate on a March quarterly cycle (March, June, September, December), with 11 of them outstanding at any given time.

The bond contract trades in 32nds of a point. One point is valued at $1,000, with 1/32 worth $31.25. However, the Chicago Board of Trade limits price movements during individual trading sessions to two points, with no limit for contracts in their delivery months. This is meant to protect investors against sudden, adverse price moves and help maintain an orderly market. When the market closes "up limit" or "down limit" the exchange expands the limit on the next day— and further after several more days of "limit" closes. To the professional, such limit days are not generally a problem. In the first place, there are not very many limit days.[1] And the money manager can trade out of a position via the cash market. Board of Trade hours are from 8 A.M. to 2 P.M. CST (or 9 A.M. to 3 P.M. EST), constituting a somewhat shorter trading day than that for investors in the cash markets.

There are transaction costs associated with buying and selling bond futures, but these are typically a fraction of those associated with dealing in actual bonds. Initial margin, which is essentially a "good faith" deposit required to ensure adherence of the long and the short to the daily cash-margin provisions of the contract, is relatively small—typically, 1.5 percent ($1,500) to 4 percent ($4,000) of the face value of the contract. A bona fide hedger, such as the holder of a cash instrument who sells bond futures against it, is subject to lower margin requirements. Investors trading spreads (long one contract month and short another) need post even smaller amounts of initial margin. Treasury bills are acceptable as initial margin, thus relieving the investor of the prospect of tying up cash in a nonproductive function.

Commissions and fees, which are paid on the round trip, may total less than 1/10th of 1 percent of the value of the contract. Comparable transaction costs for the purchase and sale of a bond can run to 2 percent of its value.

For a portfolio manager, utilizing bond futures rather than trading the portfolio may obviate another, more subtle, kind of cost. Let's go back to an example from Chapter 6. The investment manager for a hospital pension fund was concerned with the near-term environment for bonds. One of the choices available, then, was to sell some of the bonds. However, that might have required moving out of a large position in one or several similar issues over a short period of time. As potential buyers became aware of significant selling activity in these issues, prices could decline. In certain environments, a *fade*

---

[1] There have been no limit-close days in 1983.

effect occurs as traders back off bids, causing the price received to be depressed further than the indicated bid.

There's another side to the coin. Once the environment for rates improves, the investment manager may choose to reestablish the bond position. But market conditions may now contribute to artificially high prices as sellers tend to raise offerings. The trading activity limited the capital risk associated with the portfolio, but at a cost that would have been avoided by using futures.

The more illiquid a particular bond, the greater the cost of cash-market activity could be. Add to this the likelihood of other trades of this type in the ongoing management of the hospital's portfolio, and the potential for substantial "active management" costs becomes significant. By limiting trading in the portfolio itself, these particular costs can be avoided. The transaction-cost savings afforded by futures give the manager a head start; often, a substantial error in the assessment of basis risk is required to negate this cost advantage (see Chapter 16).

Delivery process

Despite the fact that substantially less than 1 percent of all contracts actually settle by delivery (the rest "cancel out" when participants in a contract effect offsetting purchases or sales), delivery terms and methods are important determinants of contract trading patterns and prices. Hedgers will not typically stay in a position and go through the delivery process. As a result, this process is important to the hedger only in its impact on pricing.

The short is given a considerable degree of control by the terms of the contract, which specifies both the deliverable issue and the delivery date within the expiration month. The short can deliver on any day—from the first business day through the last business day—of the delivery month. The short does so by giving notice two days before delivery to the exchange's clearing corporation. The next day, the exchange notifies the broker of the assigned long.

Longs are assigned chronologically, with those positions first established being assigned first. The long should be informed early in the morning that he will receive delivery on the next day, based on the prior day's settlement price.

Two things should be noted from the long's point of view. To begin with, until the end of the second day, the long can only guess which bond will actually be delivered. It could be an 8 percent bond or a 14 percent bond, with very different dollar exposures. In the second place, because the short can deliver on the first business day of the month, a long can be assigned and forced to take delivery of a contract if it is owned at the close of the notice day, which can be two days prior to the first calendar day of the month.

Decisions concerning which bond to deliver and when involve economic considerations. The cheapest-to-deliver bond may not be the same at expiration as at the start of the contract; and, depending upon yield-curve conditions, delivering an issue early in the expiration month may be more profitable than delaying delivery.

Let's say the yield curve is inverted. The current interest-rate environment is, therefore, one in which short-term rates are higher than long-term rates. A short, financing a cash instrument until delivery, will generally find it advantageous to deliver early in the contract-expiration month because financing rates are higher than the return on the instrument he is financing.

Conversely, when the cost of financing (short-term rate) is below the return on the cash instrument, the short will tend to deliver later in the expiration month.

Cheapest to deliver

Because it is also to the advantage of a short to deliver the instrument that reflects the lowest available cost to him, long-term Treasury bond contracts will tend to trade based on the expectation of the cheapest-to-deliver bond being, in fact, the bond delivered. Cheapest to deliver refers not to market yield but to the relative market value of deliverable issues vis-à-vis the contract delivery price, as dictated by an 8 percent bond of similar first call.

The terms of the bond contract assume an 8 percent coupon, and the prices quoted for these contracts reflect this. A June 1983 contract trading at a price of 75, for example has a cash-equivalent value of 122-5/32.[2] Because a Treasury bond with any coupon is deliverable (assuming it fulfills the maturity requirements outlined above), the delivery price to be paid, which is based on the settlement price of the contract on the day the short gives notice multiplied by the applicable published factor, will depend on the specific issue delivered to satisfy the contract. Delivery factors are published for each contract period, based on the potential delivery of specific bonds of various coupons and maturities. This facilitates determination of equivalent prices.

A delivery factor is that adjustment which, when applied to the price of the futures contract, gives the appropriate value for a deliverable bond with a coupon of other than 8 percent. Hence, a 14 percent bond has a June 1983 factor of 1.6286. That is, the delivery price of the 14 percent bond, if it is delivered in satisfaction of the June 1983 contract, will be 1.6286 times the price of the bond future.

---

[2] This assumes that the 14 percent Treasury bonds of 11/15/2011-06 are the cheapest to deliver.

These factors, published by the Board of Trade, are purely mathematical and are calculated as follows:

1. Assume the existence of a bond with an 8 percent coupon selling at par with the same first-call date as the bond actually being considered for delivery.
2. Calculate the price at which the deliverable bond (with a coupon of other than 8 percent) would have to sell to yield 8 percent at first call.
3. Divide that price by 100, the original price of the deliverable bond.

In practice, these published factors are simplified to the extent that they assume delivery of a bond on the first day of a contract expiration month and assume that the bond matures on the first day of the first month of the quarter of its maturity or call. This rounds down the factors to the nearest full quarter. An example is shown:

U.S. Treasury Bond Futures Conversion Factor to Yield 8.000%

Coupon Rate:	14%	14⅛%	14¼%	14⅜%	14½%	14⅝%	14¾%	14⅞%
Term								
15	1.5188	1.5296	1.5404	1.5512	1.5620	1.5728	1.5836	1.5944
15-3	1.5229	1.5338	1.5447	1.5556	1.5665	1.5774	1.5883	1.5992
15-6	1.5277	1.5386	1.5496	1.5606	1.5716	1.5826	1.5936	1.6046
15-9	1.5316	1.5427	1.5538	1.5649	1.5759	1.5870	1.5981	1.6092
16	1.5362	1.5474	1.5585	1.5697	1.5809	1.5921	1.6032	1.6144
16-3	1.5400	1.5513	1.5625	1.5738	1.5850	1.5963	1.6075	1.6188
16-6	1.5444	1.5558	1.5671	1.5785	1.5898	1.6011	1.6125	1.6238
16-9	1.5481	1.5595	1.5709	1.5823	1.5938	1.6052	1.6166	1.6280
17	1.5523	1.5638	1.5753	1.5869	1.5984	1.6099	1.6214	1.6329
17-3	1.5558	1.5674	1.5790	1.5906	1.6022	1.6138	1.6253	1.6369
17-6	1.5599	1.5716	1.5833	1.5949	1.6066	1.6183	1.6299	1.6416
17-9	1.5633	1.5750	1.5868	1.5985	1.6102	1.6220	1.6337	1.6455
18	1.5672	1.5791	1.5909	1.6027	1.6145	1.6263	1.6382	1.6500
18-3	1.5705	1.5823	1.5942	1.6061	1.6180	1.6299	1.6418	1.6537
18-6	1.5743	1.5862	1.5982	1.6102	1.6221	1.6341	1.6461	1.6580
18-9	1.5773	1.5894	1.6014	1.6134	1.6255	1.6375	1.6495	1.6616
19	1.5810	1.5931	1.6052	1.6174	1.6295	1.6416	1.6537	1.6658
19-3	1.5840	1.5961	1.6083	1.6205	1.6327	1.6448	1.6570	1.6692
19-6	1.5875	1.5998	1.6120	1.6243	1.6365	1.6487	1.6610	1.6732
19-9	1.5903	1.6026	1.6150	1.6273	1.6396	1.6519	1.6642	1.6765
20	1.5938	1.6062	1.6185	1.6309	1.6433	1.6556	1.6680	1.6804
20-3	1.5965	1.6089	1.6213	1.6338	1.6462	1.6586	1.6711	1.6835
20-6	1.5998	1.6123	1.6248	1.6373	1.6498	1.6623	1.6748	1.6873
20-9	1.6024	1.6149	1.6275	1.6400	1.6526	1.6651	1.6777	1.6902
21	1.6056	1.6182	1.6308	1.6434	1.6560	1.6686	1.6813	1.6939
21-3	1.6080	1.6207	1.6334	1.6460	1.6587	1.6714	1.6841	1.6967
21-6	1.6111	1.6239	1.6366	1.6493	1.6621	1.6748	1.6875	1.7002
21-9	1.6135	1.6263	1.6390	1.6518	1.6646	1.6774	1.6902	1.7030
22	1.6165	1.6293	1.6422	1.6550	1.6678	1.6807	1.6935	1.7064
22-3	1.6187	1.6316	1.6445	1.6574	1.6703	1.6832	1.6961	1.7090
22-6	1.6216	1.6346	1.6475	1.6605	1.6734	1.6864	1.6993	1.7123
22-9	1.6238	1.6368	1.6497	1.6627	1.6757	1.6887	1.7017	1.7147
23	1.6265	1.6396	1.6526	1.6657	1.6788	1.6918	1.7049	1.7179
23-3	1.6286	1.6417	1.6548	1.6679	1.6810	1.6941	1.7072	1.7203
23-6	1.6313	1.6444	1.6576	1.6707	1.6839	1.6970	1.7102	1.7234
23-9	1.6333	1.6464	1.6596	1.6728	1.6860	1.6992	1.7124	1.7256
24	1.6359	1.6491	1.6623	1.6756	1.6888	1.7021	1.7153	1.7286
24-3	1.6377	1.6510	1.6643	1.6776	1.6909	1.7042	1.7175	1.7308
24-6	1.6402	1.6536	1.6669	1.6803	1.6936	1.7069	1.7203	1.7336
24-9	1.6420	1.6554	1.6688	1.6822	1.6956	1.7089	1.7223	1.7357
25	1.6445	1.6579	1.6713	1.6847	1.6982	1.7116	1.7250	1.7385
25-3	1.6462	1.6596	1.6731	1.6866	1.7000	1.7135	1.7270	1.7404
25-6	1.6485	1.6620	1.6755	1.6891	1.7026	1.7161	1.7296	1.7431
25-9	1.6502	1.6637	1.6772	1.6908	1.7043	1.7179	1.7314	1.7450
26	1.6524	1.6660	1.6796	1.6932	1.7068	1.7204	1.7340	1.7476
26-3	1.6540	1.6676	1.6812	1.6949	1.7085	1.7221	1.7358	1.7494
26-6	1.6562	1.6699	1.6835	1.6972	1.7109	1.7245	1.7382	1.7519
26-9	1.6577	1.6714	1.6851	1.6988	1.7125	1.7262	1.7399	1.7536
27	1.6598	1.6735	1.6873	1.7010	1.7148	1.7285	1.7423	1.7560
27-3	1.6612	1.6750	1.6888	1.7025	1.7163	1.7301	1.7439	1.7577
27-6	1.6633	1.6771	1.6909	1.7047	1.7185	1.7323	1.7462	1.7600
27-9	1.6646	1.6784	1.6923	1.7061	1.7200	1.7338	1.7477	1.7615

Factors provide the means for calculating the value of a bond at delivery. Because these factors adjust all bonds to the 8 percent bond, the prices derived from them represent *equilibrium delivery prices*, or those prices at which the short would be indifferent with regard to which bond he buys to deliver.

Market prices will vary from equilibrium delivery prices primarily because the market sets different values for various coupons at different yield levels. As yields rise, for example, the value of premium bonds will tend to change at a different rate than will that of discount bonds.

Differences between these equilibrium prices and actual cash-market prices determine which bonds will be less or more attractive to deliver at different times. Because contract prices will tend to track the movement of the cheapest-to-deliver issue, calculating equilibrium delivery prices of deliverable issues and evaluating market values of these same issues are important first steps in understanding how a contract trades.

Let us assume that only two long-term Treasury bonds existed in the cash market: the 9-1/8 of 5/15/09-04 and the 14 of 11/15/11-06. If the current price of the June 1983 bond contract were 75, which bond would be the cheapest to deliver—and, consequently, influence the bond contract price?

The factor for the 9-1/8 percent bond (1.1128 multiplied by the bond contract price of 75) yields a delivery price of 83.46. The factor for the 14 percent bond (1.6286 multiplied by the bond contract price of 75) yields a delivery price of 122.15. If actual cash bond prices for the two issues equaled the calculated delivery prices, the short would be indifferent with regard to delivery of one bond or the other.

On the other hand, let us assume that cash bond prices are different. The 9-1/8 percent bond sells at 84, and the 14 percent bond sells at 122. Now the short has to make a decision. If he delivers the 9-1/8 percent, the long will pay him 83.46 when, based on the market price, the bond is worth 84. It is thus to the short's advantage to deliver the 14 percent bond. In this instance, the 14 percent has become more desirable to deliver because, by purchasing and delivering the 9-1/8 percent bond, the short would lose money. (If the short already owned the 9-1/8 percent, he might swap into the 14 percent or cover the contract position and sell the 9-1/8 percent and still do better than he would delivering the 9-1/8 percent in satisfaction of the contract.) The short can deliver the 14 percent if he owns it—or purchase and deliver it—at a slight gain. The relevant figures could be as follows:

			Delivery value		Market price		
Bond		Factor	Price	Yield	Price	Yield	Gain to short
9-1/8	5/15/09-04	1.1128	83.46	11.074	84	11.00	(.54)
14	11/15/11-06	1.6286	122.15	11.292	122	11.31	.15

June 83 futures price   75

The cheapest-to-deliver bond, then, is the 14 percent. Price activity in the futures contracts would follow movements in the price of this bond as long as it was expected to remain the cheapest to deliver.

Changes in the yield relationship between two deliverable bonds may affect the decision as to which bond is cheapest to deliver. In the previous example, a spread of 31 basis points existed between the 9-1/8 percent and the 14 percent. But what if yields have since increased and the yield spread has narrowed to, say, 17 basis points?

Let's say the 14 percent bond, now yielding 11.68 percent, has a market value of 118.46. Let's say, further, that there is a more rapid drop in the price of the 9-1/8 percent bond, now yielding 11.51 percent, to 80.40. The price decline of the 9-1/8 percent is sufficiently large to induce a short to deliver the bond in satisfaction of the futures contract in preference to the 14 percent. This is shown as follows:

	June 83 futures price 72-8/32				
	Delivery value		Market price		
Bond	Price	Yield	Price	Yield	Gain to short
9-1/8	80.40	11.51	80.40	11.51	(.00)
14	117.67	11.77	118.46	11.68	(.79)

Clearly, the best position for the short would be to deliver the 9-1/8 bonds.

By considering various price levels at which a given bond future could settle at expiration and calculating the associated cash-equivalent value of deliverable issues using delivery factors, an equilibrium table is constructed to provide a matrix of those values at which all bonds would be equally desirable to deliver.

The basis trade[3]

Knowing which bond is likely to be delivered is helpful in the construction of a hedge. In a perfect market, the price action of this cheapest-to-deliver bond (divided by its delivery factor) is the primary determinant of the price action of the futures.

Let's say you have now purchased the cheapest-to-deliver cash bond and wish to sell futures to offset price movement in the cash instrument and create a short-term yield.[4] It is necessary to sell a

---

[3] Basis means two different things in futures trading. Basis, as in basis risk, refers to the differing price action of a hedged asset (a corporate bond, for example) and the cheapest-to-deliver Treasury bond. A basis trade, on the other hand, refers to the cash-futures relationship, which can be arbitraged to create a short-term rate of return.

Basis = Price of future X Factor for cash bond — Price of cash bond

Basis trades are also referred to as cash-and-carry positions.

[4] For a detailed description of the mathematics of calculating the short-term rate created (implied repo rate) see Appendix III.

principal amount of futures contracts equal to the appropriate factor for each $100,000 par value of cash bonds. This can be best understood by looking at what would happen if only one contract were sold for each $100,000 par value.

Assume that the 14 percent is the cheapest to deliver and that the current bond futures contract is selling at 75. If the contract price were 75 at expiration, you would anticipate payment of 122.145 to close out your short position with delivery of the 14 percent (75 × 1.6286), or $122,145 for $100,000 principal value.

But what if the delivery price were something other than 75? If, over the life of the contract, the futures have appreciated to 76-16/32, the new delivery price (76.5 × 1.6286) would be $124,588 per $100,000 par value. You would have already paid $1,500 in variation margin to maintain your short position, leaving a net delivery price of $123,088. This is higher than the anticipated delivery price of $122,145.

The key to the discrepancy between actual and anticipated delivery price is the effect of the factor on variation margin. Price changes prior to contract settlement at expiration are paid in cash, without the application of a factor; at expiration, however, the value of the contract, which reflects the same price changes, is adjusted by the factor. Accordingly, the anticipated delivery price will deviate from the actual delivery price by the relevant factor unless this is built into the basis trade. In this instance, you came out ahead. You received $123,088 for your short position when you expected only $122,145. Had the market moved the other way, you would have paid the difference.

Had you sold 1.6286 futures contracts for $100,000 each in underlying instruments, $2,443 in variation margin ($1,500 × 1.6286) would have been posted. The result:

Delivery price ($76,500 × 1.6286 contracts)	$124,588
Variation margin ($1,500 × 1.000 contracts)	− 1,500
Variation margin ($1,500 × 0.6286 contracts)	− 943
Anticipated settlement price	$122,145

Shorting an additional .6286 futures contracts facilitates attainment of the price originally anticipated—and the yield associated with it. In a perfect market, then, the ratio of contracts per $100,000 principal amount hedged will equal the relevant delivery factor for the basis trade.

Because the number of futures sold for the basis trade is defined as a specific factor, a change in deliverable instruments will distort the accuracy of this weighting. A change in cheapest to deliver, based on market level and yield spreads, happens infrequently; and the impact of such a change on contract price levels, while not significant for a hedger over the long term, can be important to the basis trader.

Cost of carry

The tendency of bond futures prices to follow the cheapest-to-deliver cash price generally requires that, in a perfect market, the futures will have converged to this cash price at expiration. Convergence occurs even in the absence of general market price moves; it is a function of cost-of-carry relationships—which, in turn, are a function of existing yield-curve conditions.

Cost of carry, as defined by interest costs, forms the basis for price variations between cash bonds and the nearest expiring contract and between bonds traded in different contract months. Cost of carry is defined as the difference between an investor's anticipated cost of financing, which will be a short-term borrowing rate, and his return (current yield) on a cash bond, which will be a longer-term rate.

Suppose a positive yield curve exists, with short-term rates at 10-3/4 percent and long-term rates (on a current-yield basis) at 11-3/4 percent. Given the chance to purchase a bond either today or three months from today at the same price, an investor would certainly choose to purchase the bond today. At these interest levels, he could borrow money at 10-3/4 percent and reinvest it in the cash bond at 11-3/4 percent. The 1 percent difference between the rates would be his annual profit. To induce the investor to purchase the bond three months from now, instead, the price of the bond would have to be reduced to a point at which its discount (the difference between price and the price in three months) would be equivalent to the gain obtainable through the purchase of the cash bond today. Arbitrage activity will tend to force this, since the arbitrageur will buy bonds and sell futures as long as a net profit exists.

The reverse is true in the case of an inverted yield curve. If short-term borrowing rates are 1 percent higher than long-term rates, an investor would choose to purchase the bond three months from now. Accordingly, the price of that bond would be bid up to a point at which the delayed purchase would no longer be an advantage.

This is the basis on which the bond futures contract will trade. The cash bond represents the spot market, and the relationship between long and short rates defines the spread between spot and the nearest expiring contract.

As a result, the nearest expiring contract tends to trade at a premium or discount to cash, depending upon the relationship of short rates to long rates. A positive yield curve will induce futures to trade at a discount to cash because, if prices were equal, it would be more profitable to be long in the cash market. Likewise, a negative yield curve causes futures to trade at a premium to cash, because equal prices would imply no cost of carry in the purchase of the future.

This premium, or discount to cash is known as a *basis spread*. It will vary according to the yield curve and the amount of time remaining in the life of the contract. Spreads will exist between the various trading contracts as well; but because rate relationships are not known, expectations are built into these spreads. For contracts expiring more than a year out, spreads tend to narrow; at that point, the impact of the yield curve is less well defined, and the curve's impact is minimized due to the difficulty of effecting an arbitrage.

Convergence

Cost of carry, then, is a function of the yield curve. Convergence, by reducing the cost of carry to zero at delivery (i.e., converting the futures equivalent price to the cash price), acts to transform the long rate associated with the futures contract today into shorter-term rates. In other words, the difference between the cost of financing and the long-term Treasury rate will be netted out through futures converging to cash.

Suppose that, as in the inverted yield-curve scenario above, short-term rates are 12-3/4 percent, and long-term rates are 11-3/4 percent. This implies that the nearest expiring future is trading at a premium to cash reflecting a 1 percent annual cost-of-carry difference. Based on $100,000 of market value per contract, this translates into an annual cost of $1,000, or $250 per quarter. Assuming the existing yield relationship holds, the spread would be $250 at a point three months prior to expiration, $125 at 1-1/2 months, and zero at expiration. With the passage of time, the value of the differential declines toward zero—and, in so doing, narrows the cost-of-carry differential.

To the investor who is short bond futures, the effect of convergence is positive when the yield curve is inverted: As the contract adjusts, amortizing the spread, its value declines to the advantage of the short.

Let's say you have hedged a bond with a current yield of 11-3/4 percent by going short an appropriate number of bond contracts and that this creates an annualized convergence gain equal to 1 percent. Your short position will, in a perfect market, converge to cash. The gain associated with this convergence is 1 percent, making the effective yield on your underlying instrument not 11-3/4 percent but 12-3/4 percent.

By the same token, a positive yield curve implies a negative impact on effective yields for the investor who is short. The investor can anticipate a reduction of the effective yield from his cash holdings by the convergence implied in the cash-futures relationship.

For the investor who is long bond futures, the effect of convergence will work to an advantage when short rates are below long rates and to a disadvantage in an inverted yield-curve environment. This yield effect cannot be neutralized by adjusting the structure of a hedge without additional risk, and should generally be considered as an independent factor in weighing the decision to use the bond contract as a risk-management tool (see Chapter 16).

Consequently, if you were facing short rates 1 percent below long rates in the instance cited above, you would expect negative yield effects from your hedge. However, if you opted to sell this underlying bond, instead, the rates available to you for reinvestment would also be lower than the long-term rate.

Whether owning the bond and shorting the relevant futures contract will be to your advantage, compared with outright ownership of short-term instruments, is a function of market conditions and the particular hedge required.

The repo market

The rate created by effecting a basis trade is called an implied repo rate. This designation derives from arbitrage activity, which depends on the repurchase market as a source of borrowing.[5]

The repo market, a large, interdealer market, is essentially a collateralized loan market. One function is to provide financing for dealer inventories. Another is to provide for the use of excess corporate cash.

Generally speaking, the repo is an overnight market, with rates fluctuating daily. (While there is a "term" repo market, it is relatively thin, i.e., not heavily traded.) An arbitrage of cash versus future contracts is usually done with the knowledge that there is risk with respect to the repo rate, because one must estimate the cost of financing bonds for the period in question.

HEDGE-RATIO CONSIDERATIONS

In a basis trade principal protection is a given and the rate of return based upon convergence is the focus. For most hedges, convergence is a given, and the avoidance of principal risk is the main focus. This difference in focus separates hedging from basis trading. And that

---

[5] The cash-futures basis, or spread, that yields the highest implied repo rate at a given point in time will be the spread between the cheapest-to-deliver bond and the futures contract. The implied repo rate represents the return on such a trade. Hence, the apparent profit on such a position is a function of the rate at which the cash bond is financed. Appendix III illustrates the calculation of an implied repo rate.

makes things a little less precise. Fortunately, the bond futures market benefits from a considerable degree of price accountability imposed by the presence of arbitrageurs in the marketplace.

The existence of a viable arbitrage market is advantageous to all market participants. It provides liquidity and maintains spread relationships between cash and futures and among the contracts traded. The price accountability gained through this mechanism thus permits an investor to design hedges more accurately.

Take the case of General Hospital begun in Chapter 6. The pension fund manager bought corporate bonds, which he now expects to decline in value by 10 points. To eliminate the principal risk of these bonds without selling them, he would like to create a contract position that will rise in value by 10 points. To do this, he must assess the movement he expects to occur in Treasury bond futures[6] when those corporate bonds decline. If he expects the contract to decline by 5 points, he would sell two contracts for $100,000 each par value of corporate bonds to offset the anticipated 10-point decline. *This change in the dollar value of a hedged asset divided by the change in the dollar value of a hedge instrument is the hedge ratio.* Arriving at changes in dollar values requires a careful analysis of yield relationships.

Analysis of yield relationships—and consequent price estimates—should be based on a number of considerations. First among these, of course, is analysis of the historical norm. Historical information will provide insight into the relationship of differing obligations. It is, therefore, a necessary starting point. But it is by no means sufficiently reliable to permit projections based solely on such analysis.

The hedged investor usually considers where the market is at any given point in time with reference to the full cycle. At the upper limit of historical observations? At the lower limit? A historical average, while relevant over the long term, may not prove sufficient for shorter-term hedges. Knowing where the obligations are currently in the cycle will help define the likely track of yields during the hedge period.

Sometimes, of course, the historical relationship may no longer be relevant at all. A change in government regulatory policy, a major corporate or municipal default, for whatever reason, things change. And the successful hedger can never take the historical data for granted. Some assumptions about the likely new yield relationships must be made.

To achieve the "most efficient" hedge,[7] the one that eliminates as much price variation as possible and comes closest to offsetting price moves in the hedged instrument dollar for dollar—periodic adjustments may be necessary.

---

[6] This move is usually calculated by dividing the change in the value of cheapest to deliver by its factor. The result is the futures equivalent price.

[7] For more precise analysis of hedge construction, see Chapter 16.

After-hours delivery risk

For investors holding long positions, the after-hours market in cash bonds is of special importance. As noted earlier, trading in futures closes at 3 P.M. (EST). Cash bonds, however, continue trading until 5 P.M.(EST). As a result, the cash market can change at any time within that two-hour interval without futures being able to adjust until the next day.

During the normal course of the contract, this presents no great problem. The futures simply open the following morning at a price reflecting the previous day's after-hours activity. However, once the contract is trading in its delivery month, the long is vulnerable to the extent that the short can choose any day to deliver. The short has until 8 P.M. (EST) on any given trading day to notify the Board of Trade of his intent to deliver. This allows the short to purchase bonds in the after-hours market and deliver them against *that* day's closing contract price. If cash bonds decline in after-hours trading, and the short buys bonds and notifies the CBT of his intent to deliver, the long will be obligated to pay the closing price for his futures—a price that has since become too high relative to the cash instrument.

Let's say a short chooses to hedge $1 million in 14 percent bonds with bond futures. The short determines the hedge ratio and shorts 16 contracts. Thus, three options are open when the contracts reach their settlement month:

1. He can close out six of his contracts and deliver against the 10 remaining.
2. He can close out all his contracts and sell the cash bonds.
3. He can purchase an additional $600,000 of 14 percent bonds and deliver against all his contracts.

In the event of a decline in the after-hours market, the third option will become attractive to the short, for he can now buy additional bonds cheaply relative to the price he will get for them.

The higher the coupon of the cheapest-to-deliver issue, the greater the risk to the long. That's because the higher coupon implies a higher factor built into the hedge ratio. The long's exposure is that much greater.

This after-hours market activity can act to inhibit the full convergence of an expiring bond contract to the cash bond value. This is even more likely at the end of the delivery month, when the contract stops trading and its price is fixed. (Not surprisingly, speculative activity is increased at this point in the trading cycle.)

BOND SPREADS

Like the cash-to-futures spread (the basis trade), the futures-to-futures spread (e.g., December 1983-March 1984) creates short-term rates, assuming a given market level. It may be a less distinct process, but it does exist. By establishing a spread (that is, being long one contract on which you can take delivery and short another into which you can make delivery), the hedger can effectively create a short-term instrument.[8] The spread in bond contracts, like the cash-to-futures spread, is a short-rate surrogate. As such, it is important to the hedger choosing to use either near or back contracts.

Understanding this relationship is especially useful when the yield curve could change. If you expect to remain hedged for a long period of time, you can put on back contracts effectively to secure today's yield curve. The risk of unknown and undesirable convergence costs resulting from rolling back a near contract hedge position can thus be avoided.

PRICING CONSIDERATIONS

Because the Treasury-bond market is so well arbitraged, it is probably as nearly perfect a market as an investor can expect. Nevertheless, there is no such thing as a truly perfect market. And there are certain short-term aspects that can make this long-term Treasury-bond market behave differently from one that is theoretically perfect.

To begin with, the futures market is, from time to time, expensive or cheap relative to cash—even after adjustment of estimated carry cost. This means bond futures tend to lead the cash market as major price changes reflect investor expectations due to the greater liquidity of bond futures relative to cash. This anticipatory nature of the market is, however, usually brought back into line quickly through arbitrage.[9]

Technical trading can also temporarily move prices out of line. Commodity mutual funds executing large stop loss orders, for example, can bring selling pressure to bear in a given contract month. Once again, it is arbitrage that accounts for necessary corrections.

Price dislocations that take place in a shifting market environment (or one that is perceived to be shifting) can be of somewhat longer duration. This might occur when Treasury offerings increase or the Federal Reserve signals an intention to change policy. The arbitrage

---

[8] Spreads do not reflect a short rate, as bills do, but rather a relationship between long- and short-term rates. Changes in market levels, independent of short-term interest-rate changes, can affect spreads. For example, if short-term rates are constant at 10 percent, whereas long-term rates are moving up (the yield curve is becoming positive), bond-market prices will move. Your spread may have been initiated at 70 on the buy side and 69½ on the sell side. If the buy side moves up to 75, the spread between the two contracts is likely to change. The constant short rate and higher principal to finance upon delivery of the first contract imply a narrower spread at this higher market level. Adjustment for this can be made, but such adjustments can be complicated and are not generally significant for hedgers.

[9] The process is a bit more sluggish when the arbitrage involves buying futures and selling cash, because of certain advantages that the short has as a result of the structure of the contract.

community begins to speculate about a change in the cheapest to deliver, depressing futures relative to cash more than would otherwise be the case. To the extent that prices are not in line with what the hedger would expect, given cheapest-to-deliver and other considerations, he might suspect this type of activity. This provides a sophisticated sort of technical indicator, which might be used to assess market direction.

If the long holds his contract until trading stops (eight business days prior to the end of the delivery month), the after-hours risk becomes much greater. The cash market could decline over the full six days, with the short choosing to deliver only at the end of such a decline. Alternatively, the cash market could post a gain after the contract stops trading. In that case, the long might pay less for a delivered bond than it is worth. In either case, by holding a contract to the very end, the long has significantly reduced his own options; he is no longer able to close out his position in futures.

In general, though, a hedger will be "out" of his contract—either by liquidating or rolling prior to the delivery month. And the effect of after-hours trading is relevant only to the extent that it affects estimated convergence. This effect is more noticeable in highly volatile markets, when high-coupon bonds are the cheapest to deliver or close to it.

The bond market is actually as nearly perfect a futures market as can be found. And the fact that some market inefficiencies do exist should not deter the potential hedger. What is important is that the hedger evaluate the impact of inefficiencies on rates of return.

8

Treasury notes

Ten-year Treasury notes are a relatively new entrant on the financial futures scene. Trading in them began on the Chicago Board of Trade in May 1982. To date, the volume of trading has been comparatively light.

They were designed to provide an intermediate-term hedge instrument free of some of the complications associated with GNMAs ("Ginnie Maes"), the other intermediate-term contract traded on the board. (GNMA contracts are discussed in detail in Chapter 9.)

The note future is essentially an "adjunct" contract, combining the credit characteristics of the bond contract (both are tied to Treasury issues) with the maturity characteristics of Ginnie Maes (both have intermediate-term maturities). Its immediate appeal was for hedging 10-year instruments and serving as an intermediate-term instrument when market conditions favored this. The note future could also be used to do spread trades aimed at anticipating changes in yield relationships. Bond-to-GNMA spreads had been a primary maturity-spread vehicle; but they incorporated an element of basis risk associated with GNMA issues as opposed to government issues.

The introduction of trading in Treasury-note futures enabled spread traders to separate sector and maturity judgments. As a result, spreads designed to profit from changes in sector relationships can now be done by taking offsetting positions in the Treasury-note and GNMA contracts. Curve trades, designed to take advantage of changes in the yield spread between intermediate- and long-term Treasury bonds can also be positioned.

CONTRACT CHARACTERISTICS

The board modeled the Treasury-note contract after the existing contract for Treasury bonds. Both are $100,000 principal value contracts assuming a deliverable issue with an 8 percent nominal coupon. As such, the same factor delivery process (including after-hours delivery consideration) occurs, with factors for deliverable issues calculated for each delivery month. Factor-adjusted settlement prices, compared with estimated market values of deliverable notes, determine cheapest-to-deliver issues; this, in turn, influences contract pricing. The contract trades in 32nds of a point—each point valued at $1,000, with 1/32 worth $31.25—and is subject to the same daily trading limits as the Treasury-bond contract. Contract mechanics are virtually the same for both.

Instruments acceptable for delivery under the contract include Treasury notes ranging in maturity from 6-1/2 to 10 years. As with bonds, the issue with the longest maturity is the one most likely to be delivered.

By making the note contract so similar to the bond contract, the board made it easy for traders already familiar with the one to participate in the market for the other. It also made the newer contract occasionally, if not often, expendable—and, with regard to pricing, somewhat undependable. Similar results may well be accomplished by trading in bonds.

Let's go back to the insurance company loan discussed in Chapter 6. If the company were seeking to lock in a 10-year rate, it would be better reflected by intermediate-term (as opposed to long-term) rates, and that would make the Treasury-note contract seem the better match. However, the bond contract may become equally useful with appropriate adjustment of the hedge ratio. In this situation, though, one would have to deal with the maturity mismatch; but this is normally manageable.

Bond versus note contract

In choosing between the use of note contracts and bond contracts, the hedger will have to weigh the contract specifications, liquidity, and yield-curve risk of each. The stated prices of bond and note contracts is different because of their different maturities. Both may offer roughly the same yield levels, yet quoted prices may be 85 for notes, for example, and 75 for bonds. This difference in dollar prices reflects adjusting to 8 percent, as called for by the respective contracts, over different maturities.

The shorter maturity of Treasury notes also influences factor settlement—which is more easily understandable if you think of the delivery factor as a premium (or discount) paid for an instrument yielding other than 8 percent. Suppose you can buy two instruments today, a 14 percent coupon with 30 years to maturity or a 13 percent with 10 years to maturity. Assume the price of each bond will yield 8 percent to first call. That price amounts to 167-28/32 for 30-year and 133-31/32 for 10-year instruments today.

How much would you be willing to pay for each of these in three months if yields stayed at 8 percent?

The passage of three months will have a greater impact on the value of the 10-year note, because it represents a larger fraction of the time to maturity than would be the case with a 30-year bond. If an investor were willing to pay equal prices this month for the two instruments, then the premium he would be willing to pay for the 10-year note next month should be less than that he would be willing to pay for the 30-year bond. In other words, the factor for the intermediate-term instrument will have declined more rapidly than the factor for the long-term instrument. For the short who plans to deliver into the Treasury-note contract, this factor slippage can be significant and will affect determinations of cheapest to deliver with greater impact than is the case with bonds. Naturally, these differences are important in determining which market best fits the individual hedger's needs. A major consideration is the Treasury's quarterly auction of notes, because the issue just auctioned is eligible for delivery and is usually expected to be the cheapest to deliver. Such an issue has a longer maturity, so it is likely to be the cheapest to deliver in almost any market environment. (There are also quarterly bond auctions, but their impact is diminished because of the relatively small difference in factor-adjusted values between outstanding and newly auctioned issues.)

In general, it will take a large difference in coupon to negate the outstanding issue's maturity disadvantage and make it the cheapest to deliver. For example, a sharp rally in the spring of 1983 caused a 10-7/8 note to be issued at the May auction. Normally the newest issue is expected to be the cheapest-to-deliver issue. However, the previous issue was a 13-3/4 note. That note traded cheaply relative to the 10-7/8 due to the 13-3/4's high premium; and this caused the higher coupon to be preferred for delivery.

Pricing note contracts

We have observed that Treasury-bond contract prices tend to track the cheapest-to-deliver issue. The fact that market dynamics tend to favor delivery of a newly auctioned issue in satisfaction of the note contract creates a particular pricing problem, because prior to each quarterly auction, the coupon for the new issue is unknown. Current yield must be used as a base for estimates, and this creates pricing uncertainty. Such uncertainty contributes to both short-side risk and hedging imprecision, because there is, in effect, no definable coupon for the contract to trade against.

If all else is constant each quarter but yields change sufficiently to warrant a new issue, trading in the first one or two contracts can be done using the following gauge of economic price relationships (or spreads): If the auction were held today—i.e., at this yield level—where should the contract prices be?

Contract pricing thus reflects the assumption of a full 10-year factor but still incorporates the uncertainty surrounding cheapest to deliver.

As an example, suppose you own a 10-year note and short the note contract to protect against a rate rise. The contract is priced off the expectation that a full-factor note (the issue to be auctioned) will be delivered. Suppose, further, that the Treasury decides to reopen last quarter's 10-year note, now a 9-3/4-year note. The reopened issue provides no factor advantage relative to the outstanding issue, and both will be subject to a higher price at delivery because of the slightly lower factor. As participants in the market become concerned about this possibility, the contract price will be bid up to reflect the higher deliverable value inherent in the deliverable note. The market has not changed, but the pricing imprecision in the Treasury-note contract has caused the contract price to move up against the short.

There is yet another "known" situation for the short who is trading in the contract. If prices have already adjusted in anticipation of a reopening, but because of market level change a new coupon and maturity is auctioned, the short will benefit to the extent that the contract price adjusts to the new bond. This situation would obviously be detrimental to the long.

The risk due to market adjustment for a reopening has at times run to about 12/32 of a point per futures contract. This must be weighed against the potential imprecision (due to maturity mismatching) of hedging with the bond contract to determine whether to use one market over the other.

Using the note contract

Because there isn't always a definable coupon on which to base contract pricing, the most useful application of this market involves shorter-term trading. For the hedger with a longer-term perspective, there is a risk entailed in rolling over from one contract to the next because of pricing imprecision in the market; the short hedger always has to take the risk of a reopening.

The uncertainty related to cheapest to deliver affects the ability of arbitrageurs to maintain cost-of-carry spread relationships in this market. Without knowing what coupon is likely to be delivered, assessing the cost of carry is necessarily inexact and structural factors in the market create more risk. Current yields provide some insight regarding the deliverable coupon, but they are only a general measure in a situation in which specific valuation would be ideal.

Of equal, if not greater, significance is the impact of this uncertainty on market liquidity. The market in Treasury notes has so far averaged only 3,000-4,000 contracts a day, slightly better than 5 percent of the contract volume in Treasury bonds.

Like bonds, the notes trade on a March quarterly cycle; but there are generally just four contracts trading at any one time, the farthest one a year out. Of these, the nearest two account for the bulk of activity in the market. The difficulty in assessing what might happen three auctions ahead makes pricing highly tenuous in the back-contract months.

In the final analysis, the Treasury-note market is largely professional. Current participants include commercials (professionals) and corporate traders (i.e., traders with short-term goals). That, plus the fact that the contract is not really a unique instrument, would tend to suggest that the hedger often could do equally well, if not better, in another market—Treasury bonds, most likely.

The applications of the bond and note markets are basically the same. There is simply less precision in notes.

9

GNMA

The existence of an established forward market based on Government National Mortgage Association (GNMA, or Ginnie Mae) certificates suggested something to the Chicago Board of Trade: namely, that a futures contract based on the delivery of a principal amount of such certificates would provide a good start for the development of a market in financial futures.

Like forward commitments in the insurance industry (delayed-delivery loans), the mortgage-forward market suffered from the fact that it was private, there was little price accountability, liquidity was limited, and no explicit guarantees backed agreements. Additional problems entailed the lack of margin rules and difficulty in checking on a party's credit. These characteristics led to situations in which traders for institutions had committed to purchase substantial amounts of forward mortgages without the knowledge of the institutions. Subsequently, the market has gone against them and the institutions have found themselves with the prospect of paying for highly depreciated securities. When questions arise as to whether the institutions will make good to the other side, there are repercussions throughout the market.

Despite such instances, the advent of futures trading in Ginnie

Maes did not portend an end to forward trading. For mortgage bankers comfortable with the creditworthiness of their customers, the forward market, although essentially unregulated, can provide a satisfactory means of securing commitments. Forward contracts might be preferred to futures because the former are priced in line with current mortgage origination rates, and because forward market participants are not required to pay margin. The futures market represents an alternative means of dealing in future mortgage delivery for mortgage bankers and other traditionally large users of the forward market. It is not, however, an alternative that has obviated the usefulness of the forward market.

THE CASH MARKET

Ginnie Maes are pass-through (principal and interest are "passed through" from the borrower to the sponsoring agency), mortgage-backed certificates with timely payment of principal and interest guaranteed by the Government National Mortgage Association. Whereas traditional corporate or government intermediate- and long-term bonds, because of their standardized terms and liquid markets, are relatively attractive investment securities, typical individual home-owner mortgages represent highly illiquid, nonstandardized instruments with a limited secondary market; thus, they carry an interest-rate premium. GNMA was created as one response to a national economic policy that favored attracting private capital to residential housing. The agency issued its first certificates in 1970, thereby opening mortgage investment to the institutional investor.

The life of a certificate starts when an issuer, such as a mortgage banker, commits to issue a FHA or VA mortgage. The mortgage banker will typically issue mortgage commitments for a number of houses and, as the mortgages are assumed by borrowers, will finance them through short-term borrowing until the necessary paperwork has been completed. Often, during this period, such an issuer will sell forward or future contracts as protection against adverse market action before he has fully documented mortgages to sell. Upon completion of the documentation, the issuer can "pool" several mortgages.

Such a pool of documented mortgages—in an amount not less than $1 million for private homes or $500,000 for project or mobile home—can be taken for GNMA certification. The pool thus becomes a Ginnie Mae pool with, as stated above, the timely payment of interest and principal guaranteed by the U.S. government. This endorsement makes GNMA a much more salable, standized instrument. GNMA subsequently will issue new certificates in minimum denominations of $25,000 original principal plus increments of $5,000.

Ginnie Mae certificates pay interest monthly, unlike bonds which usually pay interest on a semiannual basis, making yields higher than equivalent bond rates. Each monthly GNMA payment contains both interest and a certain amount of principal payment. Because total payments are constant—and calculated to pay off the mortgage over 30 years—the principal component rises as a percentage of total payments as the years go by.

Each pool of GNMA mortgages has a stated maturity of 30 years, but otherwise is distinct. The amount of money originally placed in the pool will differ, as will the rapidity of principal repayment. With government and other agency bonds, there is a fixed maturity and/or call date at a set price. GNMAs, however, are always prepayable at the mortgagee's option. In a period of falling rates, homeowners will tend to prepay mortgages somewhat faster than they will in a period of rising rates. In addition, during periods of greater housing mobility, one would expect a higher rate of prepayments than would be the case when mobility is restricted.

When the agency was created, it was assumed that certificates would be prepaid, on average, during the 12th year. Actual experience has shown an average prepayment rate significantly more rapid than that. Given the secular trend toward higher rates during the past decade, the more rapid "paydown" (prepayment), probably reflects both greater mobility among homeowners due to job changes, and the increasing ability to afford new and better housing.

Ginnie Maes have successfully bridged an institutional investment gap and made mortgages more salable to institutions; however, they should and do carry interest-rate premiums because of:

1. Greater administrative problems relative to normal Treasury instruments. (The monthly receipt of changing amounts of both principal and interest creates bookkeeping complications.)
2. The relative difficulty of secondary trading in these issues, compared with other government issues, despite some $135 billion of GNMAs outstanding.

Maturity uncertainty, together with the effects of the housing cycle on supply and demand in GNMA markets, causes GNMA rates to fluctuate more than intermediate-term Treasuries over the business cycle. This makes the timing of the effects of these "special" factors difficult to gauge. In periods of greater activity in mortgage origination, there is a constant flow of newly-created mortgages. This generates selling in futures or forwards, placing Ginnie Mae yields under pressure relative to Treasuries. In times of high housing demand, savings and loan institutions may sell GNMAs from their portfolios to fund new mortgages, thus further increasing relative rates.[1] Also, during periods of rising rates, prepayments become less likely and

---

[1] The broader range of activities recently made available to savings institutions might dampen the institutions' impact in this regard.

Ginnie Maes tend to trade on longer maturity assumptions. Conversely, in periods when interest rates are lower, Ginnie Maes tend to trade on the assumption of more rapid paydowns. These characteristics tend to influence the prices of GNMA futures.

CONTRACT CHARACTERISTICS

The board's Collateralized Depository Receipt (CDR) GNMA contract was introduced in 1975. It was the first successful interest-rate futures contract. In addition to attracting investors previously trading in the forward market, GNMA futures began to attract others who viewed it as a vehicle for hedging or substituting for price risks within government or other fixed-income markets.

Whereas many early traders in GNMAs used the market largely to effect tax spreads, other market participants saw the GNMA contract as a potential intermediate-term vehicle. With an average life of somewhat more than seven years, Ginnie Maes complemented the later-arriving Treasury-bond (long-term) and Treasury-bill (short-term) contracts.

Actual and potential users of the GNMA futures market include mortgage bankers, savings and loan associations, real estate investors, builders, and others whose primary business involves rate exposure in the mortgage market or whose investment activity entails mortgage-rate risk. Also, as mentioned above, GNMA futures can be used to hedge against price risk in other assets.

The GNMA contract is a much more complicated trading instrument than the Treasury-bond (or Treasury-note) contract. Although contract characteristics as well as pricing and delivery-notice procedures are the same as for bonds. Ginnie Mae's liquidity is perhaps one-tenth that of the bond contract. The contract trades on a March quarterly cycle, with the short choosing what to deliver and when. The GNMA contract stipulates delivery of $100,000 principal value of GNMA certificates with an assumed coupon of 8 percent. Adjustments are made by a factor to compensate for delivery of certificates with interest rates other than 8 percent. The contract trades in 32nds of a point, with the dollar equivalent of one point being $1,000.

The delivery process

The application of GNMA delivery factors differs procedurally from that of bond factors. Whereas current settlement prices were adjusted by the factor to effect delivery of a constant principal amount of bonds ($100,000), settlement price is kept constant for delivery of Ginnie Maes; and the principal amount of GNMA certificates to be delivered by the short is made equivalent to $100,000 of 8 percent by application of the relevant factor. Accordingly, if the June 1983 contract settlement price is 72-16/32, the long would pay $72,500 for the GNMA certificates delivered (subject to accrued interest and the 2-1/2 percent rule explained below) regardless of which are delivered. The par value that the short must deliver depends on which issue he opts to deliver. For a 13-1/2 percent GNMA with an associated factor of .707214, the short must deliver $70,721.40 principal amount for which he will be paid $72,500.

As is true in Treasury bonds, there is usually a cheapest-to-deliver issue. For the short to break even in the instance cited above, he must be able to buy 13-1/2 percent GNMAs at a price of 102.515 (72,500 ÷ 70,721.40 X 100). In other words, the price of the GNMA (102.515) times the relevant factor (.707214) should at least equal the futures price (72-16/32) for the short to break even. Multiplying by the appropriate factor the prices at which various coupon Ginnie Maes can be purchased, and comparing this amount with contract prices, will determine the cheapest-to-deliver—which, in general, will be a higher-coupon GNMA.[2] If current GNMA yields are lower than the cheapest-to-deliver high coupons, hedgers may face substantial basis risk.

The short need not necessarily deliver Ginnie Maes of a single coupon to satisfy the terms of the contract. He could deliver $50,000 of 8 percent equivalent 13-1/2 percent with a factor of .707214 ($35,360.70 par value) and $50,000 of 11 percent with a factor of .817349 ($40,867.45 par value) or any other combination which amounts to $100,000 equivalent value.

Delivering exactly the dollar amount of Ginnie Maes dictated by the relevant factor could put significant pressure on the short. It would require finding a precise combination of outstanding par amounts; and, while investors occasionally do mix deliverable certificates, it is almost impossible to match the value precisely. As a result, the Chicago Board of Trade has built a 2-1/2 percent tolerance into the deliverable value allowed, so that a short can deliver between $97,500 and $102,500 par amount of 8 percent GNMA or equivalents. Within this tolerance, variations from the $100,000 total are settled in cash.

This rule provides needed flexibility. But, because of the lack of factor adjustment on the portion settled in cash, it also affects the potential gain or loss to the short and can influence the instrument a short chooses to deliver and the contract price.

Suppose, as above, a short delivers 13-1/2 percent GNMAs in satisfaction of the June 1983 contract settling at 72-16/32. Based on the 2-1/2 percent rule, 13-1/2 percent GNMAs with a par value ranging from $68,953.37 (97,500 X .707214) to $72,489.44 (102,500 X

---

[2] One important point is that these factors reflect the assumption that GNMA prepayment will take place by the 12th year (despite a stated maturity of 30 years). As discussed in the cash-market description, the prepayment rate will vary, and contract prices will reflect this. Thus, with application of the factor at delivery, the return implied by the 12-year assumption will not necessarily be captured: prices will shift to reflect differing prepayment rates.

.707214) can be delivered. Suppose the short can find and deliver $71,500 par amount of 13-1/2 percent. He owes $70,721.40 par amount. So the long must make a cash overage payment in addition to the settlement price of $72,500. The market value of the overage is $798.18 [(71,500 − 70,721.40) × 1.02515, where 1.02515 is the market value of 13-1/2 percent GNMA]. But this is *not* the amount paid by the long. Instead, the excess principal is converted to its 8 percent equivalent value and compared with $100,000 to calculate the overage payment:

$$(A) \; \$ \; 71,500 \div \$70,721.40 \; = \; \$101,100.93$$
$$(B) \; \$101,100.93 - \$100,000 \; = \; \$ \;\;\; 1,100.93$$

In this instance, the short gains to the extent that he can make the cash overage as high as possible. The total payment by the long equals $73,600.93 (72,500 + 1,100.93). The market value of the 13-1/2 percent GNMAs delivered by the short is $73,298.23 (71,500 × 102.515), resulting in a delivery gain to the short of $302.70.

Which certificates are available and in what combinations will dictate the degree to which a short can gain from this cash-settlement procedure. (Because the short controls the transaction, this procedure will presumably always result in a gain to the short.) Potentially, the combination of several coupons could maximize such overages; however, perhaps for administrative reasons, only one coupon is generally delivered and almost never more than two.

The long can in part be protected from substantial overage payments by demanding that each contract be settled separately. The short will be forced to find separate pieces of deliverable GNMAs to satisfy each contract and potentially reduce the cash payment to be made.

The CDR mechanism

At contract expiration, board rules call for deliverable instruments to be placed in a depositary bank rather than have the short directly deliver GNMAs to the long. Through a person called an *originator*, the short delivers to such a depositary bank $100,000 of GNMA 8 percent or equivalent. In turn, the long receives a Collateralized Depositary Receipt (CDR) from the depositary, and this can be converted into actual cash GNMAs on demand.[3]

The originator has the right to place any Ginnie Mae on deposit and to change the CDRs composition within a 12-day period following notification, provided there is always $100,000 of 8 percent or equivalent. The holder of a CDR receives interest monthly, at a rate of $635 per receipt. From the time he notifies the depositary of an

---

[3] Conversion takes 15 days after request by a CDR holder.

intent to convert, a long is entitled, retroactively, to the interest payable on the GNMA certificates subsequently delivered.

The CDR mechanism has some structural problems. Without an originator, a short cannot make delivery in satisfaction of the GNMA contract. The fact is, however, that there aren't many originators because of some potentially significant disincentives. Primary among these is the fact that, upon turning over the certificates, the short is paid and incurs no further risk. From that point on, the originator has full responsibility for maintaining the $100,000 equivalent principal amount with the depositary bank. Any paydown of principal that occurs while the CDR is outstanding (which could be indefinitely) must be replaced on an 8 percent equivalent basis with additional principal, by the originator. Briefly, the originator must purchase the deliverable GNMAs from the short and maintain their equivalent par value until the associated CDR is converted, even if a premium GNMA is paid off at par.

Originators are aware of this risk and take it into account when originating CDRs for premium GNMA pools with the potential for rapid paydown. This influences contract values.

The CDR mechanism poses potential problems for the CDR holder, as well. If a rapid-paydown GNMA is deposited as collateral, the CDR holder must rely on the ability of an unknown originator to replace any lost premium value. This is not guaranteed by the board, and only minimal margin is required of an originator. While these problems are more theoretical than real, and the CBT probably would protect the CDR holder, fiduciaries should be aware of these problems prior to taking delivery of a CDR.

Contract trading and pricing

Because the premise of a Ginnie Mae contract is a deliverable instrument with a 30-year maturity prepaid in the 12th year, and because the paydown can vary, contract trading can be affected significantly. In the first place, both changing maturity assumptions as well as supply and demand variables will have an impact on GNMA rates (which will fluctuate more than those of intermediate-term Treasuries over a business cycle). This will be reflected in contract pricing. Second, it becomes important to note, when paydown factors calculated for different GNMA pools (based on the amount of principal outstanding as of the first of each month) are available. In the period after May 31, 1980, there were reports of instances in which a few unwary buyers purchased GNMA cash pools of 13-1/2 percent builder loans with very high paydown factors. According to these reports, a significant percentage of principal was prepaid during the month of purchase. Because some purchases were made at prices approximating 113 percent of par, an immediate loss was realized when the principal payment for June was received.

Paydown factors should become available to the financial community on the fifth business day of the month. The movement from one month to the next is not always small, and investors should be aware of this risk, because prices will adjust in relation to changes in these factors. Likewise, there is the possibility of the cheapest-to-deliver issue being paid down or otherwise becoming unavailable. When this happens, contract prices will shift to reflect a new set of cheapest-to-deliver assumptions.

All these variables, combined with the unique nature of each outstanding GNMA pool, cause the pricing of GNMA futures to be more imprecise than pricing of Treasury-bond futures. This is reflected in the relative arbitrage opportunities of the two markets. Bonds have a well-established repo market and instant homogeneity of coupons and maturities; consequently, they are much more easily arbitraged than are Ginnie Maes, for which a fairly involved evaluation must be made to determine what package of deliverables is cheapest. There is a repo market for GNMAs, which helps arbitrage commercials keep the market in line. The rates available will be a function of the relative liquidity and marketability of the instruments offered as collateral. Because Ginnie Maes lack the homogeneity of Treasury bonds, repos are more difficult to do and carry a higher effective cost.

Characteristics of the GNMA cash market and the CDR mechanism contribute to the relative imprecision of pricing in this contract, compared with Treasury-bond futures.[4] After evaluating these factors, the hedging procedure used in GNMA futures is not unlike that for Treasury bonds. The contract tends to trade in line with a cheapest-to-deliver issue; and constructing a hedge involves evaluation of contract price activity vis-à-vis the cheapest to deliver and relating this to movement in the hedged asset.

For private mortgage holders, there is an advantage with regard to matching in the use of Ginnie Mae futures. For other investors, this contract can at times provide a reasonable short-term hedge instrument. The fact that the GNMA is not a very good delivery contract is, however, an important consideration, as this makes it somewhat more difficult and less precise to trade than other financial futures.[5]

---

[4] One additional arbitrage complication arises from the fact that an outstanding GNMA cannot really be shorted. It is distinct from other GNMAs; so the short could not be readily replaced. This also serves to limit arbitrage opportunities. A forward GNMA can be shorted against a long contract, but this introduces additional basis risk.

[5] Pending approval by the Commodity Futures Trading Commission, the CBT will begin to trade a new GNMA II future contract. This contract allows for delivery of actual GNMA and GNMA II certificates, as opposed to a CDR. Delivery may occur on the last three days of the delivery month. Delivery price is established in a manner similar to that for bonds, i.e., adjusting the futures settlement price by a conversion factor for the delivered coupon. To insure that the contract price will track current production of GNMA pools at the current market rate—making a cash-futures relationship more predictable—a 102.5 price cap and a six-month delivery "window" allowing for delivery of coupons in effect and issued within six months prior to and including the delivery month is specified. Final settlement will incorporate the 2½ percent variance allowed in the GNMA-CDR contract. If this GNMA II contract is successfully introduced, it could prove to be a valuable tool for hedgers.

10

Treasury bills

In 1976, the International Monetary Market (IMM) inaugurated trading in Treasury-bill futures—and, in so doing, established a market with potential applications for every money market participant. By mid-1982, the bill futures market was one of the largest, with daily volume averaging slightly over 30,000 contracts, although, in 1983, as short-term rates became less volatile, contract volume declined.

Trading has been far greater in bill futures than in either of the other two short-term markets: bank CD futures (with about 20 percent to 40 percent of the bill volume) and Eurodollar futures (with only about 10 percent to 20 percent of the bill volume.)

Numbered among the hedgers in this market are those investors whose cost of money is pegged to short-term rates. These include bank liability managers, corporate treasurers, and money managers affiliated with other financial and nonfinancial concerns with earnings linked to money market rates. The bill contract can be important in the management of asset/liability gaps and can provide the flexibility for banks to write fixed-rate loans. However, the fact that lending and borrowing rates of actual hedgers may track (but not mirror) Treasury-bill rates creates a basis consideration risk.

CONTRACT CHARACTERISTICS

The IMM's contract calls for the delivery of $1 million face value of 13-week Treasury bills. The deliverable supply of bills generally includes the last three months (the "tail") of a one-year or a six-month bill and the 13-week bill auctioned on the Monday prior to the contract settlement date. The contract-settlement date cycle has recently been changed specifically to accommodate the delivery of a one-year bill's tail. This helps avoid short squeezes because deliverable supply is increased by the amount of the previous one-year bill auction. Because arbitrage can be set up out to the fourth bill contract, liquidity in back contracts may improve. However, contract settlement dates, which used to be roughly the same for each delivery month, now vary from one delivery month to the next, and this causes overlaps and gaps in the periods the contracts cover.

Contract	Period covered Delivery date — Deliverable bill		Number of days (gap)/overlap
March '83	3/24/83	6/23/83	14
June '83	6/09/83	9/08/83	7
September '83	9/01/83	12/01/83	(21)
December '83	12/22/83	3/22/84	7
March '84	3/15/84	6/14/84	7
June '84	6/07/84	9/06/84	(21)
September '84	9/27/84	12/27/84	7
December '84	12/20/84	3/21/85	

The contracts are no longer as contiguous, as they once were, and those gaps and overlaps cause a timing problem for hedgers. Contracts trade on a March quarterly cycle with eight contracts generally outstanding. As with other futures, liquidity tends to be greater in the front contracts; but, for hedging relatively small amounts ($5 to $10 million), back-month liquidity is sufficient. Furthermore, liquidity problems tend to be a one-time concern—namely, when the investor is setting up the hedge—and can usually be circumvented at a give-up of just a few basis points.

Deliverable issues

Unlike that of bond, note, or Ginnie Mae contracts, T-bill futures' pricing entails a discount-adjustment mechanism. Accordingly, the price to be paid for the cash bill upon delivery is calculated based on the contract price at settlement. The bill-contract discount can be quickly calculated, because contract prices are quoted on an index

basis. A quote of 90.00 on the IMM indictes a 13-week bill for settlement at a 10 percent discount:

$$100.00 - \text{Index level} = \text{Discount}$$
$$100.00 - 90.00 = 10.00$$

A rise in the index indicates a decline in yields. This inverse relationship causes the index to move like the dollar price of a Treasury-bill,
rather than like the discount on Treasury bills quoted in the cash
market. Increases in the index, therefore, result in gains for the long
and losses for the short; decreases in the index result in gains for the
short and losses for the long.

The minimum price change for bills is one basis point, referred to
as an "01." Although the contract calls for delivery of 13-week bills
to facilitate trading, the value of each 01 is set at $25.[1]

$$\$1,000,000 \times .0001 \times 90/360 \text{ days} = \$25$$

If the contract price increases by 10 basis points, from 90.00 to
90.10, the long's profit would equal $250 per contract. The T-bill
contract is, in many ways, easier to understand than those described
in previous chapters. Essentially, there is only one deliverable issue.
According to contract specifications, the deliverable bill is the one
that matures 13 weeks after contract expiration. Hence, the complications related to factor and delivery mechanisms do not exist.

The question naturally arises as to why there is only one deliverable issue. As noted above, the deliverable supply will consist of:
(a) the just-auctioned 13-week bill, or (b) the tail of either the six-
month or the one-year bill. Because a bill is a discount instrument
that pays both interest and principal upon its maturity, the time period and the associated rate will be the same for any of the above
bills, making them indistinguishable. If any of these is being delivered
into the June contract, a trader knows he or she is buying or selling
the rate for the discrete period of time covered by the deliverable
bills' 13-week time span between June and September.

Treasury-bill futures involve a discrete deliverable instrument. This
tends to make them less disciplined, relative to each other, than are
either the bond or the GNMA contract. Each bill contract calls for
delivery of a specific bill—namely, the one that matures 13 weeks
after the delivery date. Thus, whereas the same bond or Ginnie Mae
could be deliverable for back-to-back contracts, the bill delivered
to satisfy a current contract will mature before delivery for the next
contract. With bond contracts, a trader could go long the front con-

---

[1] The 13-week bills are almost always 91-day instruments, which would imply a slightly
higher 01 value ($25.27). However, for most applications, this difference is not significant.

tract (June, for example) and short the subsequent contract (September) with the ability to take the delivery of a bond in June and redeliver the same bond three months later; the difference in contract prices would be primarily a function of anticipated cost of carry. On the other hand, the bill delivered into one contract is not deliverable into a subsequent contract. This makes relationships between contract months somewhat less definable.

Cash-futures relationship

As long as a trader can buy a cash instrument and sell futures with the intention of delivering, a primary cash-futures arbitrage will maintain relative price discipline. This can be done by purchasing the deliverable tail of the six-month bill and shorting the first bill future. As with bonds, the purchase of a cash instrument and sale of the appropriate future create a rate of return that can be compared to alternative investments of equivalent maturity. This type of transaction creates a synthetic short-term security: If the cash bill is held through delivery, the investor will earn the approximate rate of return expected when the position was put on.

Consider the market conditions prevailing in mid-1983:

June 9 cash bill	Discount 7.92
September 8 cash bill	Discount 8.02
June contract	Discount 7.94
Contract price: 92.06	

An investor could buy the September 8 bill and sell the June contract, intending to deliver on June 9. This creates a Treasury-bill position with effectively the same maturity as the June 9 Treasury bill, but at a yield approximately 50 basis points higher (see Appendix IV).

The return on this synthetic short-term security is assured only if the position is held through contract delivery. One variable not present in bonds is that if the investor chooses to reverse the position prior to delivery, the net return will be affected by market level as well as by spread changes. The market-level impact is due to the fact that the contract covers a static 90-day period with an 01 value of $25, while with the cash bill there is longer duration until delivery date. Hence, the value of the 01 is greater on the September 8 bill than it is on the contract.

This type of trade might well appeal to institutions wishing to create better yields than those available on equivalent Treasury bills. However, because this is still a Treasury-bill position, the yield created will not necessarily be higher than that available from other instruments that carry credit spreads, such as a certificate of deposit.

A second method of cash-futures arbitrage can involve the purchase of 13-week "when-issued" bills to be rolled forward to eventually own a deliverable issue. Each week, usually on Tuesday, the Treasury announces its intention to auction 13-week and 26-week bills on the following Monday for settlement the Thursday following the auction. Dealers can begin late that same Tuesday to trade in a when-issued market, which is a market for issues to be auctioned the following week. The price differential between the current 13-week bill and the when-issued bill is a function of the dealer's cost of carrying bills in inventory. The arbitrage—which keeps the spread between the Treasury-bill market and its future in line with short-term rates—is easily affected because of the leverage of the when-issued market, the bill market, and the futures market.

Suppose there were a difference of 100 basis points between the when-issued 13-week bill and the front bill contract. By determining the number of times that the arbitrageur would have to roll when-issued bills to end up owning the deliverable issue, the arbitrageur can calculate how many basis points per roll he can afford to give up before giving away the whole spread.[2] If, in this case, the issuance of a deliverable 13-week bill were 8 weeks away, the arbitrageur could afford to sell the previous week's bill and buy the new "when-issued" bill at an average cost of 12.5 basis points a week and come out even. This 12.5-basis-point give-up on the roll may be compared to a dealer's anticipated carry profit for one week.

There are difficulties in this arbitrage as well, most of them involving the uneven degrees of supply and demand for cash bills versus when-issued bills, repo rates, and market factors in the bill contract. For example, money-market fund activity affecting demand and the amount of Treasury issuance, which will alter a given week's supply of bills, can distort the price relationship between current and when-issued bills. This when-issued arbitrage-style trade is usually positioned against the front contract, which has the greatest liquidity. Retail participation and speculative activity can move the contract price, disturbing the cash-futures relationship and creating risk and opportunity for the arbitrage trader.

Thus, discrete deliverable issues make the role of arbitrage less well-defined in the bill market; and pricing relationships tend, at times, to be less precise.

A BASIC HEDGING EXAMPLE

Capitol Leasing Corporation is a major source of computer equipment available for rental in the New York metropolitan area. In

---

[2] The roll transaction is effected on a spread basis by closing out the position in the bill, which will be paid for on a Thursday, and simultaneously reestablishing the position in the 13-week bill most recently announced, which will not be paid for until the following Thursday.

December, Capitol Leasing plans to enter into an unusually large 18-month lease. The company knows both its equipment and its financing costs through March 15. After that, financing costs are an unknown. They may be higher; they may be lower; or they may remain the same.

Capitol Leasing knows the computer business and how to fix competitive rates associated with equipment costs. Because financing costs are variable, writing large lease agreements puts Capitol at risk to the extent that rates might rise and make those agreements unprofitable. Unwilling to risk an increase in interest rates, Capitol hedges.

Capitol's loan is going to be set for a three-month rate. The shorter loan period focuses on the near end of the yield spectrum, and this puts the emphasis on Treasury bill futures—or on one of the other short-term futures.[3]

To write an 18-month computer lease—from December 1983 through June 1985—Capitol needs to borrow money to finance its equipment. The financing is structured to cover three-month periods, with interest rates adjusted in December, March, June, and September. It is also pegged at 150 basis points above the 90-day Treasury bill rate on each rate reset date.

On December 15, Capitol shorts one March 1984 bill contract at 10 basis points above current bill rates. By buying back the March contract when it terminates on March 15, 1984, the company's base borrowing rate will be 10 basis points above the current bill level for the March through June period covered by the contract.

Suppose the current Treasury bill rate is 9 percent and the March contract rate is 9.10 percent, while Capitol's borrowing rate is 10.50 percent. As is true in all futures, the price of the bill contract will converge to the cash-market Treasury at contract expiration (see Chapter 6). If rates do not change at all, the contract will come down to 9 percent at expiration, and the short March position will decrease in value by 10 basis points.

March position at outset	9.10%
March position at expiration	−9.00%
Basis-point loss	.10%
Capitol's borrowing rate	10.50%
Basis-point loss	+ .10%
Effective hedged rate	10.60%

If rates go up to 10 percent, Capitol's December-March borrowing rate would increase to 11.50 percent, but the net hedged rate would be unchanged.

---

[3] Most of the procedural hedging considerations are the same for Treasury-bill, domestic bank certificate of deposit, and Eurodollar contracts. As a result, methodologies applicable to all three—as well as characteristics and hedging considerations specific to bills—will be discussed in detail in this chapter.

March position at expiration	10.00%
March position at outset	− 9.10%
Basis-point gain	.90%
Capitol's borrowing rate	11.50%
Basis-point gain	− .90%
Effective hedged rate	10.60%

Of course, if rates fall, the value of the hedge position will decline. Regardless of interest-rate moves, Capitol's borrowing rate for the last three months remains at 10.6 percent. This is now a given, rather than an unknown, factor in calculating the cost of doing business. By using the Treasury-bill contract, the company has established a financing rate today based on rates in the futures market for the second three months of the lease. By shorting subsequent contracts, the rate for the remaining term of the leasing agreement can be established without being subject to the risk of a major change in interest rates.

In the case of Capitol's loan, the company established a rate 10 basis points higher for the second three months, as compared with the current rate. Before putting on the hedge, Capitol would have evaluated the futures market rate; if the cash-futures spread had been 200 basis points, creating a three-month loan rate of 12.5 percent rather than 10.6 percent, the relative merits of putting on the hedge would have had to have been more carefully considered. Essentially, the hedge has helped Capitol achieve its objective of *eliminating the risk* inherent in variable borrowing costs.

Constructing the bill hedge

Mechanically, T-bill hedges are easy to construct. Each basis-point move in a bill contract results in a $25 change in value. Dividing the dollar variation (caused by any given basis-point change) anticipated in the item being hedged by 25 yields the number of contract basis points needed for the hedge. Dividing this total number of basis points required by the movement expected in 13-week bills during the relevant period gives the hedge ratio. This method isolates the cash-futures spread discussed in the following section from the principal rate movement on which the hedge is based (see Chapter 16).

$$\text{Number of contracts} = \frac{\text{Dollar variation in hedged item}/25}{\text{Basis-point move in 13-week cash bill}}$$

If Capitol Leasing finances $1 million, and its annual rate is 10.5 percent, the dollar variation caused by a rate increase to 11.5 percent (100 basis points) would be $2,500 for three months.

$$1\% \times \$1,000,000 \times 90/360 = \$2,500$$

The rate is pegged to the Treasury-bill rate, so the contract basis point move will presumably be the same: 100 basis points. Using the preceding formula,

$$\frac{\$2,500 \div 25}{100} = 1 \text{ contract}$$

By shorting one contract, Capitol Leasing can protect against movement in the Treasury-bill-determined financing rate for the months.

How would this analysis change if Capitol's financing were based on a three-month CD rate, instead? A change of 100 basis points would still imply a dollar variation of $2,500 per quarter. How much the contract moves would depend on the relationship of CD rates to bill rates. If it is determined that the cash bill will shift by 90 basis points, then 1.11 contracts would be shorted to protect against a shift in financing rates.

$$\frac{\$2,500 \div 25}{90} = 1.11 \text{ contracts}$$

In establishing the hedge, four major variables must be taken into account: the cash-futures spread, duration mismatch, basis, and variation-margin impact. These considerations are further illustrated in Chapter 17.

Cash-futures spread

Initially, Capitol Leasing Corporation's three-month loan cycle covered the same time periods as those of the contract, and the loan rate varied with the 90-day Treasury-bill rate. By selling bill contracts that directly matched the loan rate and contract time period, the hedge rate was easy to define—in that example, at 10.60 percent. Each contract position would be reversed when the contract had fully converged and its price equaled the 90-day bill rate. The hedge rate becomes more difficult to define when the hedge period does not match the contract cycle and exact convergence cannot be assumed. If the 90-day rate reset dates were changed from the futures cycle to the 15th of January, April, July, and October, Capitol would be exposed to some yield-curve risk stemming from the cash-futures relationship.

		Loan reset period						
		Period 1				Period 2		
Dec.	Jan.	Feb.	March	April	May	June	July	Aug.
	December contract			March contract				
		Contract Period						

In general, when the time period involved in hedges does not correspond exactly to the time period available in futures contracts, the potential for a hedge-rate variance must be considered.[4]

The cash-futures spread is a key element in determining the final rate realized on the hedge. This spread is created by the changes in bill contract prices relative to the 90-day Treasury-bill rate. Because we first assumed that hedges would be reversed when the contract price had converged to cash and this spread was zero, the spread became a known entity. Thus, Capitol's hedged rate for each period was the rate on the appropriate bill contract when the hedge was put on.

Once the loan agreement was changed to the January cycle, Capitol had to be concerned with interim changes in the cash-futures spread. This price spread is determined by carry cost and time. It will be affected by changes in market level and the yield curve. If market conditions remain similar to those at the time Capitol put on the hedge, the contract price will converge to cash in a fairly consistent fashion. However, changing market conditions will affect this convergence process. Suppose that, when Capitol shorted the June 1984 contract, its discount was 20 basis points higher than the cash discount for the current cash bill price of 9 percent. (That is, Capitol was attempting to establish a borrowing cost of 10.7 percent for the period from May through August.) Capitol could cover the contract on the reset date of May 15. If the contract had fully converged and cash 90-day bills had declined to 8 percent, the net loan rate for the period would be:

June contract at outset	9.20%
June contract at expiration	− 8.00%
Basis-point loss	1.20%
Capitol borrowing rate	9.50%
Basis-point loss	+ 1.20%
Effective new rate	10.70%

Suppose, however, that the 90-day rate was, in fact, 8 percent when the contract was offset; but, because of a more positive yield curve, the spread between the cash market and the June contract remained at 20. The net loan rate for the period would then be:

June contract at outset	9.20%
June contract at expiration	− 8.20%
Basis-point loss	1.00%
Capitol borrowing rate	9.50%
Basis-point loss	+ 1.00%
Effective new rate	10.50%

---

[4] Because contract delivery dates have recently been changed, creating a noncontiguous string of contracts, the problem of matching contract timing to the loan structure must often be considered.

Duration mismatch

Before Capital entered into the permanent financing agreement previously discussed, they were financing for variable 60-day periods at a rate linked to the 2-month Treasury bill. A hedge was put on for this period as well as for the longer-term agreeement. Capitol's strategy varied slightly to cope with the imprecision of hedging 60-day borrowing with a 90-day rate contract. Because this interim financing was for 60 days, each basis-point change in rates would affect Capitol's cost by $16.67 per million ($25 × 60 ÷ 90 days). Therefore, only two-thirds as many bill contracts are needed to cover this period and compensate for the duration mismatch.[5] Because the loan rate is now linked to the 60-day bill rate, but the contract trades to the 90-day Treasury bill, the final hedge rate would also be affected by changes in the relationship between 60-day bills and 90-day bills. Such yield-curve risk is minor when compared with the threat of absolute changes in market levels. In actual applications, this mismatch can be minimized.

Basis

Basis refers to divergence between the rate on the contract and other market rates to which the loan agreement is pegged. If Capitol's loan is tied to rates other than 13-week Treasury-bill rates, then basis risk would be taken into account. The example of a CD-based loan led to a hedge of 1.1 contracts. The judgment concerning relative movements of CD and bill rates implicit in this calculation will affect the accuracy of the hedge; willingness to take on such basis risk will depend on the alternatives available to the hedger. Sometimes, due to the relationship between the contract rate and the rate to be hedged, managing the basis can be part of a hedge strategy.

One commercial bank, for example, put on a hedge in bills knowing they had to issue CDs to fund a fixed-rate loan. But they built in a differential of roughly 250 basis points between the two and used a one to one hedge ratio. This was acceptable in the loan pricing, given market conditions at the time. The prospect of the spread being at 250 basis points for the entire term of the loan was unlikely. If rates declined, the bank would have gained to the extent that spreads would narrow. And that, in fact, is just what happened (see Chapter 17).

---

[5] If the duration of the hedged item changes daily, as would be the case with the hedge of a 26-week bill while the contract's 13-week duration remains constant, the hedge must be periodically revised. This is because the constant move of the cash bill toward maturity affects its 01 valuation.

We calculated the value of an 01 for a 13-week instrument at $25. The comparable value for a 26-week issue would be $50. For each day such a cash bill moves toward maturity, the 01 decreases in value by $0.27 − 0.28. This constant decrease will have an impact on the numerator of our hedge ratio formula, and the appropriate contract weighting will decline accordingly (see Appendix IV).

Variation margin financing

As is true in any futures transaction, the hedger must consider the effects of gains or losses from financing variation margin. For shorter-term hedges, variation margin is typically not significant; but, for longer-term positions, its effect must be weighed against that of other hedging variables. For example, the commercial bank referred to in the previous section took into consideration the fact that gains or losses in financing variation margin would tend to offset any gain or loss in the spread between bills and CDs.

Deferred-month hedges and stacking

In the preceding section, the time periods of the contracts sold closely matched the time periods to be hedged. Sometimes, either due to liquidity or spread considerations, hedgers choose to stack their position by selling or buying all front month contracts with the intent of rolling into the contract that directly covers the time period of the hedge at a later date.

Consider the following situation

	Contract price	Equivalent bill discount
Cash bills		10.00%
December contract	90.00	10.00
March contract	90.00	10.00

An issuer of CDs wishing to hedge rates for a period of six months has two alternatives—short one December and one March contract (the better time-period match) or short two Decembers and roll one forward into March when the December contract expires. What is the risk of each alternative if rates decline to 8 percent and stay there?

Alternative A

Short 1 December contract at 90.00, buy in at 92.00
Short 1 March contract at 90.00, buy in at 92.00

The average loss from the hedge position is 200 basis points. However, this will be made up in lower CD issuing rates. In this case, the hedger knows the rate level, regardless of change in cash rates.

Alternative B

Short 2 December contracts at 90.00
Offset 1 December contract at 92.00
Offset 1 December contract at 92.00, rolling into 1 March contract at 91.70
Offset 1 March contract at 92.00

Alternative B exposes the investor to yield-curve risk. As rates come down, the yield curve becomes more positive, as reflected in the new December-March spread of 30. For the first period (the period covered by the December contract), the hedger has a 10 percent rate; the 200-basis-point loss on futures is offset by lower CD issuance costs. For the second period, however, there is the additional expense of rolling into the March position—in this case, 30 basis points. Therefore, 10.30 percent is the best the hedger can do now. By *stacking* front contracts, the hedger has increased costs, on average, from 10.00 percent to 10.15 percent.

Stacking contracts—as opposed to selling a strip of contracts covering the hedge time period—involves decisions pertaining to the yield curve. The most conservative hedge would involve using a strip, regardless of spreads and the yield-curve scenario. To cover a two-year loan, for example, the hedger would be assured of a given rate by shorting all eight contract months, calculating the average give-up or gain from the spreads, and basing the loan on this value. Stacking may be desirable if the yield curve is so positive that the hedger feels the strip can more favorably be set up at a later time. This is less of a hedge, though, and more of a yield-curve judgment.

The experience of one major bank is classic in this regard. The bank undertook to hedge against short rates to offer fixed-rate loans in the summer of 1982, when the yield curve was inverted. To set up the hedge, they stacked the front contracts with the intention of rolling them into subsequent contracts. At this point in time, shorting a strip of contracts would have secured a rate below current rates, on average, because of the yield curve. The implication of stacking was that the yield curve would become *more* inverted—that the bank would gain by rolling into subsequent contract months rather than shorting them all now. With short rates at all-time highs, this was an unlikely scenario.

In fact, the yield curve reversed at that point and became positive. The bank then had three choices: cover the contracts and give up on the hedge; roll only to the next contract, which would have cost the bank a substantial number of basis points; or short a string of contracts at that point, which would have locked in this unfavorable yield-curve penalty for the life of the loan.

What went wrong? The bank's managers may have simply made a bad bet on the yield curve. Perhaps they did not realize that shorting the front contracts gave them level protection—but no yield-curve protection for the remaining period of time. Ideally, short positions should have been taken in all available (and liquid) contract months at the outset to ensure that the anticipated borrowing rate would be protected.[6]

In short, then, the hedger concerned with short-term rates can do most of what he wants to do by using bill futures. There are some exceptions, of course. Banks, for example, would like the ability to cover longer-term loans with this market. But it is generally recognized that the bill contract is a valuable tool. The rapid growth of the market in bill futures since its inception in 1976, attests to this.

[6] As discussed in Chapter 17, if for liquidity or other reasons stacking is to be done, the simultaneous purchase of bill spreads, can offset at least some portion of the spread risk as gains or losses in the spread positions offset changes in the roll cost.

11

Certificates of deposit

The CD contract lends itself to cash-management applications as well as some banking applications. It also tends to provide a better match for private rates than does the Treasury-bill market. Nevertheless, this contract remains very much the stepchild of the bill contract: It simply hasn't evolved into the big market some people expected.

Initially, three exchanges applied for, and gained approval for, trading CD futures. And, in 1981, within just a few months of each other, the Chicago Board of Trade, New York Futures Exchange, and International Monetary Market all unveiled their versions of CD futures contracts.

The IMM contract was ultimately successful—though to a lesser degree than its sponsors had hoped. For one thing, the International Monetary Market was the only exchange that had the advantage of bills trading on the premises. (The CD and bill pits are actually adjacent to one another on the IMM trading floor.) Then, too, it had a late-month delivery contract[1] that coincided with the delivery timing of its Treasury-bill contract. And, finally, the IMM undertook an aggres-

---

[1] Following cash market convention, CDs are designated as either early- or late-month instruments. As implied, late-month instruments mature in the latter half of the month, while early-month contracts mature in the first half.

sive marketing program for the CD contract aimed at maintaining the exchange's top position in money-market contracts.

Not suprisingly, trading in bill-CD spreads creates much of the liquidity in this market. Still, liquidity is very much confined to the front two contracts (out of four that are listed for trading). In 1983, average daily volume of CD contracts ran about 3,000 to 4,000 — slightly less than 25 percent of T-bill volume.

Actual and potential market participants would include institutions or corporations that want to use the contract as a cash-management tool; banks using asset/liability gap management to help adjust their CD portfolios; and variable-rate borrowers, including issuers of commercial paper (depending on spreads between CDs and commercial paper).

CONTRACT CHARACTERISTICS

The IMM contract calls for delivery of $1 million par value of CDs with approximately three months to maturity and trades on a March quarterly cycle. Like the bill contracts, CD futures are quoted off an index, with an 01 (worth $25) as the minimum trading unit. Unlike the bill contracts, CD futures are not discount instruments. They are 360-day, coupon-bearing instruments selling on a repo equivalent (360-day-year) yield. Thus, 100 minus the index level relates to a yield level in CD contracts. A quote of 90.50, for example, implies a yield of 9.50 percent.[3]

Contract deliverables

The deliverable CD must be issued by a top-tier bank, usually no more than three months prior to the delivery date. The term "top tier" refers to those banks with the best credit ratings; and their CDs are nearly interchangeable in the secondary market, where they generally trade on a "no-name" (anonymous) basis. These top-tier names trade at near equivalent yields; the money market jargon for this group of CDs is "on the run." However, for a given maturity or for credit reasons, some of these banks' certificates may trade slightly rich or cheap relative to others in the cash market.[3] This will have a bearing on what will be delivered into the CD contract. For, as with Treasury bonds, there is a cheapest-to-deliver cash instrument and that is the deliverable-grade CD with the highest yield.

---

[2] Because CD yields are calculated on a 360-day "year," they vary slightly from bond equivalent yields (365 days) often quoted for T-bills.

[3] Maturity considerations can, at times, be important. Usually, though, they are less significant than credit characteristics.

Generally speaking, a change in cheapest to deliver is not a dramatic influence. The IMM maintains a committee for selecting the deliverable names from one contract to the next. That selection is made about a week before the first delivery date of a contract. For that reason, credit risks that arise during contract trading can be accounted for.

In the summer of 1982, Continental Illinois National Bank and Trust Company was among the top-tier banks. Due to credit-related problems, however, the bank's CD rates diverged from those of others on the deliverable list. Had its name remained on the run, the CD futures contract would have traded in line with Continental's higher yield rather than the more expensive CDs. This would have been to the distinct disadvantage of holders of long positions in CD futures. Instead, Continental asked to have its name withdrawn from the list of deliverable certificates; and market price levels, more accurately reflecting the top-tier credit, were maintained.

Unlike the T-bill contract, which has one delivery day and one fixed-maturity deliverable instrument, CD futures have a range of delivery dates and a variable deliverable maturity. A delivery period, rather than a single day, makes this contract like the bond contract. As with bonds, the short determines what to deliver. Delivery may begin on the first business day after the 14th calendar day of the month. It ends on the final business day of the delivery month. Consequently, CDs delivered at the beginning of the period may have 3-1/2 months to maturity, whereas those delivered at the end of the period may have only 2-1/2 months to maturity. This variability is built into the contract to ensure an adequate deliverable supply and avoid squeezes.

The delivery period for the CD contract, in contrast to the bill contract, allows hedging with almost no time gaps. This is an advantage for the hedger contending with specific reset dates on a loan, for example, or for asset/liability gap management.

Because various deliverable CDs have slightly different maturities and coupons, each will have a slightly different 01 value—and, as a result, a most economical delivery day. The contract will converge to the appropriate deliverable CD. And, except when potential liquidity problems occur, a short can maintain his position through the end of the month. If a long is not planning to stay in a contract for delivery, he will likely be out before the delivery period begins.

As with other futures markets, the nature of the deliverable instrument has an impact on arbitrage opportunities and thus on cash-futures price accountability. Cash CDs are heterogeneous, each having its own coupon, maturity, and credit. With so many different deliverables, it becomes difficult to determine precisely where the contract will sell relative to cash. Also, given the choice of delivery dates and the fact that trading in CDs is based on yields—that take in accrued interest, which changes daily—the return on a cash-and-carry rate-of-return trade created by buying a deliverable CD and selling CD contracts, can vary greatly.

The spread between bill and CD contracts is well-traded. This intermarket trading helps maintain CD contract liquidity.

CONSTRUCTING THE HEDGE

Hedging in the CD futures market is much the same as hedging in the T-bill futures market. The same variables must be considered. In addition to variation-margin financing, these are:

Duration mismatch. The hedger must account for the varying dollar effect an equivalent yield change would have on the hedged item, relative to the contract. Say, for example, you want to hedge a 45-day commitment. The 45-day rate is such that a one-basis-point change in rate would serve to change interest costs by approximately $12.50 per million. You would have to sell one CD contract for every $2 million commitment.

Cash-futures spread. The CD contract covers a discrete period of time from the delivery date (when cash and futures converge) through the maturity date of the deliverable CD. Hence, while the December contract trades to reflect a 90-day period ending in the last half of March, the hedged item might cover a slightly different period of time (such as the 90-day period ending in the middle of April). Prior to the delivery period, the price of a CD futures contract will differ from the price of the anticipated cheapest-to-deliver certificate of deposit by an amount predominantly reflecting cost of carry. The hedger will set a target based on rates available in the futures market, taking into account the fact that the contract will converge to cash on the delivery date. Until that date, a spread between the futures market and the cash market will exist, creating some imprecision if the hedger chooses to close out the hedge prior to convergence.

Basis. The yield movement of the hedged item and the contract may diverge, resulting in some variance in the hedge results. For example, the asset or liability to be hedged may be set at some rate other than the CD rate but related to it While the two rates move in the same direction, the price or yield spread between the cash position and the futures contract might vary. This, of course, would affect the net result of the hedge.

Basis risk: An illustration

As in all futures markets, the hedger should be aware of trading problems that could have a negative impact on the success, or even the feasibility, of a hedge. A good example is the case of the Darnton Group, a financial intermediary that in January 1982 borrowed money for five years for lending purposes. Their borrowing rate was tied to the prime, an administered floating rate, and the group had the option of locking in a term rate at the end of any year. Darnton made a market decision that rates would decline—and, taking no steps to protect themselves against a rate rise, lent funds at a fixed five-year rate. Subsequently, rates moved against them. And Darnton became increasingly nervous.

With the prime up substantially, Darnton chose to look into CD futures. They were unable to short the prime directly, but they wanted to protect against rates going any higher. However, CD rates had moved even more rapidly upward, affecting the spread between a bank's cost and return on funds. Whereas a normal spread between the two rates at these yield levels might have been three or four points, it had narrowed to 1-1/2 points. This meant that the prime could rise with no accompanying movement in CDs; on the other hand, CD rates might decline substantially before banks lowered the prime. Or CDs might fall while the prime remained unchanged. Such a situation made a CD hedge relatively unattractive for the Darnton Group. On the other hand, the situation would have been quite attractive for hedgers going long the CD contract because there was a good chance then that basis risk would have worked for them rather than against them. While the prime rate did decline CD rates came down faster and the hedge would have only aggravated Darnton's problems.[4]

A HYBRID HEDGE

The use of CD contracts in combination with T-bill contracts can compensate for the relative problems of each contract. Let us say, for example, that you wanted to hedge a two-year commitment funded at the 90-day CD rate. Selling CD contracts to cover the life of the commitment would seem a natural strategy. However, CD futures are currently traded only in the first four contract months, and liquidity in the last two contracts is limited. One could hedge the liability to be incurred in the first year by selling the front two or four CD contracts and cover the remaining period by selling T-bill contracts of corresponding maturity.

To adjust for any variation between bills and CDs, three alternatives are available: (1) short the bills at a favorable spread to CDs;

---

[4] The Darnton Group could have gone forward with this hedge, if they felt strongly that rates *would* continue to climb, adjusting their hedge ratio to reflect the CD-prime relationship. If they believed that CDs would move up half as much as the prime, they could have shorted twice as many contracts. If rates came down, however, their risk would have been that much greater.

(2) stack forward CD contracts; or (3) adjust the hedge ratio for any divergence between bills and CDs (selling perhaps 1.1 bill contracts for every contract bought). Undertaking the first two alternatives is largely a function of market conditions. The third alternative can be undertaken at any time (see Chapters 10, 17, and 23).

The bill contract provides better back-month liquidity, whereas CD futures match the underlying commitment. If one is short back-month bill contracts during a period when market conditions are favorable, the hedger can switch over from bills to CDs and lock in the benefit (see Chapter 17). That's one of the advantages of this type of strategy.

12

Eurodollars

The Eurodollar time deposit contract is perhaps the least complicated of the three short-term contracts. Introduced by the IMM in December 1981, this contract was the first cash-settlement instrument; as such, it paved the way for introduction of stock index contracts.

Because it calls for cash settlement, there is no actual deliverable—and, hence, no physical delivery. The price at expiration is settled by a dealer survey on the level of the 90-day Euro time-deposit market, which is equivalent to the London Interbank Offered Rate (LIBOR). While an arbitrage trade can be simulated for this type of instrument, it is difficult to do.

CONTRACT CHARACTERISTICS

Like the other money-market contracts, the Eurodollar contract is for 90 days; it trades on a March quarterly cycle; and it is priced off an index, with 100 minus the index level relating to the underlying Eurodollar yield. Contract size is $1 million, so that the value of an 01 is $25—in keeping with those of the other money-market contracts.

There are four contracts currently traded, with liquidity greater in the front contracts. Contract settlement date is the second London business day before the third Wednesday of the contract month.

With regard to average daily volume, Eurodollar contracts trade more lightly than do CD contracts, which, in turn, trade more lightly than Treasury-bill contracts. While CD contracts posted daily volume of roughly 25 percent of T-bill futures in 1983, Eurodollar contracts traded about 15 to 20 percent of the volume in T-bills futures. Liquidity is aided by spread tables against both bills and CDs.

The Eurodollar contract tends to trade parallel to a comparable maturity CD, subject to the influence of reserve requirements for domestic CDs and political events. For this reason, there are few substantive uses of this market beyond those for CDs.

HEDGING

The applications of this market are much the same as those for the CD futures market. Banks, in particular, for whom Eurodollars represent an alternative source of funding, might find the use of the Eurodollar contract attractive. The large participants in this market are, in fact, major international banks. A common use of this contract is for creating a synthetic longer-term Eurodeposit (see Appendix V).

Hedging considerations associated with this contract are similar to those outlined for bill and CD futures. They include duration mismatch, cash-futures spread, basis, and variation-margin impact. (See Chapter 10 for a discussion of Treasury bills.)

Spreads between Eurodollar and CD contracts are well traded, and the two rates tend to move pretty much in tandem. If the yields implied in a March CD contract rise relative to a March Eurodollar contract, a spread trader can buy the CD contract and short the Eurodollar contract in anticipation of a subsequent narrowing of the spread. There are exceptions, of course. Cheapest-to-deliver changes can affect the CD side, whereas world events may move the Eurodollar side. But, in general, the two will move together.

A direct arbitrage of Eurodollar contracts to cash is difficult, if not impossible, because of the non-negotiable nature of Eurodollar time deposits. Because contract prices tend to move in line with CD and bill contracts, which are arbitraged to cash, a good measure of pricing discipline prevails.

Eurodollar contracts, like CD contracts but unlike the bill contract, are contiguous. This makes it easier to set up a hedge with regard to timing, because there are no gaps or overlaps. Using the two contracts— much the same way one might use the hybrid CD-bill hedge—can help to improve liquidity. And trading in a cash-settlement instrument does away with the uncertainty related to a cheapest to deliver.

13

Stock indexes

A cash stock index[1] is the underlying "instrument" for stock-index contracts; it represents a composite of stock prices. A trader in such an index purchases or sells the weighted price and dividend activity of those stocks. Thus, someone purchasing the component parts of the S&P 500 index is doing more than making an investment based on market direction. The investor has bought the volatility of a specific group of stocks.

A stock-index future is the obligation to purchase or sell the underlying index at an agreed-upon price and time.

CONTRACT CHARACTERISTICS

Three separate stock-index contracts began trading in the first half of 1982: the Value Line Index on the Kansas City Board of Trade (KCBT), the S&P 500 Index on the Index and Options Market (IOM) of the Chicago Mercantile Exchange, and the NYSE Index on the New York Futures Exchange (NYFE). By the middle of 1983,

---

[1] We refer to a stock index as a "cash stock index" or a "cash index" to differentiate between it and the stock-index future.

with less than one year of trading, volume in these contracts had grown so rapidly that the S&P 500 alone ranked among the top five contracts available for commodities trading, and the value of stock represented by the combined trading of these contracts often approached the value of trading on the New York Stock Exchange.

In 1983, the IOM introduced a contract of smaller denomination, based on the S&P 100. It trades in line with the S&P 500, but it has a lower value.[2]

The immediate appeal of these contracts appeared to some observers to lie with speculators, because the leverage inherent in the contracts makes it possible to "play" the market with relatively little capital. However, the liquidity, cost effectiveness, flexibility, and anonymity of these markets—together with the fact that they offered the first real substitute for market-index fund investments—began to encourage more conservative types of hedge applications.

As an investment alternative to a cash-index position, a stock-index future has the potential for a more attractive rate of return, and it often provides more flexibility. Managers of equity portfolios, large or small, can use stock-index contracts to increase or decrease the systematic risk (general market risk) inherent in their positions; to transact future equity purchases or sales at current market levels; and to create a stock-based money-market instrument.

Each of the three major contracts is written on a broad-based market index. The S&P 500 Index contract is based on the Standard & Poor's 500 Stock Price Index, which is a market-weighted index with each company's stock represented in proportion to its respective market value. The S&P 500 is a widely recognized measure of the general market, commonly used as a benchmark of institutional performance. And any money manager who says that he has outperformed the market is, in all likelihood, gauging his performance against either the S&P 500 or the Dow Jones Industrial Average.[3] Volume in S&P 500 Index futures has thus far outpaced that of both the other stock indexes combined. Its wide recognition among institutions may lend support to the use of this contract for hedging purposes.

The S&P 100 contract is also based on a market-weighted index. As mentioned before, it tends to be easier to follow, because it comprises only 100 stocks. Currently, initial margin requirements for speculators in these contracts are $6,000 for the S&P 500 and $3,300 for the S&P 100. A hedger's rates are lower.

The NYSE Index is based on the market-weighted average value of

---

[2] The S&P 100 was created by the Chicago Board Options Exchange (CBOE) as a base for a competitive but similar index to the S&P 500. Subsequently, the IOM and CBOE agreed to reciprocal trading privileges.

[3] The Chicago Board of Trade has tried to offer a futures contract based on the DJIA, but has been stalled by court suits instituted by Dow Jones.

common stocks listed on the New York Stock Exchange. As created, the NYSE Index is valued at approximately half that of either the Value Line Index or the S&P 500 Index. Whether intentionally or not, such a size discrepancy biases the use of this contract toward retail rather than institutional use. With an initial margin requirement of $3,500 per contract, participation by the small investor is facilitated; however, the need for substantially more contracts to hedge a given dollar position may discourage institutional participation.

The Value Line Industrial Composite Index, on which the Value Line contract is based, differs in one notable way from the S&P and NYSE composites. It is an equally weighted geometric average of the return on approximately 1,700 stocks. This equal weighting works to minimize the effect of market capitalization; hence, it is a more volatile contract, trading more like over-the-counter (non-exchange-traded) stocks than the other indices. For certain applications, this emphasis may be preferred by the money manager. Initial margin is $6,500 per contract.

Liquidity in the three older contracts is good, led by the S&P 500 contract trading roughly 35,000 contracts worth $3 billion daily in mid-1983. Average daily volume of NYSE Index trading involves more than 15,000 contracts valued at $725 million; and nearly 4,000 Value Line contracts trade each day, with total value of approximately $360 million.

Each of these contracts trades on a March quarterly cycle. The NYSE Index currently trades in six delivery months; the S&P and Value Line contracts are available in four delivery months. For all indexes, liquidity tends to be limited to the front contracts.

As with other futures, changes in the price of stock contracts are marked to market daily, based on closing prices, and, through the transference of variation margin from accounts showing a net loss to accounts showing a net gain, the system is balanced out each day. On the final day of trading, the value of a stock contract is set to the cash index level as of 4 P.M. (EST). The final mark to market for that day is calculated, and transference of funds completes the cash-settlement procedure.[4]

The three original index contracts are set up so that an 01 change is equivalent to $5; and the minimum price fluctuation, or "tick," is 05 ($25). For the S&P 100, an 05 tick is valued at $10. The index numbers quoted for stock futures are comparable to the underlying cash indexes.

When an investor buys or sells a contract, he is trading a given

---

[4] The last day of trading varies from contract to contract. These days are set out in the table on page 111.

value of the underlying index. For the three older contracts, this value is equivalent to the index level multiplied by $500. (For the S&P 100, $200 times the index level represents the underlying value.) If the S&P contract is priced at 169, it represents $84,500 of the stocks included in the Standard & Poor's 500. A price rise to 170 translates to a change to $85,000 in underlying value.

In multiplying its index by $500, the New York Futures Exchange created a contract whose mechanics were consistent with the two other stock contracts—although, as mentioned, the resulting value is only about half of either the S&P 500 for Value Line indexes. (Had the NYSE chosen to use a factor of $1,000, these three contracts would have been roughly the same size.) The lower value and lower margin thus required draw slightly different participation. The underlying value of the S&P 100 contract, on the other hand, has purposely been kept low (approximately 40 percent that of the S&P 500) by using the $200 rate to calculate its value.

Prior to termination of each contract, prices are established by open outcry in the trading pit. If the cash S&P is at 169, for example, it is possible for the future to be trading at 170, or, in some cases, at 168. The premium or discount of the futures to cash has so far been largely a function of investor-paced sentiment, and of the fact that this is the fastest medium through which traders can react to changing information. Contract pricing will not go unreasonably out of line with the cash market because of the attraction of these markets as an alternative for cash traders.

The stock contracts tend to trade with respect to their underlying indexes; but they can also react sympathetically to general market indicators—including, at times, the debt markets. The spread between the Dow Jones Industrial Average and the respective indexes may, at various market levels, influence the contract-pricing pattern. At the start of a stock market rally, for example, the DJIA might increase at a faster rate than the S&P 500. If market participants believe the rally will become more broadly based, then buying pressure will begin to build in the S&P contract, temporarily widening the spread between this contract and its underlying index.

CASH SETTLEMENT AND ARBITRAGE

The cash-settlement characteristic of stock-index futures has caused a great deal of stir, despite the precedent set in the trading of Eurodollar contracts. Traditionally, futures contracts have been satisfied by physical delivery of the underlying asset. The delivery capability of Treasury-bond and other contracts creates the opportunity for rate-of-return arbitrage, which serves to keep cash-futures spreads in a reasonably predictable relationship. The more limited arbitrage opportunities in stock contracts, due to cash settlement, have probably created the perception that these are more speculative vehicles.

Physical delivery of securities is not a feasible alternative to cash settlement in the stock contracts. The cost and difficulty of buying the securities represented by the indexes would be too great. Shares of an appropriate index fund, or a smaller group of stocks that mirror price activity in the relevant index, represent alternative delivery possibilities. However, the potential for market manipulation or a short squeeze would adversely affect contract pricing. The underlying stock indexes are designed to represent sufficient volume and size to preclude manipulation; and cash settlement circumvents any delivery problem.

Interestingly, in those markets in which there is a deliverable instrument, only a fraction of all contracts settle by the taking or making of delivery. It is unclear, therefore, how cash delivery in and of itself makes stock-index futures any more speculative than other futures. In fact, the inefficiencies that exist in other futures—such as after-hours risk (bonds and notes) and cheapest to deliver (bonds, GNMAs, notes, CDs)—are attributable to the delivery process. Cash settlement avoids such complications.

The absence of a deliverable in stock-index futures inhibits precise arbitrage. Increasingly, attempts to create smaller portfolios of stocks, the price activity of which matches that of an index, indicates one way in which professional arbitrageurs attempt to play a role in stock-contract pricing.

Options (the right to buy or sell an index at a specified price within a specified time) on cash indexes, which began appearing in 1983, provide another means of arbitraging. Using Chicago Board Options Exchange (CBOE) options on the S&P 100, for example, artificial longs or shorts can be created against a contract position.[5] If the contract or options are out of line when the position is initiated, this will result in gains for the arbitrageur. Greater participation by institutions mindful of rate-of-return considerations would aid in aligning prices with the underlying indexes.

Whether or not such practices will grow sufficiently to override the prevailing influence of investor sentiment on contract pricing remains to be seen. In any case, thanks to forced convergence at settlement, contract prices cannot move away indefinitely from the underlying cash index. Each higher market level will see additional sellers coming into this market. Selling contracts as an alternative to

---

[5] An artificial long is created by buying a call (right to buy) and selling a put (obligation to buy) at the same strike (specified price); an artificial short entails buying a put and selling a call at the strike price.

selling in the cash market would be stimulated if the contract rises relative to its cash index. This will tend to correct contract pricing.

USING INDEX CONTRACTS

Basic long- and short-term hedges using stock futures may be undertaken to achieve a better rate of return on a stock position or to protect the value of a portfolio in a declining market. Or they may be used to take advantage of the flexibility, cost, and efficiency of these markets. Often, when the market is moving rapidly, it is better to establish a general market position and adjust in or out of specific stocks later. Stock futures provide an attractive vehicle for this purpose. If you don't know which stocks to buy, want to buy stocks that have run ahead of the market, or want to buy stocks lacking liquidity, then establishing a long futures position can get you into the market today.

Futures also afford ease of execution, compared with transactions in cash equities. As one trader in these markets said, having just sold 700 contracts, "Where else can I trade $60 million worth of stocks so quickly, and with no impact on the market?" (That particular trade was the equivalent of selling nearly 1 million shares of AT&T stock, which certainly could not have been done so advantageously.) This ease of execution is relevant particularly on the short side, because no borrowing of stock is necessary and there is no uptick rule.

Example: A long position

The purchase of an S&P Index contract as an alternative to buying the S&P Index cash portfolio can often be initiated to create an attractive rate of return. Assume that you were able to purchase an S&P 500 portfolio in the cash market on June 16 at a price equivalent to 169, and planned to hold this investment until September 15. The cost of such a purchase would be $84,500 ($500 × 169). Based on an analysis of ex-dividend dates, for the period through September 15, dividend income would be projected to equal $928.60.

Stock value × Annual dividend yield ×
Percentage ex-dividend during period = Dividend income
$84,500 × 4.2% × 26.165% = $928.60

Alternatively, you might purchase an S&P contract when the cash-index price was 167. Like other futures, stock-index contracts are designed to be volatility-related only; they neither pay a dividend to the long nor require any dividend payment from the short. Because they reflect the level of the cash index at expiration, however, the value of the contract is effectively reduced by the dividend. Owning the contract, therefore, implies a decrease in value equal to the dividend income $928.60, which the owner of the cash index would have received.

However, $84,500 remains available for investment in T-bills, Eurodollars, CDs, or any other short-term vehicle (subject to margin and liquidity reserves). Let's say that, through an alternative use of funds, you attained an average yield of 9 percent. That would amount to $1,922.38 in interest earned during the same period—for a net dollar gain of $993.78. If market levels remained unchanged, the purchase of the S&P contract would imply outperformance of the cash portfolio by some 4.65 percent on an annualized basis, or 1.18 percent for the period. Because any change in the market would be equally reflected in both these investments, purchase of the stock contract would be more attractive. In addition, transaction costs would be lower in futures.

Buying the stock-index contract at parity (a price equal to the cash-market index) you would have earned a premium value representing the difference between short-term investment rates and the dividend yield. Pricing disciplined by such rate-of-return calculations would imply that the contract would be bid up to a premium equal to the incremental returns generated by the contract over the cash index. In this example, the breakeven premium would be 1.99 points. At a contract price of 170.99 and a cash-index price of 169, you would thus be indifferent to a choice between the two investments (see Chapter 21).

Inasmuch as any alternative use of money provided returns superior to dividend yields, the contract would tend to sell at a price higher than the cash-market level if tax-exempt index funds were the controlling influence in the market. Because the market is not as price predictable as other contracts at the moment, and because the contract market tends to react faster than the cash market, at times contracts have sold at a discount to the cash index. Investor sentiment may move the contract to these levels, despite the expectation of a premium based on implied rates of return. Two other reasons exist for the contract to sell at a discount from rate-of-return-calculated levels: there are some technical advantages to creating a short position by selling futures rather than in the cash market and what some believe is the negative impact of the 60-40 tax treatment for futures (see Chapter 25), which could be highly beneficial but which might also force an investor to take a long-term loss.

Example: A short position

Equity Investors Corporation manages a $50-million portfolio of stocks they expect will outperform the market. Anticipating a general market decline, Equity decided to sell stock futures. With regard to both cost and ease of execution, the futures contract would often provide an attractive hedge. If the S&P 500 cash index were at 165, for example, the equivalent stock value for each contract would be $82,500. Equity would sell 606 contracts to cover the current market value of its $50-million stock investment.

Determining the hedge ratio for this application is generally a straightforward matter. A dollar balance between the cash index and the stock portfolio is calculated and a number of contracts sold to match off the dollar value being hedged against the dollar value represented by the index.

$$\frac{\text{Portfolio market value}}{\text{Cash index market value}} = \frac{\$50,000,000}{\$82,500} = 606.06 \text{ contract}$$

Suppose that Equity Investors put on this short hedge and the market subsequently declined by 5 percent compared to a portfolio decline of 2.5 percent in value. Having shorted 606 contracts would have earned Equity $2,499,750:

$$
\begin{aligned}
165 \times 5 \text{ percent} &= 8.25 \text{ points} \\
8.25 \text{ points} \times 606 \text{ contracts} &= 4,999.50 \text{ points} \\
4,999.50 \text{ points} \times \$500 \text{ per point} &= \$2,499,750
\end{aligned}
$$

The portfolio would have posted a loss of $1,250,000, resulting in a net gain on the hedge of roughly 2.5 percent. Had the market rallied by 5 percent and the stock position value increased by 7.5 percent, the return to Equity Investors would still have equaled 2.5 percent. In both instances, systematic risk/reward was hedged out and unsystematic risk/reward was retained.

By shorting futures against the stock position, Equity Investors gains from the relative performance of the stock; any premium in the contract price when the position was initiated accrues to them, and dividends on the stock are earned, as well. This type of hedge can also be viewed as a stock-based, short-term money-market alternative, because the investor is not in a position to benefit from or be hurt by general market risk. In effect, the investor has created a periodic-return vehicle that should be compared to money-market alternatives on a gain/risk basis.

To the extent that the stock contract is trading away from the cash index (i.e., at a premium or a discount), an adjustment will be made to the portfolio's rate of return. Note, however, that often no adjustment for basis risk is warranted if the portfolio manager seeks to benefit from any variation between the general market and his portfolio.

It is possible that a portfolio which is attractive as a long-term investment may be too illiquid to sell near term when it might underperform. In that case, a money manager might choose to create a hedge ratio that attempts to compensate for some of the unsystematic risk represented in his holdings. Toward this end, using the *beta* which measures the volatility of the stock portfolio relative to the market could compensate for price volatility of that particular portfolio. In certain cases, there is enough liquidity to simply sell stocks, this alternative may be preferable to substantial short-term unsystematic volatility—the greater cost notwithstanding.

Options: An alternative to futures

In addition to selling futures, Equity had other alternatives available to protect capital: sell equities to raise the proportion of cash in their account; go short calls or long puts in the option markets, either on specific stocks or in the new stock-index option markets; or create, through options, a synthetic short by going short a call and long a put at the same strike price.[6] They have already decided against selling equities or utilizing options on specific stocks because they would like to capture the relative performance of their stocks— that is, eliminate the systematic (market-specific) risk while keeping the unsystematic (portfolio-specific) risk. Thus, Equity Investors must weigh the use of futures against the use of options on indexes or the creation of synthetic shorts.

Futures are often compared unfavorably with options as high-risk vehicles. This is because the risk for the buyer of an option is limited to the premium; with futures, that risk can be unlimited. For certain speculators, this may be true. However, the reverse is frequently true for the hedger.

Futures are often, in fact, *less* speculative than options. The hedger is already long or short the other side of the risk. Because the price action of the futures will be offset by that of the hedged item, there is no net gain or loss. The purchase of a put or sale of a call represents new market decisions—that, for a certain price, the hedger can be protected from adverse movement while benefiting from favorable movement over a defined period of time.

Because the writer of an option will, over time, earn a rate of return from his sale, buying put options to reduce risk will be successful only if done periodically and timed correctly. This introduces a new, more complex risk/reward analysis over a specific time, than is required for futures hedging. Selling calls represents a decision that premium income more than offsets the general downside risk for a

---

[6] In this case, if stocks rally, the hedger is adversely affected by the short call; but, if the market declines, his long put increases in value. The net result is the same as a short position.

given period. But a seller who is concerned about the market prospects over the short run, as is Equity, assumes all the systematic downside risk in his long stock position beyond his call premium (the amount received for selling the call) with limited upside potential.

The risk/reward opportunities afforded by options should be weighed against alternative opportunities in light of one's objectives. Figure 13-1 compares alternative strategies—being long an index put, being short an index call, and being short futures—as hedges for a stock position with the stock index at a current price of 100. In all cases, the investor bears the risk/reward prospect of his stock's performance relative to the market index.

If all positions are held to expiration, in the event of a decline in the stock index price to below 96, the best strategy would have been to short futures. However, the call writer would receive maximum gains should the index remain between 96 and 108. Hedging with puts allows the greatest upside participation in the event that stock-index prices rise above 108. The result with futures is always the same, as Table 13-1 shows.

If one considers the possibility of terminating the hedge prior to expiration, a "delta" factor (the options hedge ratio measuring price change relative to the instrument on which the option is written) must constantly be applied and hedge ratios consistently changed. Option prices do not move evenly with underlying values, due to

FIGURE 13-1 Strategy comparison (call premium of 4. put premium of 4)

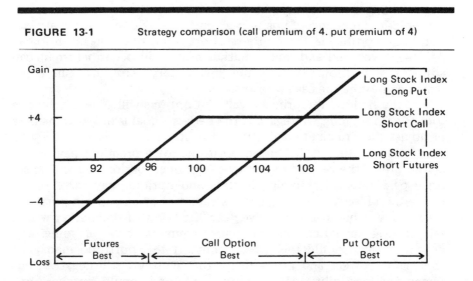

TABLE 13-1

	Gain or loss		
Price of stock index	Strategy I (futures)	Strategy II (short call)	Strategy III (long put)
88	0	−8	−4
92	0	−4	−4
96	0	0	−4
100	0	+4	−4
104	0	+4	0
108	0	+4	+4
112	0	+4	+8

changing market levels, volatility estimates, and time. Futures, after consideration of the cash-futures spread, move on a one-to-one basis with the underlying index.

If Equity Investors could not trade in futures, but were allowed to trade in options, they could create a synthetic short by buying a put and selling a call at the same strike price. If the market declines, their put increases in value; but, if the market rallies, the hedge works against them. The net cost of such a position will usually be arbitraged so as to be in line with the premium or discount between the stock-index future and the cash index. The value of the position will also change very much like that of the future. For accounts that cannot trade in futures but can trade in puts and calls, the synthetic short may be viewed as an alternative. However, as is not true of futures where the position cannot be terminated involuntarily, with a call the holder can change a position at any time. Because there are certain timing problems, the synthetic short could find that his short call has been exercised and that a market move will occur before he can adjust his position. Thus, some involuntary exposure can exist, which cannot be the case with futures.

For the hedger, the primary value of options will generally be as a tool for fine-tuning strategies. If the hedger's goal is often to insulate or adjust the principal volatility of a portfolio, futures can easily be used to meet this goal. Option positions for a premium paid or received affect the rate of return over a defined period and within set price parameters. Combining futures and options may serve to enhance the effectiveness of a given strategy. For example, a portfolio manager who has a very negative near-term view of the market would sell futures, avoiding any premium payment but foregoing any potential gain should the market rally. If this portfolio manager's analysis is correct and prices drop, the manager, still negative, but seeing the possibility of an interim rebound, could purchase call options to capitalize on the possible interim rally while preserving the hedged position.

The disadvantage of options is that the investor, to a large extent, must be right on market timing. As a result, futures tend to be less speculative for the hedger than are options. Futures isolate market risk and allow the hedger to manage this risk. Clearly, if one is correct on timing the potential for attractive gains relative to risk exists with options.

14

Options on futures

Until 1982, there was a ban on the sale of any type of commodity option. In lifting this ban, the Commodity Futures Trading Commission (CFTC) laid the foundation for a pilot program that allows any existing exchange to apply for the right to trade options on any one of the futures contracts already traded on that exchange. The first approved options began trading in the fall of 1982: Treasury-bond futures on the Chicago Board of Trade; gold futures on the Commodity Exchange (COMEX); and sugar futures on the New York Coffee, Sugar and Cocoa Exchange. Early in 1983, options on the three stock-index futures—S&P 500, Value Line, and NYSE—became available.

The Value Line Index option has been discontinued, and the S&P 500 and NYSE options on futures have been outdistanced by equity options on cash indexes (see Chapter 13), primarily the Chicago Board Options Exchange (CBOE) option on the S&P 100. The dominance of that option seems to be due both to the CBOE's greater experience with equities and to the fact that the S&P contract is not unique. (CBOE volume, for example, runs to the equivalent of 8,000 futures contracts a day and continues to grow.) On the other hand, options on bond futures appear to be more successful in the fixed-income area.

OPTION BASICS

Options on futures combine the potentially limited risk inherent in listed options and the homogeneity and infinite supply of futures. They represent a different type of risk/reward vehicle for the money manager seeking to hedge positions.

Two types of options can be bought and sold: **puts** and **calls.** The purchaser of a put option has the right to sell the underlying futures contract at a specified price over the life of the option. The purchaser of a call option has the right to buy the underlying futures contract, also at a specified price, during the life of the option. The price at which the future can be bought or sold is called the **strike price.**

The buyer of an option is the one who can exercise the option. If the buyer purchases a call, he may choose to be assigned a long futures contract; if he buys a put, he may choose to acquire (exercise for) a short futures contract. It is this right that distinguishes a long position in options from a long futures position, the latter entailing an *obligation* to acquire if the position is not liquidated.

The amount paid for the option is called the **premium.** The amount of money that could be made by exercising that option at current market levels represents the **intrinsic value** of the option.

Option pricing is a function of the intrinsic value of the contract and the **time value** (premium minus intrinsic value), which reflects the perceived volatility of the underlying market. Because an option involves time value, which, by definition, will be zero at expiration, it is known as a **wasting asset.** (Futures, by contrast, are not wasting.)

Suppose a June 74 call on a bond contract was purchased at 2-30/64[1] when the June contract was valued at 75-16/32. This option has an intrinsic value of 1-32/64.

$$\text{Contract value} - \text{Strike price} = \text{Intrinsic value}$$
$$75\text{-}16/32 - 74 = 1\text{-}32/64$$

As noted, the intrinisc value is less than the premium paid and the difference is referred to as the time value.

$$\text{Premium} - \text{Intrinsic value} = \text{Time value}$$
$$2\text{-}30/64 - 1\text{-}32/64 = 62/64$$

If the price of the underlying future remained constant at 75-16/32, the time value would diminish—reaching zero at expiration of the option—and leave only the intrinsic value as the option value. The buyer of this option at 2-30/64 needs a market rise to make a profit. Specifically, if the market went above 76-15/32, this option would

---

[1] Options on bond futures trade in 64ths of a point, compared with 32nds of a point for the underlying contract.

show a profit for the buyer and the 62/64 previously representing time value would have become intrinsic value.

In deciding on the purchase of an option, the length of time left until expiration and the strike price of the option are important considerations. Premium costs are typically higher on options with more time remaining until expiration. With time, there is greater opportunity for the market to move in the right direction—and far enough in the right direction—for the option to become profitable. In addition, those options with strike prices *in the money* will command higher premiums than those trading *out of the money*.[2]

CONTRACT CHARACTERISTICS

An option on a Treasury-bond future represents the right to buy or sell one bond contract with a face value of $100,000 of 8 percent deliverable Treasury bonds at a specific price for a set period. At any time during the life of the option, the buyer may exercise the option to take on a position in a Treasury-bond futures contract—either long (call option) or short (put option). If the option is exercised, the seller must assume an opposing bond-contract position. The procedure is straightforward for both the option writer and the option buyer: Upon notice of exercise, the Chicago Board of Trade Clearing Corporation assigns a long futures position (if the option is a call, for example) to the buyer and a short futures position to the option writer, or seller, both at the option strike price.

Unlike the futures market, in which delivery notice is chronological, options-on-futures assignments are made at random. And, unlike the cash options market, options on futures are marked by an unlimited deliverable supply, because the board can simply create a long and a short future at the same price upon notice of exercise. Contract prices are then adjusted automatically to the current price by variation margin.

Options are available on the same quarterly cycle as the underlying futures. In the case of bonds, options may be written on the first three contract months.

One important distinction between the option and the bond future is that, although the June option is written on the June contract, for example, the option actually expires in May. In the case of bonds, this arrangement was made to avoid the complications of having an

---

[2] The strike price of an in-the-money (above market price) call option is less than the current futures prices; the strike price of an in-the-money put option is greater than the current futures price. Conversely, the strike price of an out-of-the-money (below market price) call option is greater than the current futures price, while the strike price of an out-of-the-money put option is less than the current futures price. An option trading at the money is selling equal to the current market price of the underlying futures contract.

option exercised when the futures contract could be delivered against.

Margin rules on options differ, depending on whether the investor is long or short. The long simply pays the premium. He will owe nothing beyond that. The option writer recieves that premium in cash. Because the writer can be assigned a contract position at any time, the initial margin requirement for a futures position must be met. In addition, the short must be prepared to meet a daily mark to market on the option position; this assures all parties that the writer could meet the variation margin call, if assigned. Because there is no transfer of funds to the option buyer, the seller can post the daily variation margin in Treasury bills instead of cash. The option writer has guaranteed the ability to meet margin, if assigned. Assuming initial margin is covered, cash may be withdrawn as the position moves in the writer's favor.

While profits on a futures position are credited daily (by means of variation margin), and a short option is marked to market daily, no cash is paid to a long until either an exercise or an offsetting transaction occurs. This will prove to be an important consideration for the investor who shorts a futures contract and buys a call, for example. If the market rises, the long call will rise in value, but the short future will decline in value. Despite the fact that these positions may match each other economically, no cash will be available (because of the appreciation in the value of the call) to be used against the margin owed on the future.

Ownership of an option on futures has substantially different risk implications than does ownership of a futures position, because the holder of a futures contract must be prepared to meet variation margin calls on his account. Offsetting an option may often prove a more manageable way of capturing gains or limiting losses. Some brokers may, in the absence of direct instruction, reserve the right to offset an in-the-money option close to its expiration because if the option is exercised for a futures position the option buyer would then be obligated to meet any variation margin call.

The price of a bond futures contract is a function of the price of the cheapest deliverable instrument, adjusted for the net cost of carry through the contract delivery period and some technical contract considerations (see Chapter 7). Because the option on bond futures is priced relative to the underlying futures—which, in turn, is a function of cash-market levels—the option is a double derivative instrument. The underlying futures price already reflects convergence. Therefore, the time value of the premium of an option should be analyzed, taking into account the convergence value of a contract. For example, if one buys an at-the-money September call in June, and the market remains virtually unchanged, the future will still increase in value in a positive yield-curve environment, transforming the call to one in-the-money.

The price (premium) of an option on bond futures, then, should reflect, in part, the cash-market assumptions captured by the current market in futures; and the difference between the current futures market level and the strike price of the option should affect the premium. In addition, both the time remaining until expiration and the volatility of the instrument on which the option is written will have an impact on its value.

The covered writing of stock options has been used by institutions to increase portfolio yield. For example, as a short-term investment, options on bond futures could be sold against the cheapest-to-deliver Treasury bond.[3] If the market rises, and the call expires in the money, the writer will be assigned a short futures position. The writer can eventually deliver bonds against those shorts or reverse his positions in the cash and futures markets.

To the extent that premium income (plus interest) exceeds other available short-term rates, the return on the bond portfolio will be increased. The risk, as is true in any buy-write option program, is a decline in the value of the bond, which could create a lower rate of return than that available from other short-term investments. Variations in the covered "write" are possible, depending on whether the option was written in, at, or out of the money. Premium income will be different in each of these cases. Buy-write strategies are discussed in greater detail in Chapter 22.

Certain types of arbitrage typically associated with cash options, particularly conversions and reversals, are more difficult to do with options on futures. In stock options, transactions such as reverse conversions are often done to create rates of return on cash generated. However, because the delivered instrument—in this case, a future, is leveraged, there is no cash coming in from it.

Moreover, the more professional nature of this market limits arbitrage opportunities; without large-scale public participation, market prices have remained closely in line with arbitrage expectations.

---

[3] A higher yield can often be attained by writing options against nonTreasury issues, but that must be judged against the basis risk assumed.

Major Contract Specifications

Debt-instrument contracts

Contract	Exchange	Contract months	Last day of trading	Trading hours (EST)	Trading unit	Minimum fluctuation	Daily limit
Treasury bond	CBT	Mar/Jun Sep/Dec	8th business day prior to the last business day of the month	9:00-3:00	$100,000 par value of 8%	1/32 ($31.25)	2 points ($2,000)
10-Year Treasury note	CBT	Mar/Jun Sep/Dec	8th business day prior to the last business day of the month	9:00-3:00	$100,000 par value of 8%	1/32 ($31.25)	2 points ($2,000)
GNMA-CDR	CBT	Mar/Jun Sep/Dec	8th business day prior to the last business day of the month	9:00-3:00	$100,000 par value of 8%	1/32 ($31.25)	2 points ($2,000)
90-day Treasury bill	IMM	Mar/Jun Sep/Dec	Business day preceding first delivery day	9:00-3:00	$1 million par value	.01 ($25.00)	60 basis points ($1,500)
CD (domestic)	IMM	Mar/Jun Sep/Dec	Business day preceding last business day of the month	8:00-3:00	$1 million par value	.01 ($25.00)	80 basis points ($2,000)
Eurodollar (time deposit)	IMM	Mar/Jun Sep/Dec	Second London Bank business day preceding 3rd Wednesday of contract month	8:00-3:00	$1 million par value	.01 ($25.00)	100 basis points ($2,500)

Stock-index contracts

Contract	Exchange	Contract months	Last day of trading	Trading hours (EST)	Trading unit	Minimum fluctuation	Daily limit
S&P 500	IOM	Mar/Jun Sep/Dec	3rd Friday of contract month	10:00–4:15	Index × $500	.05 ($25)	None
NYSE Composite	NYFE	Mar/Jun Sep/Dec	Business day prior to last business day in the settlement month	10:00–4:15	Index × $500	.05 ($25)	None
Value Line	KCBT	Mar/Jun Sep/Dec	Last business day of the contract month	10:00–4:15	Index × $500	.05 ($25)	None
Options on futures:							
Treasury bond	CBT	Mar/Jun Sep/Dec	1 PM EST on 1st Friday preceding by at least 5 business days the 1st notice day for the Treasury bond futures contract	9:00–3:00	One Treasury bond futures contract of the specified month	1/64 ($15.625)	2 points ($2,000)
S&P 500	IOM	Mar/Jun Sep/Dec	3rd Friday of contract month	10:00–4:15	One S&P 500 futures contract of the specified month	.05 ($25)	None

PART THREE

Hedge strategy design

15

Introduction to hedging strategies

Until now, we have concentrated on contract mechanics and characteristics, citing various hedging strategies as part of our discussion of each contract. Going one step further, let us now take a more detailed look at the implementation of hedging strategies. While each has its own peculiarities, certain methodologies and patterns are repeated.

For each strategy, the variables described in Chapter 6—principal protection, convergence, contract characteristics, and variation-margin financing—will be important to varying degrees. The relative importance of the variables is a function of the goals of each strategy. Moreover, the length of time involved in a hedge is itself important.

For shorter time periods, basis risk is typically of greater concern; for longer time periods, convergence and variation-margin financing may have greater impact on hedge results. Similarly, the greater the time frame of the item being hedged, for example, a 15-year versus a three-month loan, the longer the period over which any deviation from expectations can be amortized. The individual user of the financial futures market will need to assess his own time frame and goals.

On the most fundamental level, hedging should serve to reduce the amplitude of risk. It is difficult, if not impossible, for the money manager to eliminate risk entirely. However, risk can be reduced to more acceptable levels through a well-conceived hedge program.

Managing volatility risk

To manage risk, a hedge must be designed first to isolate principal volatility; all other variables can be treated as costs of doing business or as explicit market judgments. The precedence of each variable will depend on the specific hedge, but the effects of the variables are interdependent.

The required degree of precision varies. A hedger attempting to create a pure rate of return to match asset earnings or liability cost may require greater precision than one using futures for temporary protection against overall market moves.

In the simplest form of a bond hedge, the basis trade (see Chapter 7), we found that the factor for the cheapest-to-deliver bond was the hedge ratio—that is, the number of contracts that should be purchased or sold to offset a principal change in $100,000 par value of the cash instrument. The hedge ratio, the number of contracts used to protect a position, should serve to maintain principal parity between the hedged asset and the futures contracts.

Only one variable need be considered to create a hedge ratio, and that is the respective price volatility of the hedged item and that of the cash instrument on which a contract is written. Cash-to-cash basis relationship is implicit in any investment decision. The decision to buy utilities instead of Treasuries, for example, contains a basis risk, but it is a hidden risk. As was true of inertia speculation, futures often highlight what is already implicit.

This basis relationship is studied to structure a hedge and determine the number of contracts required to offset the principal volatility of the hedged cash position. To the extent that the relationship changes unexpectedly, the gain or loss from the contract position will not offset the change in value of the cash position, and the hedge ratio will be imprecise. This potential for basis risk may work to the benefit or detriment of the hedge. Hedgers may also try to take advantage of changing sector relationship and a positive basis change, while still protecting against general market moves.

To assess basis risk for a particular strategy, the relationship between hedged cash position and the cheapest-to-deliver cash instrument must be considered. Once the hedger has gauged the basis relative to cash, the way the contract moves relative to its cash market can be fitted into the equation.

Typically, basis risk is assessed in terms of yield changes. Such yield changes must then be translated into dollar changes to arrive at a hedge ratio. Basis risk and hedge ratio imprecision are usually evaluated in terms of the hedger's alternatives for acting upon a market decision.

Convergence

A common misconception concerning futures is that hedging can allow for ownership of a cash instrument—removing any existing principal risk—while still allowing the investor to recieve the full yield associated with it. What is not taken into account in this view of the hedging process is the effect of convergence.

Convergence is the process that equilibrates the value of the futures contract to the value of the deliverable issue at expiration. This price difference indicates whether a contract is trading at a premium or discount relative to the underlying cash instrument.

The cost or gain from convergence is partly a function of the hedge ratio because calculations are made on a per-contract basis. Accepting convergence as a rate of return adjustment is consistent with isolating principal risk in the hedge ratio.

A hedge ratio can be adjusted to compensate for convergence, but this amounts to making a judgment on the yield curve. If the judgment is correct, then the investor stands to gain: the investor's assessment of the relationship between long- and short-term rates has been proved right (see Chapter 16).

One other significant aspect of convergence is that it can be measured and thus accounted for at the onset of the hedge. Assuming a contract is held through the end of its trading period, full convergence can be calculated and its cost or benefit defined. While this convergence may represent a cost or benefit it may not necessarily be a net cost or benefit, if it is factored into product pricing. Knowing what to anticipate in terms of convergence is essential to the analysis of a hedge.

If a loan is to be issued at a fixed rate with variable funding, convergence cost is known at the time the loan is made. Competitively, such cost can often be passed on to the borrower; or alternatively, any pickup may also have to be passed on to the borrower. If this is not done, the maker of a fixed-rate loan must understand that he is initiating a transaction at a different gross margin than the cash market would indicate (see Chapter 17).

Understanding convergence is important for the general bond-portfolio hedger to the extent that it aids in determining whether or not a contract is trading at a fair price relative to the cash market. For the bond portfolio or general bill hedger, who is directly concerned with the periodic return on a position, it will prove important in assessing the expected result of a hedge.

Contract characteristics

The hedger should be aware of contract specifications that will affect pricing efficiency and the structure of a hedge. Contract technicalities that ultimately affect price are measured along with convergence. For a bond-portfolio hedger protecting against changes in market direction, understanding these technicalities and the anticipatory nature of the market will help in implementing hedge strategy. For the product portfolio hedger, these factors will affect interim return.

Variation-margin financing

Like convergence, variation margin is unique to futures, and the associated potential financing effect can be treated as an adjustment to the rate of return.

Suppose you have designed a perfect hedge. You own a cash bond and are short the appropriate number of futures contracts. The market then rises, and your cash bond appreciates by $10. Your short futures position declines by a matching $10. Your net gain/loss is zero. But, unless you choose to liquidate your bond and satisfy the $10 margin call with the proceeds from it, you must meet the margin call with cash from another source.

The use of cash for this purpose implies either a direct borrowing cost or an opportunity cost for the hedger. The amount of deviation from a projected rate of return this might cause depends on the financing rate and the length of time for which this margin must be financed, you stop financing only when you choose to unwind the position, selling the bond in this case and applying the proceeds either to pay back the loan or to return cash to its previous use. At this point, the variation-margin balance is recaptured. What cannot be recaptured is the financing effect from that cash balance. This is a problem of cash-flow timing.

In evaluating hedge applications, it will become obvious that different variables are emphasized in different situations.

Nevertheless, the hedger starts with the same basis formula in each case: Assess the risk of doing nothing, assess the risk of other alternatives, and compare them to the risk inherent in using futures.

In defining the risk inherent in using futures, one must define the variables and the probable range of expected results utilizing the key variables; calculate a hedge ratio and define the basis risk; determine the cash-futures relationship and, therefore, the convergence impact; and analyze the possibilities for variation margin.

16

Creating a hedge

Many hedge applications have similar characteristics. As an introduction to the more individualized applications, this chapter is concerned with the analysis of hedges to protect against changes in general market levels in two areas: debt markets and money markets. Debt-market hedges are generally created with instruments having longer maturities. They rely principally on the Treasury-bond contract. Money-market hedges, generally related to maturities of less than one year, employ primarily Treasury-bill and/or CD contracts.[1]

As examples of the general hedge for debt markets, we have chosen the hedge of an existing cash bond portfolio, and the hedge of anticipated pension receipts; for a hedge involving general money-market moves, we have chosen to look at the situation of a savings institution trying to hedge its liability costs.

HEDGING A BOND PORTFOLIO

Using futures contracts to manage risk in a bond portfolio is a cash-market alternative. It is a way around the need to sell bonds.

---

[1] There is some overlap. Instruments ranging from one to three years may, at times be managed with a series, or strip, of Treasury-bills and/or CD contracts covering the range of the contract periods.

Just how good an alternative the futures market represents is a function of several variables:

What are the transaction costs of hedging versus trading in the cash market?

To what degree is the price relationship between the futures market and hedged portfolio predictable?

Do you want to disturb your portfolio?

Is the market for a specific issue too illiquid for frequent buying or selling?

Do you have an accounting or tax reason for holding a bond rather than selling it?

The short hedge is a risk-managment tool for general bond portfolios; one of the ways it can be used is to unwind a long bond position, or reduce the bond's maturity by partially hedging.

Suppose you own an issue that is particularly illiquid and you expect it to decline in value with the general market. Selling this bond in the cash market and planning to purchase it again at a later date may prove difficult and relatively expensive. The short futures position protects against the market decline and essentially shortens the maturity of your portfolio, but does not have an impact on the market for a specific issue. This allows you to retain the bond that was purchased for specific reasons, while insulating the whole portfolio against market risk.

The short hedger is often a portfolio manager who, as an alternative to hedging with futures, would consider selling bonds and investing the proceeds in short-term instruments to avoid a period of temporary market risk. As a result of convergence, the hedged position, like the cash alternative, will provide a shorter-term rate of return on the hedged asset for the period of the hedge. As a result, this strategy tends to be used over relatively short time periods.

Developing a hedge ratio

Typically, in a shorter-time-period hedge, basis risk will be the focal point of the portfolio manager's attention. The basis relationship between a specific bond and the general market vis-à-vis principal changes in futures prices is managed with a hedge ratio.[2] The hedge ratio seeks to equate dollar changes in bond prices with dollar changes in futures prices. In practice, a variety of techniques can be used to

---

[2] This technique for calculating a hedge ratio can be applied for a portolio, given its average coupon and maturity, or by using a single bond with price activity that replicates the portfolio.

actually calculate a hedge ratio. The first step is to determine the relationship between the hedged bonds and the long-term Treasury market by analyzing price and spread history. Often, a hedge ratio is derived based solely on this historic price correlation, and the success of the hedge strategy will depend upon whether these past patterns are repeated during the hedge period. A hedge ratio can also be derived based on measuring the dollar effect of *anticipated* yield and spread changes. This method also uses price history as a guide to what these spread relationships will be over time and at different market levels. The latter approach tends to be more projective. The hedge ratio is ultimately derived based on the anticipated change from current market relationships. This tends to make the hedge ratio more consistent with the portfolio manager's normal decision-making process.

Table 16-1 describes the calculation of a hedge ratio using changes in the futures equivalent prices for the most deliverable Treasury bond rather than actual changes in the futures price. This allows the creation of a hedge ratio based solely on principal valuation changes and allows the convergence effect to be treated separately. To segregate these effects, the price used for the December future is not an actual market price; instead, the futures equivalent of the price of the cheapest-to-deliver bond is substituted. The difference between the futures equivalent price and the contract's market price will equal the convergence gain or loss per contract.

The hedge analysis, which works off the current Treasury bond, builds in an adjustment for the expected cheapest-to-deliver bond at different market levels to determine the contract price as a futures equivalent value. In the case of a market rally to 11.20, a price increase of 8.77 points on the 14 percent of 11/2011 would probably make this bond cheapest to deliver. As such, the contract will trade in line with the 14 percent, and the futures price would be calculated as the bond price divided by the factor for the appropriate contract month (122.971 ÷ 1.6238 = 75.727). When the hedge was initiated, the 14 percent was not the most deliverable bond, the 9-1/8 percent of 5/2009, selling at $78,519, was. The short hedger would now benefit from the change in the cheapest-to-deliver issue. As the market declines, a low-coupon bond is likely to remain the most deliverable issue, and the contract price would be based on a lower coupon bond, such as the 9-1/8 percent. For example, as the yield on the 14 percent increases to 13.20, it is assumed that the 9-1/8 percent would be most deliverable at a 12.90 yield to maturity (see Chapter 7). The dollar price on the 9-1/8 would equal 71.86, for a December 83 futures equivalent value of 64.64 (71.86 ÷ 1.1117). The change in value per contract is taken consistently as the futures equivalent price.

The hedge ratio calculation is based on the expected changes in

TABLE 16-1 Hedging analysis—Southern Bell 12-7/8% of 10/2020

Price of hedged issue	Yield	Price of 14% of 11/2011	Yield	Current price spread	Current yield spread	Dec 83 future price
97.14	13.25	114.20	12.15	−17.05	1.10	70.63

Hedged issue		14.00% of 11/2011		Yield spread	Hedged issue price change from today	Projected future price	Change from today	Optimal hedge ratio
Price	Yield	Price	Yield					
110.788	11.600	127.018	10.800	0.800	13.648	78.220	7.595	1.797
105.421	12.200	122.971	11.200	1.000	8.281	75.727	5.102	1.623
100.530	12.800	118.212	11.700	1.100	3.390	72.796	2.171	1.562
91.958	14.000	109.599	12.700	1.300	−5.182	67.231	−3.394	1.527
87.885	14.650	105.695	13.200	1.450	−9.255	64.644	−5.981	1.547
87.587	14.700	105.695	13.200	1.500	−9.553	64.644	−5.981	1.597
83.605	15.400	101.326	13.800	1.600	−13.535	61.769	−8.856	1.528
79.717	16.150	97.216	14.400	1.750	−17.423	59.122	−11.503	1.515

the market and changes in the spread between the hedged issue and the deliverable bond. If the yield on Southern Bell deteriorated by 140 basis points and the spread to Treasuries widened to 145 basis points, a short 15.5 contract position would be required to offset the loss on a $1 million par value bond position. However, if yields improved by 105 basis points (from 13.25 to 12.20) and the spread narrowed, the loss on 16.2 contracts would offset the gain on Southern Bell.

The portfolio manager would look at a range of possibilities to choose a hedge ratio; that ratio can be set for an entire portfolio, given the manager's estimate of its performance relative to Treasuries. Hedge ratios will vary depending on where the market is when the hedge is initiated and expectations of market direction. Given the cases analyzed and probable occurrence, a hedge ratio of 1.55 is selected.

Table 16-2 shows the effect of using a less-than-perfect hedge ratio for the various market scenarios assumed. Evaluating these potential costs of imprecision can help the portfolio manager select a minimal-risk hedge ratio. Even if the hedge ratio chosen does not achieve a perfect match between the contract and hedged asset, there is usually room for some error because of the transactions cost advantage offered in futures.

Table 16-2 indicates the net gain or loss per million dollars par value based on the 1.55 hedge ratio and on some potential market

TABLE 16-2   Error Tolerance Matrix (per million hedged) *

Hedged issue Gain (loss)	Futures position Gain (loss)	Net hedged position Gain (loss)
1. $136,480	($117,723)	$18,757
2. 82,810	(79,081)	3,729
3. 33,900	(33,651)	249
4. (51,820)	52,607	787
5. (92,550)	92,706	156
6. (95,530)	92,706	(2,824)
7. (135,350)	137,268	1,918
8. (174,230)	178,297	4,067

*Hedge ratio = 1.55.

outcomes. Take, for example, the sixth case in which the market declined and the manager was underhedged. Table 16-1 indicates a gain of 5.981 points per short contract; resulting in the $92,706 gain. Thus, a net loss of $2,824 was realized. This imprecision should be compared to the cost involved in selling the Southern Bell position and repurchasing it when the manager's market judgment turns optimistic.

The extent of basis risk that a hedger will tolerate can be assessed in terms of the cost of using the cash market alone to protect portfolio value. For highly liquid bonds, the cost of using futures can be directly equated to cash-market transactions cost. For less liquid bonds, the hedge ratio is harder to determine, but the cost of doing business in the cash market is higher.

Often, a portfolio manager will choose to manage the basis through the hedge ratio. For example, if a bond were expected to outperform the general market, a manager could underhedge to protect against general market level but maintain the benefits for which the bond was purchased.

Hedge ratio imprecision may not necessarily have a significant impact. A portfolio manager may know that he wants to hedge 25 percent of the portfolio. If the hedge is off by as much as 1-2 percent, the manager can still be well within acceptable tolerances.

Take the case of the Merrimac Fund, which was concerned with hedging a junk bond portfolio comprised of low-rated and even unrated bonds from smaller, less liquid issues. The advantage to owning these bonds is their high return. But, if possible, selling and buying back the bonds to avoid temporary market risk can be a very expensive proposition. Alternatively, the illiquidity of the issues can be handled through hedging. If the Merrimac Fund anticipates a market move, this can be incorporated into the hedge ratio; but, because the spread between junk bonds and Treasuries is not as dependable as other relationships, the hedge may be less accurate. Still, because the cash alternative is costly, the benefit from hedging can be quite high.

Basis risk is essentially a cross-market consideration. To deal with it when setting up a debt-market hedge means analyzing the same variables which would be assessed when working in the cash markets. Once a set of assumptions related to basis risk has been established decisions are made concerning the unique variables of futures, the convergence spread, contract characteristics, and variation-margin financing.

Convergence

Convergence, while relevant, is often not as large a consideration in this instance as in others, primarily because the alternative activity (selling a bond) involves temporarily receiving a short-term rate upon reinvestment and the yield-curve effect of convergence is overwhelmed by the anticipated market move. Assessing the cash-futures relationship is important; for example, if excessively cheap contracts are sold, the short hedger could face an undue loss with no gain on the cash side, particularly if the contract is not held to expiration.

The debt-market general hedge is one instance in which it is sometimes desirable to adjust for the effects of convergence. This is because the application results from a market decision. Because the hedge is put on as a result of a shift in market expectations, the bond manager may choose to incorporate this type of direction-sensitive adjustment. The portfolio manager could adjust the hedge ratio to reflect a yield curve consistent with such a market projection. How much it will cost if market expectations turn out to be wrong can be evaluated.

Assume the future is selling at 71.5 and is expected to converge fully to a price of 72. Assume also that, to hedge the anticipated decline in the cash market, 10 contracts are required. Due to the positive yield curve, however, the short hedger faces a convergence loss. If the market declines by 4 points and the contract price is 68 at the end of the period, the hedger would have a $40,000 loss on his cash position but only a $35,000 gain on his futures—for a $5,000 net loss on the position. We have stated that this loss should actually be assumed and the hedge based on the future equivalent price, here 72.[3] . If the

---

[3] For example, if the hedge is against $1 million par value 12 percent bonds, the analysis of the three-month hedge would include a reduction in the effective bond yield from 12 percent to 10 percent due to convergence.

Bond principal:	
Gain on future	$40,000
Loss on bond principal	($40,000)
Net change	0
Income effect	
Interest income	$30,000
Convergence cost	($ 5,000)
Net income	$25,000
Effective yield	10%

hedger decides that he wants to try to avoid the $5,000 yield impact of convergence loss, he could increase the hedge ratio to 1.14. In this case, the $35,000 gain on futures would be increased to $40,000, and the gain on futures would equal the loss on the cash position. The risk inherent in this position, however, becomes clear if prices increase.

Suppose cash-market prices increase, and the futures converge to a price of 76. At this point, the hedger will find that he has a loss on futures (from 71.5 to 76) of 4.5 points per contract. With 11.4 contracts, this is a $51,300 loss, $11,300 greater than the $40,000 gain on the cash position.

Adjusting the hedge ratio has accentuated the hedger's market judgment. Even after accounting for the inherent yield-curve cost of $5,000, the hedger has worsened his position by $6,300. Also, the hedge ratio required to compensate for convergence was set for a 4-point move in the cash market. If the hedger is right on direction but not on the amplitude of a market move, the adjusted hedge ratio will not precisely compensate for convergence.

	End of period					
	Future = 68			Future = 76		
Number of contracts sold at 71-16/32	Gain (loss) cash	Gain (loss) future	Net	Gain (loss) cash	Gain (loss) future	Net
10.0	($40,000)	$35,000	($5,000)	$40,000	($45,000)	($ 5,000)
11.4	(40,000)	40,000	—	40,000	(51,300)	(11,300)

Contract characteristics

For a general market-level protection hedge, expected to be kept in place for a relatively short period of time, a portfolio manager will tend to use the contract that most closely matches the characteristics of his portfolio. The manager of a mortgage portfolio would probably use the GNMA contract; but he must consider the contract's pricing, which is often strongly influenced by delivery considerations. The manager of an intermediate-bond portfolio would often prefer to use the note contract, although he must carefully consider its peculiarities. And, like a bond hedger, he would have to judge the degree of after-hours protection implicit in the contract price.

Variation-margin financing

Variation-margin financing is a function of three factors: the average market move during the period of the hedge, the amount to be financed, and the length of time involved. Generally, there is no need to adjust for potential variation-margin financing costs in the hedge ratio when dealing with a short time frame because margin financing will have a negligible effect on the hedge results.

ANTICIPATING PENSION CONTRIBUTIONS

The short general portfolio hedge is the "sell" equivalent of trading in cash. The "buy" equivalent is the general anticipatory hedge. Going long futures effectively allows the portfolio manager to buy bonds before cash is available. The manager expecting a decline in interest rates is positioned to gain on futures if rates do decline while the hedge is in place. If rates increase, the loss on futures is made up by purchasing bonds at a more attractive cost than is available at the time. Futures have allowed the portfolio manager to separate the rate decision from the timing of cash flow. Monitor Pension Accounts has contributions coming in three months from now. But current yield levels meet actuarial requirements, and the pension managers foresee a decline in yields.

The manager's first alternative, which is the most common, is inertia speculation: Monitor sits tight and hopes the market will be as attractive in three months as it is today. The second alternative is to use futures to "buy" the market today. By going long these contracts, Monitor won't be hurt by a market rise over the next three months.

The analysis of the general anticipatory hedge is essentially the same as that for the short general portfolio hedge. To assess basis risk, Monitor must determine what type of bonds it would buy if it could establish a position today. A somewhat less rigid analysis of basis risk than that required for the short hedge will likely result. Monitor may know only what sector it would like to buy (telephones) but not the specific issue (Southern Bell). As market conditions change, Monitor may find the issue hedged against has become unavailable or unattractive. Adjusting for basis risk, then, will not necessarily imply an exact match between the futures and the bond eventually purchased.

If, given yield-curve conditions, convergence would have a negative effect on the short hedge, then it would have the opposite effect here—enhancing the general anticipatory hedge.

MEASURING HEDGE PERFORMANCE

Performance measurement is often important to the debt-market general hedger.[4] The existence of futures in a portfolio tends to

---

[4] For hedge accounting and tax treatment, see Chapters 24 and 25.

make the manager's performance more visible. The relative impact of a hedge is more apparent when the alternative means of principal protection was to sell out part of the position at a known cost. For accurate measurement, certain items must be considered.

Matrix pricing. Many bond managers rely on matrix pricing tapes for specific bond quotes. Matrix pricing creates prices for specific, and possibly illiquid, bonds based on estimated yield spreads to more active bonds. All issues included in the matrix may have updated prices but still reflect the spread relationship implicit in the pricing tape. The price of the bond being hedged may not accurately reflect the current market relationship, leading to a distortion in the hedge results. This is especially apparent when the hedge is correctly positioned for a change in the spread relationship between a particular bond and Treasuries. Being aware of these considerations, and adjusting for them when measuring hedge performance, will lead to a more accurate assessment of the hedged position.

3 o'clock versus 5 o'clock. Because bond contracts stop trading two hours before the cash market stops, any moves in the cash market after trading ends in futures will not be reflected until the market opens the next day. As a result, using the cash-market closing price of the bond will distort assessing performance of the hedge. (Some managers are trying to build a data base to compensate for this timing distortion.)

Bid/asked spread. Monitor sells a bond today and buys it back tomorrow. If the market has not moved, the fund receives the bid price today and must pay the asked price tomorrow. But what if Monitor hedges the bond, instead.

A common error in assessing the performance of the hedge is to look at the price of the bond (the asked price) and roll in the difference between this price and the bid when measuring the hedge. This bid/asked differential is not paid by the futures hedger who maintains the cash bond position. Including this transaction cost distorts the hedge results. The portfolio manager should measure the cash bond's performance on a comparable basis (bid to bid or asked to asked) when measuring the gain or loss relative to the futures position.

A LIABILITY HEDGING PROGRAM

Both the short general portfolio hedge and the long general anticipatory hedge deal with long-term investments and thus, the longer-term contracts: bonds, notes, or GNMAs. Hedges of general market levels of short-term contracts, in contrast, often arise out of asset/liability gaps or general liability cost management considerations.

Olympic National Savings Bank has long-term, fixed-rate mortgages outstanding at an average 9-1/2 percent rate. If its cost of funding is

9-1/2 percent, Olympic National breaks even.[5] A decline to 8-1/2 percent in funding costs would imply a 1 percent gain. On the simplest level, Olympic National's business involves speculating on the cost of money (yet another example of inertia speculation). By using futures, Olympic National can sharply reduce the speculation inherent in its business.

The primary judgment involved in this type of hedge—the direction of rates—is not new to the bank. If liability costs are currently below the rate of return represented by the Olympic National's mortgages, or if they are above, but at a tolerable level for a defined period of time, the bank may want to protect against rates rising. At whatever rate level, the bank must decide, as a result of its own market judgment, cash-flow projections and constraints of the contract market, when to put on a hedge, how to design it, whether to put on the hedge at different levels to hit a target average cost, and how long to hedge for. Rather than absolutely defining the rate that the bank will receive, this type of hedge serves to protect against the effect of general market moves on the banks cost of funds.

The primary problem for Olympic National and other savings banks is that, whereas the Treasury-bill rate was a good proxy for deposit costs in the past, government policies adopted to help savings banks attract deposits have made funding costs more uncertain and volatile. The customer has many options among deposit rates: the four-week average or the most recent six-month or three-month Treasury-bill rate, the various time-deposit rates, and the money-market deposit-account rate. One must assume the customer will always choose the most attractive rate, leaving the bank with the highest cost of funds.

As a result, savings banks employing a liability-cost hedge cannot target a particular period with certainty, but are concerned with general market rates for the expected level of deposits. This is less precise than hedging a cost based on a specific bill rate for a known period of time. However, if bill rates were to jump to 12 percent from 8 percent, all rates should move. In this sense, the hedge is more a yield-level hedge with which the bank expects to protect itself from drastic changes in levels.

Convergence is of primary importance in determining the rate received. If a hedge is held until contract expiration, the hedger will receive the rate on the contract when the hedge was initiated. To assess convergence, spreads are considered. If a spread between the current 13-week bill rate and the contract covering a three-month period in the future is 25 basis points, in addition to any move in cash bills, the contract will move by 25 basis points by its expiration. This implies a convergence cost or benefit (depending on the yield

---

[5] For purposes of illustration, all other costs are omitted.

curve) of 1 percent annually. Hedging for three months, then, would get the bank the current rate, plus or minus 1 percent annual convergence.

Rates can be hedged by stacking all in the front contracts, which not only provides more liquidity but in some yield-curve environments, can provide a more attractive rate.

The risk is that the yield curve will shift. Going short a strip of eight consecutive contracts, for example, will create a two-year hedge. In this case, the risk of a shift in the general yield curve is mitigated. However, given the general nature of the hedge program, stacking may be preferable more often than in other cases (see Chapters 10 and 17).

There is no real basis risk in the sense of the debt-market general hedge examples. What does exist for a savings bank is the problem of timing mismatch. Hedges are set up to cover specific time periods. But deposits may not coincide with these periods—or, if they do, they may be difficult to measure. Because deposit flows are hard to gauge, the savings bank simply can't be that precise on what they are hedging.

If certain large deposits are known to be coming due and will be renewed, contracts can be established, to specifically protect against their costs. For example, Olympic knows that a $10 million deposit is going to be rolled over on December 21, 1983, for a period of three months.[6]

A short of 10 bill contracts would protect against rate changes during that period. Assume that today 90-day bills are at 9 percent and the December contract could be sold at a 9.40 percent discount. If the liability cost changes in line with T-bill rates, Olympic's liability cost for the three months beginning December 21 would be 40 basis points higher than today's level reflecting the bill contract's full convergence. If, however, the deposit being hedged were to be rolled on December 9, the spread between cash and futures would not have fully converged. Generally, the shorter the time period until contract expiration, the lower the spread uncertainty. However, in addition to the time factor, significant changes in the yield curve will have an impact on spreads. When the contract is closed out, if the spread between 90-day bills and the December contract is such that the future is 10 basis points higher, Olympic's cost of money will be 10 basis points lower than it would have been on December 21 because convergence would only cost 30 basis points.

Two characteristics differentiate Olympic's general-liability hedge from the hedges previously discussed. First, this type of hedge is more *rate* sensitive. The goal is to reduce volatility on the liability side of

---

[6] December 21 is the date on which the December T-bill contract stops trading.

the bank's asset/liability equation. Second, there is really no cash alternative, except matching assets and liabilities. The choices, then, often involve doing business with volatility or trying to manage that volatility.

A sample hedge program

Suppose that in March of 1982, Olympic National decides to begin hedging its $100 million of 9-1/2 percent mortgages for one year. Rates are at 12 percent. While Olympic does not want to lock in a loss, its losses will be worse if rates increase sharply. Rather than hedging the whole position at once, Olympic scales into its futures position.

At the completion of the program, Olympic will be short 100 contracts in each of four contract periods. It is assumed that the period prior to the hedge program is already funded. For illustrative purposes, it is also assumed that the contracts are evenly allocated to each period, Olympic needs to scale into 400 contracts. Contracts will be covered when they are the front month and liabilities are incurred, such that rate protection is no longer required for that particular time period. In other words, Olympic will cover its June bill contracts just prior to contract expiration and simultaneously issue a 90-day time deposit at the current market rate. The change in value of the 100 June contracts will offset the cost of the time deposit.

The goal of the hedge program is to establish a reasonably defined cost of funds for the hedge period. As demonstrated in Table 16-3, this rate is achieved upon completion of the program. *Sale rate* refers to the weighted average of the rates on the four contract months to be sold. If rates continue to decline, increasing numbers of contracts can be sold to bring down the overall hedge rate until the fixed-rate loan portfolio is hedged. As the program is in progress, Olympic will run a deficit balance in its variation-margin account, and negotiable funds must be available to meet margin calls.

Olympic anticipates a decline to 8-1/2 percent, but not being able to predict that decline with certainty starts to hedge earlier, starting such a program when rates are at 12 percent. If rates turn upward before the program is finished, Olympic will regret not having had a more aggressive program, but obviously the program will have been beneficial. If rates decline as the hedge is put on, lower rates keep getting averaged in as more contract positions are added. In this way, the bank can still achieve an attractive *average rate* from the hedge. Under the most favorable circumstances, a large variation-margin call would be anticipated.

Olympic assumes that rates will reach and remain at 8-1/2 percent and that the cost of variation margin will not be significant. If from

Table 16-3   Hedge program schedule

New	Total	Sale rate	Average rate	Variation-margin balance
25	25	12.00%	12.00%	$ 0
25	50	11.50	11.75	31,250
25	75	11.00	11.50	93,750
30	105	10.50	11.21	187,500
50	155	10.00	10.82	317,625
60	215	9.50	10.45	511,500
90	305	9.00	10.02	779,375
95	400	8.50	9.66	1,159,000

the time the program is completed, half (200) of the contracts were outstanding for a year, the average adverse margin payments will be half of $1,159,000, or $579,500. If this is financed at a cost of 9-1/2 percent, it would cost $55,000 per year. For $100 million of liabilities being hedged for a year, this is not material. Each change of 100 basis points in average rates would change the variation-margin balance by $500,000 and the financing effect by $47,500 per year.

Liquidity can be difficult in the distant months, but with some minor price penalty, Olympic can sell contracts (see Chapters 10 and 17). However, it may be difficult to trade out of these quickly. The assumption is that these will be held until liabilities are incurred against them and they have, therefore, become closer to the front contracts.

Olympic has spread this position throughout a year. If rates continue to decline, lower rates can then be realized on new contracts sold. Thus, if rates stay low, Olympic sees its liability costs declining, though more slowly than the cash market. But it will have been protected.

17

Fixed-rate loans

The use of financial futures written on Treasury bills, CDs, or Eurodollars can make it possible for a bank with variable funding costs to offer fixed-rate loans, thus giving a competitive edge to those banks which can take advantage of such flexibility.

Hedging with these money-market contracts whose price activity reflects the bank's cost of funds, allows a loan rate to be extended based on money-market conditions when the liability hedge is put in place. To protect its cost of funding, the bank will sell contracts to cover the term of the loan. Because trading volume in deferred-month contracts is limited, this hedge strategy is usually most meaningfully applied by small and medium-sized banks with fewer alternatives for laying off interest-rate risk than larger banks with more diverse portfolios.

Many customers prefer to minimize their rate risk by taking fixed-rate loans, but the optimal situation for a bank is to earn a spread over its variable cost of funding. By setting up a hedge program, the bank can calculate a base rate for fixed-rate loans that will encompass the potential costs of the hedge along with the bank's profit spread. And an institution offering fixed-rate loans often puts an asset on its books that it couldn't otherwise offer without the credit risk inherent in variable rates when rates rise substantially.

DEFINING HEDGE MECHANICS

The hedge is set up to protect the quarterly funding costs incurred close to each contract expiration date. Money-market contracts are sold against liabilities representing the source of funding (which will be incurred at a later date) in an effort to match the existing asset to those liabilities today. The existing asset—the loan—is priced at some spread off the funding cost set up by the hedge, and any imprecision from hedging or pricing will adjust the profit spread.

Part of setting up the hedge, then, involves developing a base loan rate that will be competitive but still afford protection against changing market relationships while the hedge is in place. It is important to note that the cost of funds and the related base rate are derived from the rates given by the futures market, *not from current cash-market rates.* Furthermore, the comparable rate is not the existing three-month rate but a one-and-one-half-year funding rate, say for a loan covering a period of one-and-one-half years. At times, the rate implicit in a strip of futures contracts is lower than the cash-market rate for the same period. In those cases, a bank can create a more attractive loan with futures than by funding in the cash market.

Any hedge strategy is a function of the market environment that exists when the strategy is implemented. The fixed-rate loan hedge generally exemplifies this and shows how the liability manager must adapt strategies.

Hyland Trust initiated a fixed-rate loan program three years ago. As the general market has changed from high yield expectations and a steeply inverted yield curve to lower rate levels and a positive curve, Hyland's hedging program has evolved.

A NEGATIVE YIELD-CURVE LOAN

The methodology for establishing fixed-rate loans varies slightly, depending on the yield curve. In a positive yield-curve environment, yield increases with maturity, whereas in negative environments, longer maturities have lower yields than shorter maturities. This influences the relationship between the cash and futures markets. In a positive yield-curve environment, it is likely that the rate created with a strip of futures being shorted will be higher than current lending rates. Clients may be willing to accept that, because of the lower absolute levels and the greater potential over time for rates to rise. When the yield curve is negatively sloped, the rates on these loans will typically be below current three-month rates but at high absolute levels.

To illustrate fixed-rate loan construction, we have chosen to first consider an example based upon an actual loan established in 1981— a time of highly inverted yield curves—and to trace its development.

At that time, the CD contract did not exist, and Treasury-bill contracts terminated on a relatively contiguous basis. After that, we will consider the creation of a fixed-rate loan during a period of positive yield curves, with CD contracts available as an alternative and Treasury-bill contracts noncontiguous.

Structuring the hedged loan

The fall of 1981 was a time of great uncertainty in fixed-income markets. Many economists were predicting increasing interest rates and a prime rate as high as 25 percent. Hyland Trust had a client in the construction business who wanted to borrow $1 million for a period of approximately 27 months. The bank was concerned that, if rates increased, the effect of a variable-rate loan on construction costs could jeopardize the project. Because the client already had a mortgage commitment, Hyland was not concerned about the effects of long-term rates. The bank wished to minimize its credit risk by offering a fixed-rate loan to the company, but it certainly didn't want to take the risk of funding the loan at higher rates.

Hyland knew it could issue a CD to fund the first three months of the loan at a rate of 16.35 percent, but it had to analyze potential costs and risks before pricing the hedged loan. Hyland could short a strip of bill contracts, which would cover the time period and principal value of the loan. And it could fix a loan rate based upon the hedged liability cost, adjusted for the market and credit spread of its CD-based funding.

Table 17-1 shows the hypothetical rate of return that would be earned for the total loan using the Treasury-bill hedge. When the loan was extended, a 250-basis-point difference between the 13-week bill rate and CD yields existed in the market and could be included in the base loan rate. By using futures, Hyland was seeking to insure a cost of money approximating 15.85 percent. This hedged cost was then adjusted for reserve requirements, for the potential costs of managing the hedged position, and finally for the bank profit and customer credit spread to set the loan rate for the client.[1]

On December 15, Hyland issues a three-month CD to fund the second period of the loan and covers the December contract. If interest rates decline and the December Treasury-bill contract goes up 100 basis points, from 86.39 to 87.39, then Hyland will have lost $2,500 on this one contract. Hyland will recapture this loss when it issues its CD at a cost 100 basis points lower than that in effect when

---

[1] This does not take into account what, in this case, would be minor timing differences, derived from the fact that the cost of funds will go down over a period of time while the loan receipts will be constant.

TABLE 17-1

Time period covered	Contract month	Treasury bill contract rate	Effective CD issuance*
12/81- 3/82	December '81	13.61%	16.11%
3/82- 6/82	March '82	13.44	15.94
6/82- 9/82	June '82	13.29	15.79
9/82-12/82	September '82	13.30	15.80
12/82- 3/83	December '82	13.29	15.79
3/83- 6/83	March '83	13.30	15.80
6/83- 9/83	June '83	13.30	15.80
9/83-12/83	September '83	13.30	15.80
Average		13.35%	15.85%

*Cash CD issued to cover September-December 1981 period at 16.35.
Assumes a 250-basis-point spread between CDs and bills.

it put on the loan. The lower funding cost offsets the loss in futures.[2]

Two things have been assumed: first, that the CD rate would remain 250 basis points higher than Treasury bills; second, that the CD issuance date would coincide with a date very close to the date on which the Treasury-bill contract stopped trading.

The Treasury bill-CD spread

Hyland did not have the opportunity to hedge with CDs. It had to make some decision on how to handle the spread between the CD market and the Treasury-bill market. The spread between CDs and bills when Hyland put on the hedge was 250 basis points. The bank was able to build this spread into its fixed-rate loan for a period of 24 months and still offer an attractive loan package.

By historical standards, 250 basis points is exceptionally wide. Hyland decided that compensating for the CD-bill spread in the loan rate was a viable strategy and an acceptable risk.

If the market rallied, this spread would likely narrow, with CDs rallying more than Treasury bills. A reduction of 100 basis points in Treasury-bill levels might occur, while CD yields might improve by 115 basis points. Thus, Hyland would face a loss of 100 basis points on the bill futures but would earn 115 basis points by issuing a lower-cost CD—for a net gain of 15 basis points.

Of course, if rates rose dramatically, Treasury bills might go up at a slower pace than CDs, exposing Hyland to some risk. However, variation-margin financing would likely work counter to the direction of

---

[2] If the yield curve warranted, Hyland could issue a six-month CD and cover two successive contracts, i.e., December and March.

the CD-bill spread. If the market rallied and Hyland were forced to pay variation margin, that cost should be mitigated by an improvement in the CD-bill spread. Just the opposite would be true if yields rose.

Hyland's other alternatives in handling the CD-bill spread was to use a hedge ratio. The greater volatility in CD rates might be managed by shorting 1.1 Treasury bill contracts for each $1 million of CDs to be hedged. If Treasury bills went down by 100 basis points, Hyland would suffer a loss of 110 basis points—which should match the more rapid decline in CD rates. However, should Treasury-bill rates go up by 100 basis points, Hyland's 1.1 hedge ratio would protect the bank against a 110-basis-point increase in CD costs. At this time, given the historically wide spread, Hyland decided to assume the risk and hedge only one contract per $1 million.

As it happened, yields improved dramatically after Hyland extended this loan. The bank financed a large variation-margin balance over this loan period, but the absolute cost of CDs declined precipitously. More important, the spread between bills and CDs narrowed to less than 100 basis points.

Despite the decline in market levels, Hyland earned a substantial profit for a limited risk, capturing the difference between the 250-basis-point spread it included in the loan and the narrowing spread in the market when the contract positions were closed out. This more than offset the financing cost of the variation margin. The decision to incorporate this spread in the lending rate thus created a highly profitable loan.

Handling longer loan periods

If the client had wanted a rate for longer than the 27-month period originally granted, Hyland could have considered it. Contracts from the December 1982 to December 1983 period were selling at approximately the same index level of 86.70—and, therefore, the same yield of 13.30 percent. If Hyland chose to, and liquidity permitted, it could have shorted an additional December 1983 contract or other distant contracts. If the bank chose to short a second December 1983 contract, it could have done so with the expectation that that contract would cover changes in yield levels for the March 1984 to June 1984 period.

Obviously, Hyland would prefer to match the time period for which the cost would be incurred by selling a March 1984 contract, but such contracts were not yet trading. By shorting the December 1983 contract, Hyland assumed that it could protect itself against changes in levels. Hyland also considered the possibility that when the March contract began trading, the bank could buy in the second December 1983 contract and sell a March 1984 contract at a narrow spread if the contract spreads didn't change.

The risk that Hyland was taking, therefore, was not one of changes in level for the period March 1984 to June 1984. The December contract gave it effective protection against that. Instead, the risk was that the December 1983 contract would not, in fact, trade at the same price as the March 1984 when the latter began to trade (see Chapter 10).

To the extent that the March 1984 contract traded at a price lower than that for December 1983, Hyland would have been adversely affected. To the extent that the contract traded at a higher price, Hyland would have been a beneficiary. The contract would tend to trade at a lower price if it were reflecting a positive yield curve. However, Hyland estimated that contracts that far out probably wouldn't reflect rate differentials greater than 20 basis points. Thus, Hyland knew that, if rates went down, it would have variation-margin financing costs to bear in addition to a loss on the roll from December 1983 to March 1984. However, it also knew that it probably would have substantial spread gains from the relationship between CDs and bills.

Hyland was aware that if rates rose, the December 1983 to March 1984 spread could move in its favor, mitigating the risk that the variation-margin financing gains would not offset the possible widening of the CD-bill spread.

If Hyland chose to extend the loan beyond 27 months—to 30 months, for example—with minimum risk, it might face an additional *potential* cost of 20 basis points for three months. On the other hand, this might turn out to be a gain.

To be prudent, Hyland could include the spread risk as a cost factor in the extended loan. In so doing, the net cost for a total 30-month loan would hardly be raised at all. By including the additional contract sold, at an assumed cost of 13.50, the rate on the loan would increase by only two basis points. However, this would enable Hyland to extend the loan with a certain degree of protection—while, in all probability, having created a loan at a higher level of profit for itself.

For Hyland, convergence is a given rather than a risk in this application. It can be measured when the hedge is put on. Because the basis risk between the CD and the Treasury-bill contract used for the hedge has been accounted for by an adjustment of the loan price and a decision to accept the risk, no adjustment to the hedge ratio is necessary. Only if contracts must be offset prior to full convergence at expiration will the actual Treasury-bill hedge rate vary from that anticipated.

Generally speaking, the closer to the contract expiration date, the closer the cash Treasury-bill rate will be to the contract price and the greater the chance that the bank will realize its anticipated hedge rate. The imprecision that would occur prior to settlement date will not necessarily be unfavorable and will primarily be a function of the yield curve. However, as long as Hyland chooses to issue CDs on or about the time the Treasury-bill contracts converge, it does not have to worry about this problem (see Chapter 10).

Variation-margin financing

As each new CD is issued, one Treasury bill is offset—reducing total exposure. If Hyland assumes that, during the 27-month loan hedge, it will have, on average, four contracts outstanding for each $1 million loan, the problem can be analyzed as follows:

In the event that rates fell, Hyland would be required to provide margin for the variation-margin account. A decrease of 100 basis points, on average, would result in a $10,000 average margin balance. If this prevailed over the term of the loan, and if the bank could finance this at a rate of 15 percent for the entire two years, the bank would have an additional expense of $1,500—or 15 basis points—a year. The bank would have to analyze this risk against the other variables of the loan.

A POSITIVE YIELD CURVE-LOAN

Hyland continued to issue fixed-rate loans as yield levels and yield-curve circumstances changed. In the summer of 1983, it was approached by a client who felt that market yields were at unsustainably low levels. Hyland was prepared to issue a fixed-rate loan—although, at these lower yield levels, it, too, was concerned about the possibility of increased funding costs over the next two years. And the fact the CDs were then only 70 basis points higher than the bill discount rate was seen as an additional concern.

Circumstances also changed within the futures markets. By 1983, futures on CDs had become available; and, while due to limited trading, they could not be used effectively beyond the first two contracts, they provided Hyland with some flexibility. However, the bank's situation was complicated by the fact that bill contracts were no longer contiguous (see Chapter 10). This meant that using bill contracts could create substantial gaps in the time periods covered by the hedge.

The rates shown in Table 17-2 prevailed in the CD and Treasury bill futures market in the middle of 1983.

Treasury bill-CD spread

Hyland could finance the initial part of a two-year fixed-rate loan at a rate approximating 9.20 percent. It realized that it could short the first two CD contracts, those being the most liquid, and avoid the

TABLE 17-2

CDs:	
Current three-month CD	9.20%
September 1983 CD contract	9.65
December 1983 CD contract	9.89
T Bills (discount):	
March 1984	9.36%
June 1984	9.54
September 1984	9.72
December 1984	9.87
March 1985	10.02

CD-bill-spread risk. However, because deferred CD futures trade with limited liquidity, Hyland was forced to again sell Treasury-bill contracts to match the remaining five contract periods. It was thus once more in a position of having to decide how to handle the spread between CDs and bills.

In the 1981 situation, Hyland felt that the 250-basis-point spread between the CDs and bills incorporated in the loan rate provided a good level of protection. However, at current levels, with a spread of approximately 70 basis points, the risk was much greater that CD yields would increase substantially more than those of bills. Accordingly, the bank was not comfortable merely hedging one to one and using the current spread in its base loan rate.

Hyland analyzed three choices.

The first was to price the loan with the assumption that CDs could be issued during the hedge period at a spread of 150 basis points, producing a rate Hyland felt was acceptable to the client, even though the rate was substantially higher than the current market rate that reflected the prevailing 70-basis-point spread between bills and CDs. This level was lower than the potential cost if yields rose substantially. Hyland knew that the first three periods were funded or hedged with CDs and, therefore, had no spread risk. As the March CD began to trade, the bank could buy its T bill and sell a CD in its place. To the extent that the CD-bill spread at that time was less than 150 basis points, Hyland would have been adding to its cushion for the following periods.

Hyland's second choice was to use more bills and hedge with a 1.1 ratio. By analyzing the likely relationship between bill discounts and CDs from current levels, Hyland might have concluded that, in the event bill rates rose CD cost would rise an additional 10 percent. Therefore, Hyland would seek to increase its hedge ratio. For every 100-basis-point move in bills, it would gain 110 basis points, protecting itself against the greater increase in CD rates. Of course, Hyland would now face a cost if rates declined but the bill-CD spread did not narrow, because, for every decline of 100 basis points in bills, Hyland would need a 110-basis-point decline in its CD cost to offset the loss on futures. While the CD spread might come in, based on historical analysis, a substantial movement seemed somewhat unlikely.

Hyland's third choice was to go short all CD contracts, utilizing September or December CDs. Instead of shorting bill contracts, it would sell five additional December 1983 CD contracts to avoid any risk in a relationship between CDs and bills. Hyland would have had to assume a "roll" cost to assess its yield-curve risk. For example, using current bill spreads as a guide, if a loan could be competitively priced assuming a 20-point spread between each contract month, Hyland could assume an average rate at which it could roll all its CD contracts as liquidity in CD contracts permits.

In the event the yield curve became more positive, Hyland would have to assume a higher cost to roll its December contracts successively to later contracts. On the other hand, if rates went up, Hyland could assume that the contract-month spread would become more favorable. Consequently, the bank would be able to move contracts back at increasingly favorable rates, thereby cutting its costs. If rates increased sharply, Hyland would have the option of transferring the CD contracts to later bill contracts at any time, taking advantage both of the higher CD rate and the more favorable pricing of the distant contracts. Should rates rise from prevailing levels, this could work out well, with only moderate risk.

Hyland could also lessen the risk of rolling the CD contract position by buying Treasury-bill spreads. If the spread between contract months became more positive, the profit on Treasury-bill spreads would have offset the cost of the roll. Of course, the possible advantage of a negative yield-curve roll would have been offset by the loss on the bill spreads.

Measuring the Treasury bill gap

As long as Hyland decided to short Treasury-bill contracts as part of its hedge, adjusting its hedge ratio or incorporating the 150-point spread in the loan rate, it would have to contend with another problem.

Treasury bills cover discrete, noncontiguous periods. As discussed in Chapter 10, bill contracts now terminate on a schedule determined by the one-year Treasury bill. Consequently, they may terminate on the 7th of one contract month and the 21st of the next contract month. This leaves substantial time periods uncovered, or substantial periods of overlap.

One way to avoid the problem—and perhaps the easiest for Hyland— would be to roll its bill contracts into CD contracts before that timing differential had any impact on the bill contract. It is unlikely that relatively short time period mismatch will affect contract pricing six months in advance. Thus, if Hyland could move its contracts from the bill market to the CD market (because CD contracts cover adjoining periods of time), it could substantially avoid the problem.

Other ways to manage the gap are much more complicated, either using when-issued Treasury bills or fractions of contracts to try to cope with timing differences.

The positive yield-curve situation thus provided Hyland with a different set of circumstances. But, analytically, the situation was essentially the same. Hyland would first consider the rate it could get based on the futures market and then weigh any basis risk or spread risk incurred because of a decision to sell bill contracts or a decision to stack contracts in the front. Any failure to match the liability-funding cycle with futures would have to be considered. And Hyland would have to analyze the potential variation-margin financing risk. Finally, if the bank were going to make a loan for longer than two years, it would have to consider whether or not it wished to stack back contracts.

INTERNAL COORDINATION

One last consideration involves the management of fixed-rate loans within a bank. Some banks have approached the subject by assuming that corporate loan officers should deal with their clients and set rates on loans. However, for a person without experience, the subject of futures can be complex. Typically, the considerations involved in making hedging decisions are very much like those made by money managers for a bank. It makes organizational sense, therefore, that those responsible for the bank's asset/liability mix and monetary activities undertake hedging activities. Just as funding liabilities are these persons' responsibilities, potential losses or gains from the hedge apply to them, as well. Hedging is centralized and there is no need to instruct a large number of loan officers in the use of futures. However, the structure of loan-takedown dates (lack of prepayment options) will be influenced by the constraints of the contract market.

How the bank makes a fixed-rate loan is less important than the competitive position it can establish by making such a loan. Those who are familiar with money-market activities can calculate rates. They, in turn, can extend rates that loan officers can, after adjusting for profit and credit spreads, quote to customers.

Creative uses of fixed-rate-loan-futures applications, therefore may allow participation by banks in areas they would not normally enter, because they can thus accommodate a customer or because they can better control credit risk.

18

Variable-rate insurance products

Many insurance companies now offer variable-rate products in response to the consumer demand created by secular increase in interest rates and the accompanying heightened rate volatility over the past few years. These products have made inroads into markets traditionally available for whole-life policies.

The goals in designing these variable-rate products are to be innovative, competitive, and highly marketable, and two basic types have evolved; the single premium deferred annuity (SPDA) and more recently, the universal life policy. There are many variations in product terms and the pricings offered; the common thread is that these products change the rate paid to the policyholder on a periodic basis, often quarterly. The rate paid is pegged either to an index established when the product is sold or to one periodically determined by the company.

The growth in these products has been dramatic. However, in the late 1970s, many companies ran into substantial problems managing their SPDA portfolios. The insurer continually faced the risk that, if its payout rate is not competitive, a policyholder could pay a "surrender charge" and cancel the policy. In addition, the tax law gave annuity holders the ability to cancel a policy with one company and move to another without having to pay taxes on accumulated interest earnings.

The need to be very rate competitive was a constant influence on investment policy and often prompted contracyclical investment decisions. When rates were low and the yield curve positive, pressure existed for insurers to buy long-term instruments to get the higher yield. If interest rates moved up from the point at which the annuity proceeds were invested, the insurer was forced to raise the policy payouts—although the principal value of the portfolio declined and its investment income was static. Failure to raise payouts would result in substantial liquidation costs as annuitants surrendered their policies. On the other hand, while rates were high and the yield curve was inverted, insurers tended to invest in shorter-term instruments to maximize current yield, foregoing the benefit of improving rates on the prices of long-term bonds. Consequently, investing for the variable-rate product was a high-risk proposition.

Variable-rate product offerings remain highly competitive and are marketed aggressively. This often results in conflicts between marketing, actuarial, and investment decision makers. For many products, profitability is strictly a function of the portfolio manager's investment skills.[1]

Futures can play a role in creating and managing variable-rate products. The holder of a fixed-income security has a constant income stream but a variable principal value; in a hedged bond position, the principal value is stabilized but, due to convergence and variation-margin financing, the income stream becomes variable and moves with the market. The variable-rate product manager has to analyze the factors involved in using futures to assess the rate-of-return potential for the hedged portfolio. The hedging strategy is tailored to the particular product specifications and to the degree of rate exposure a portfolio manager chooses to assume. Many companies link product payout to indexes expected to exceed the three-month Treasury-bill rate. The need to invest for these rates forces the manager to use innovative portfolio-management techniques.

The factors that will influence the periodic return on a hedged bond portfolio are the same as those considered for a general hedge, but the focus of the analysis is different. Convergence, which adjusts the earnings on a long-term bond position to a shorter-term rate, is a dominant variable in creating periodic return. The bond portfolio will often be hedged over the product's life, and basis risk is limited

---

[1] For example, "safe" product rates based on the three-month Treasury-bill rate, but which change monthly, involve a difficult management problem. While the difference between a 90-day rate and a 30-day rate is usually not dramatic, neither is the rate of return differential the company can hope to earn. On a risk-adjusted basis, this strategy can often be hazardous.

in comparison to the shorter-term portfolio hedge (see Chapter 16). The basis relationship may change over the cycle, but unexpected variations do not usually have a compounding effect on overall product return. The impact of variation-margin financing will vary depending upon the type of product, the length of time between payout resets, and the nature of the bonds hedged. The anticipated effect of each component can be quantified and used to adjust the coupon earnings on the bond portfolio. The company can then estimate its periodic return on the product portfolio, which can be compared to the payout rate required. Below, the principal types of variable-rate products are discussed.

UNIVERSAL LIFE

Empire Life Insurance Company has decided to offer a new universal life policy. The universal product is attractive to policyholders due to its flexibility. The client may deposit various amounts of premium income and determine that a segment will be devoted to an insurance premium while the residual amount earns the payout rate for the period. Interest on the cash excess accumulates tax-free until it is withdrawn or used to cover the premium payments. The use of the interest on this cash balance effectively converts the insurance premium to a pretax cost.

Based on actuarial and marketing considerations, Empire Life decided that an indexed universal life policy with a payout rate pegged to the five-year Treasury note would be a competitive product that could be managed without excessive risk. The five-year rate will be adjusted by a set amount to cover product operational costs. Empire is considering a product with a payout rate reset quarterly at 100 basis points less than the current yield of a five-year Treasury note.

Empire has been analyzing the relationship between this rate and various investment strategies to determine its risk and potential profit spread. When the yield curve is positive, Empire could maximize its yield by buying long-term instruments; but if rates rise, the company will lack the income to increase payouts and could suffer substantial losses if cancellations force the sale of securities. Buying a short-term instrument to match the quarterly rate reset is another alternative. Although the risk is limited, often these will not provide an acceptable return.

Empire is also examining the returns that could be created by managing a bond portfolio with futures. This strategy will often provide a better rate of return than will short-term instruments, though not as good as the return from long-term bonds. The flexibility, limited risk, and other advantages afforded by a futures strategy may prove attractive, all the more so because the strategy permits Empire to maximize product sales to the benefit of the entire company.

In the case of fixed-rate loans, Hyland Trust Company looked to the futures market to create a currently defined rate of return for specific time periods in the future (see Chapter 17). The goal of Empire's hedge is similar, but the strategy and management are different. Empire will sell futures with a view to creating investment returns which will vary constantly with its payout rate by controlling the market volatility of a long-term bond portfolio. Hyland's basic funding cost was established to match a fixed-loan rate when the hedge was put on. Empire's strategy requires more active management than was true for Hyland. But the focus still centers on protecting the profit spread.

By creating a hedged portfolio that takes advantage of the credit spread between long-term Treasuries and the highest yielding, acceptable nonTreasury bond, Empire assumes that over a period of time, its portfolio earnings will be satisfactory. If the yield curve inverts and portfolio return becomes far out of line with the payout rate, some funds can be put into Eurodollars or other acceptable short-term investments. Empire also has the option at any time to hedge only part of its portfolio, thus creating any desired level of market exposure. Most important, in the event that it does face some redemptions, Empire will be protected at all times against the adverse impact of a forced liquidation of bonds.

Empire's first step is to put together a public bond portfolio[2] with an acceptable credit rating, one that will provide the greatest after-tax income to the company.[3] The variable functions related to cross hedging with futures can then be analyzed. These functions include (a) setting a hedge ratio to minimize principal variability and evaluating the basis risk,[4] (b) looking at convergence, including contract characteristics, to determine the likely impact of any cash-futures price adjustment of the contract and, (c) estimating potential variation-margin financing benefits or costs. The effects of these variable functions can be measured to determine the expected portfolio income and to provide a reasonable estimate of periodic rate of return.

In seeking to protect its principal value, Empire will analyze the expected performance of its portfolio relative to the Treasury market

---

[2] Empire might also hedge fixed-rate private placement loans in this investment portfolio, taking advantage of the relatively higher yield, as well as the rate variability and liquidity provided by futures.

[3] Tax considerations can vary substantially from company to company and from year to year. In some years, certain companies will prefer to utilize premium bonds while other companies will prefer to have discount bonds or preferred stocks, depending on their aggregate tax situation. For that reason, we have not considered potential tax-financial accounting timing differences. For a discussion of the tax implications of futures, see Chapter 25.

[4] For a detailed description of calculating a hedge ratio, see Chapter 16.

to set up its hedge ratio using a surrogate bond or average portfolio characteristics to describe its anticipated portfolio performance. In setting its hedge ratio, Empire would ignore the effects of convergence or variation margin at the outset, and base its hedge on the future equivalent value of the most deliverable Treasury bond. (Compensating for convergence in the hedge ratio would lead to market-level risks, which Empire is trying to avoid in product portfolio management.)

Unlike the portfolio manager protecting against intermittent market moves, Empire is looking at a longer-term strategy. Its hedge ratio is set in keeping with this longer-term market perspective and may not capture smaller cyclical changes in basis spreads. To the extent that the hedge ratio proves inadequate during one quarter, it may prove to be profitable in the next quarter.

Empire will probably make relatively few adjustments to its hedge ratio. Such adjustments could result from a new investment philosophy or from major shifts in the market, either of which would affect the performance of the portfolio relative to that of the Treasury market. If, for example, Empire bought current coupon telephone bonds (with a five-year call) during a period of high yields and rates subsequently declined precipitiously, the callable bonds would begin to underperform Treasuries. Depending on cash-market yield spreads, Empire might swap the cash bonds if they were expected to continue to underperform or adjust its hedge ratio to reflect the change in the projected relationship between its portfolio and Treasuries. In either instance, Empire is able to update its hedge strategy to accommodate market conditions.

The risk of changes in the basis relationship might be considered when pricing the product. Empire could accrue a quarterly expense to cover potential hedge imprecision. For example, Empire might set up a reserve to cover potential basis cost. If no basis cost has been incurred at the end of several quarters, Empire might stop accruing for the potential loss. In fact, if Empire's cash portfolio outperformed the futures position (after a satisfactory reserve has been established), a basis gain might be taken into profit. In this manner, the company can establish its product pricing with some protection against basis risk becoming an unexpected cost.

Once Empire has protected its capital position, adjustments to periodic income due to convergence and variation-margin financing are considered.[5] These adjustments help Empire maintain a level of income that will vary in line with the general market and, consequently, in line with the payout rate on the universal life policy. The

---

[5] Accounting treatment for hedged positions has been evolving as the use of futures becomes more accepted. Acceptable accounting methods are being reviewed by the Financial Accounting Standards Board (see Chapter 24).

primary adjustment factor Empire considers is convergence, calculated as the difference between the actual futures price and the future equivalent value at the time the company establishes a position.

Let's say the future is selling at 16/32 below its equivalent value during the initial period hedged with the first contract. Empire must take into account that for each future sold it faces a loss of $500.[6] This cost—or in the case of a negative yield curve, this benefit—is treated as the major adjustment factor between the long-term rate being secured on the income from the cash bond and the short-term rate being created through the use of futures. The impact of convergence is affected by the hedge ratio, which, in turn is a function of the asset's dollar volatility vis-à-vis that of futures. Empire can calculate the convergence effect for subsequent periods in terms of the spread at which the contract position is rolled to the next reset period.[7]

Empire has to be aware of the particular characteristics of the contract it is using to estimate the convergence effect. Most product portfolios are hedged with Treasury-bond contracts, and the after-hours delivery problem will have to be assessed. To be conservative, for the initial period, Empire could assume that the future will converge fully to cash. In fact, due to the after-hours delivery mechanism, the future may stay below its cash equivalent value. (Generally, having the future remain at a discount to cash is a one-time benefit.) To the extent that contracts are rolled, after-hours delivery is not necessarily a major factor because the price of the contract to be bought as well as sold on the roll will involve some degree of after-hours price adjustments. However, the front contract tends to be affected more than the price of the second or third contract will be. The significance of after-hours delivery lies in the combination of cash-futures relationship when Empire first shorts a future and when it finally closes out the futures position.

Variation-margin financing is not usually significant if it is accounted for quarterly with the product reset. The longer the period between the pricing reset and the greater the market move, the more impact upon return this financing is likely to have.

Although Empire can evaluate each of these risks, because they are

---

[6] Empire evaluates the price of the cheapest-to-deliver bond and compares that to the price at which the contracts were sold. For example, Empire sells September contracts at 74-16/32 when the 14s are the cheapest to deliver, priced at 122. The September factor is 1.6265. The price of the 14s (122) divided by its factor (1.6265) equals 75, the future equivalent value.

[7] At the end of the September period, for example, Empire will buy in its September contract and sell December contracts. This roll is done as a spread (see Chapters 5 and 7), and creates the adjustment to income for the next period. If the price of the December contract is 12/32nds lower than that of the September contract at the time of the roll, a cost of $375 per contract for rolling the short position would reduce the income for the September to December period.

interdependent, computer programs have been designed to help analyze the probable rates of return for hedged portfolios. The output shown in Table 18-1 describes some base case assumptions related to a product portfolio hedge. The impact of each variable on the periodic rate of return is calculated. This example leads to a rate of return of 9.633 percent on the bond portfolio. It assumes no basis gain or loss, a convergence loss of 12/32 per contract, a hedge ratio of 1.3 contracts per $100,000 par value of bonds owned, and an average adverse yield change of 75 basis points. This return is compared to Empire's alternative investments and quarterly product cost. A domestic CD for a comparable period of time would have yielded 8.75 percent. The product payout, set at 100 basis points lower than the rate of a five-year note, equaled 9.16 percent.[8]

The effects of basis, convergence, and variation margin can only be estimated at the beginning of each payout period. These factors can be assessed at various levels to determine their impact on income and on the sensitivity of a hedged portfolio's return. Empire can analyze the payout on a five-year Treasury less the 100-basis-point policy rate, at different market levels and using matching yield-curve assumptions, create a set of probable returns for the hedged portfolio. This analysis can be used to create a matrix of forecasted earnings for the hedged product over a period of years.

Empire realizes that one of the advantages of hedged portfolios backing variable-rate products is the flexibility to change investment strategy. Cash bonds can be sold and futures purchased at any time for any portion of the portfolio to maintain virtually 100 percent of the original principal.[9] Therefore, Empire could maximize yield and shift to a short-term instrument, such as Eurodollars or preferred stocks, should that be a more advantageous strategy. As a practical consideration, for market reasons as well as tax reasons, it is often not feasible to liquidate entire portfolios and repurchase them. Thus, while Empire has that option, it should initially consider how futures will affect its results under various conditions.

SINGLE PREMIUM DEFERRED ANNUITY

Empire is also considering an SPDA product. Such products are somewhat more difficult to manage than universal products, because holders of SPDAs have traditionally been more aggressive in canceling their contracts. This was prevalent during the late 1970s and early

---

[8] Matrixes showing variations from the base case yield are given in Appendix VI.

[9] If this is done at a time other than the end of a contract period, the return for the period may be somewhat different from that projected, depending upon any difference between the rate of convergence assumed when the hedge is initiated and the cash-futures spread when the hedge is reversed.

TABLE 18-1

BOND PRICE AND YIELD INFORMATION

TIME PERIOD OF ANALYSIS FROM 12/07/82 TO 3/07/83
CASH BOND MATURITY DATE: 12/01/12   COUPON: 12.125%.   YTM AT START OF ANALYSIS: 12.170%
THIS IMPLIES CASH PRICE OF: $ 99.64   ACCRUED INTEREST AT START OF ANALYSIS : $ 2020.83
AND ACCRUED INTEREST AT END OF ANALYSIS OF: $ 3233.33
GIVES INTEREST DURING PERIOD OF: $ 30312.50 (0. COUPON(S) + END ACCRUED - BEGINNING ACCRUED

AVERAGE YTM CHANGE OF: -75.00 BASIS POINTS GIVES NEW AVG. YTM OF   11.420%
AND AVERAGE PRICE BASED ON NEW YIELD OF: $ 105.95

CONVERGENCE INFORMATION

CONVERGENCE OF: -12.(32NDS), AND HEDGE RATIO OF: 1.300
GIVES CONVERGENCE AMOUNT OF: $ -4875.00 OR AN ANNUALIZED: -1.953%

BASIS RISK INFORMATION

END OF PERIOD BASIS RISK OF: 0.0000%
MEANS DOLLAR CHANGE OF: $ 0.00 OR AN ANNUALIZED   0.000%
AVERAGE BASIS RISK OF: 0.000%

VARIATION MARGIN INFORMATION

AVERAGE OVERNIGHT FINANCING RATE: 8.503%
AVERAGE VARIATION MARGIN BALANCE: $ -65552.58 (BASE CASE)   STARTING BAL: 0.00

MATRIX ANALYSIS INFORMATION

MATRIX INTERVALS OF: 25.00 BASIS PTS. AVG. YTM CHANGE   AND 25.000 FOR FINANCING RATE
MATRIX INTERVALS OF: .2500% FOR AVG. BASIS RISK AND   .2500% FOR END OF PERIOD BASIS RISK
CONVERGENCE INTERVAL OF: 2.(32NDS)

OUTPUT SUMMARY

BASE CASE: 9.633

* ANALYSIS PER $1. MILLION PAR CASH BOND POSITION

1980s as rates rose sharply and cancellation penalties became minor compared with the yield advantages of switching to a new annuity. In addition, SPDAs often are sold through brokers who have the incentive to make policyholders aware of competing products. The fact that the tax code allows one to switch policies without penalty minimizes the rate advantage, creating a "hot" money product.

Companies are pressed to offer increasingly attractive rates and terms. The typical SPDA, to be competitive, sets an attractive rate for one year and institutes a surrender charge. Following this period, intervals at which the interest rate paid is reset vary; they can be one year or less. Also, the surrender charge often decreases with time. The SPDA payout rate is often based on an index of bond yields. Because the product buyer is sophisticated and can switch without penalty, the indexed rate must be attractive. Fairly large amounts of money are deposited at the outset; typically, more than with universal life policies which usually require a continual deposit of premium.

The insurer is constantly faced with the problem of maximizing yield and must generally be more aggressive about market-risk exposure than with universal life products. The use of futures will give Empire added flexibility in terms of the degree of market risk and product size that it chooses to accept.

Empire will decide how much of its portfolio to hedge and will define the appropriate hedge ratio based on future equivalence value. The periodic cost arising from convergence, contract characteristics (or contract rolls), and variation margin are calculated to set up a potential return for the product the company is offering.

To minimize product-management risk the hedge strategy is set up to match the product's terms as closely as possible. If Empire's SPDA rate is guaranteed for the first year, deferred-month contracts would be sold and the convergence effect, based on when that contract terminates, would be known. The convergence effect would be based on the price difference between the futures equivalent value of the cheapest-to-deliver bond and the actual price of the fourth or fifth contract, depending upon the timing of the payout reset. If Empire projected that the slope of the yield curve would change to its benefit, it could stack and hedge with the first or second contract and roll into successive contracts, introducing an element of yield-curve risk.

The most conservative strategy would be to use the contract that matches the first payout reset date and assume convergence as a given in setting a competitive rate. If, with a positive yield curve, the spread between the future equivalent value of the deliverable bond and the fourth contract is 32/32, a convergence cost of $1,000 per contract sold would be assumed. If Empire chooses to hedge with the front contract, the cash-futures spread relative to the first contract is 11/32 ($343.75 per contract), and the incremental spread between each of the successive three contracts is 7/32, Empire must be able to roll its hedge back at an average spread of better than 7/32 to improve its position. Empire's convergence exposure will change with yield-curve changes—a more positive yield curve being adverse. In addition, the yield-curve effect tends to flatten out for the deferred contracts, with the spread between the first and second contracts generally wider than that between the fourth and fifth contracts. Consequently, if market levels are unchanged and the yield curve doesn't shift, it is probable that the total cost of rolling for the year will be greater than the cost incurred by matching dates in the present.

Managing a contract position in this manner is like stacking in the fixed-rate loan hedge. This introduces into SPDA profit analysis a risk/reward element based upon expectations of yield-curve changes. One advantage of futures is the degree of this yield-curve risk that can be tailored to part or all of the total position. In the event that there is an improvement in spreads, the position can be rolled to the fourth contract at any time to take advantage of transitory positive movements. A convergence allowance can be built into the fixed rate, extended for the first year; any gain over that reserve accrues to the company's benefit. In the shorter variable-rate segments, most of the gain or loss from convergence should match the product price and thus is ultimately borne by the client.

Variation-margin financing is more of a problem for calculating a one-year rate. The rate extended cannot truly account for variation margin because market direction for the period is unknown. A certain penalty can be assumed in product design by taking variation-margin financing as an adverse factor; or variation margin can be analyzed, along with basis risk and convergence, to make an aggregate rate assessment, as often some factors can offset others.

There are various sophisticated methods of trying to minimize variation-margin impact. These include shorting a slightly lower than optimal number of contracts with the expectation that the unhedged asset position will compensate for variation-margin financing gains or losses.[10] Other dynamic hedging techniques have been developed which tend to be complex and require constant monitoring. Buying a small number of call options on bond futures to protect against substantial adverse margin costs can also be considered. As bond prices increase, these calls will appreciate in value, mitigating the financing

---

[10] The extent that the market moves up will create a variation-margin financing cost; this would be offset by gains in the cash market that are greater than losses in the future market because the future position is somewhat smaller than otherwise would be expected. Likewise, if the market declines, variation-margin financing gain would be expected to compensate for the underhedged position. This is a fairly complex subject, because results are dependent upon levels in the market on average over the entire period for variation margin, but only at the end of the period for closing out the undershorted position.

cost on the variation-margin deficit incurred on the futures position. If bond prices decline, the cost of the calls will be offset by the variation-margin financing gain.

Empire, in seeking to enter rapidly growing but highly competitive product areas, can look at futures as a tool that will provide a range of choices and substantial flexibility without exposure to extremely high risk. Empire knows that in a given period, it may not have the highest rate of return. It expects that it can be competitive over any period of time; and it hopes that the penalties and customer relations are such that one or two periods of less-than-maximum yield offerings will not result in cancellations.

The fact that one can manage a $500-million product and assume the volatility risk of a smaller product takes on particular significance for this type of portfolio management. By having the principal risk under control, Empire can afford to sell a great deal more insurance than it otherwise could, providing substantial benefits to the company. It knows that it will not face substantial capital losses, and that the company's basic health and security cannot be impaired. Redemptions can be managed without major problems to the company.

19

Managing rate commitments

PRIVATE PLACEMENTS

Financial intermediaries are constantly faced with the problem of accommodating clients' rate expectations and takedown timing needs with their own funding availability as well as cost and rate projections. Private-placement hedge strategies can help to match the sometimes divergent preferences of customers and lending institutions.

Private placements are typically of shorter maturity than long-term bonds and of longer maturity than commercial loans. Usually written by insurance companies for corporations, they are unique and highly illiquid. Private-placement agreements that are flexible enough to attract clients without involving unwanted rate exposure, can be difficult to negotiate. Hedging with futures can make this more manageable.

Capital Insurance is an active participant in the growing, highly competitive market for the medium-size corporate private loan placement business. The company wants to maximize its position in writing loans but recognizes the risks inherent in this client-oriented business. As a means of smoothing out its timing problems and managing its private-placement portfolio, Capital is considering the futures market. Four basic cases are apparent.

1. Capital has money available today but no client to take down the loan at the current market rate. Going long futures will help to protect a desired spread.
2. Capital has funded a placement, but the client, expecting rates to decline, would like a floating-rate loan. Capital not only obliges but also gives the client the right to convert to a fixed rate at some later date—protecting its spread by going long bond futures.
3. A client requires a forward commitment on a loan but at a rate set today. Capital makes the commitment but hedges its exposure to an increase in its funding costs by going short bond contracts.
4. Capital has funds available today at a floating rate, but the client wants a long-term, fixed-rate loan. Capital offers the fixed rate and protects its future cost of funds by going short bond contracts.

Using futures will give Capital a way to separate the timing of rate decisions from its actual flow of funds. This gives the company the flexibility to meet client requests without endangering its profit spread.

Future loan takedowns

Capital has $10 million available to lend. It has an actuarially defined annual return requirement for its funds. It is interested in lending this money for approximately 15 years. Capital believes that, with the long-term Treasuries currently yielding 11.50 percent, it should be able to write loans at 13.50 percent. Unfortunately, Capital's clients are not now interested in borrowing money with the desired maturity. Capital considers going long bond futures to protect the spread that would be available today if it had a client.

In analyzing its futures hedge, Capital reviews the basic ingredients that go into all hedges: hedge ratio and basis risk, convergence—including the specific contract considerations—and variation-margin financing effects.

Capital's hedge-ratio and basis-risk analysis focuses on preserving a certain rate of income over the 15-year period of the proposed loans. A precise hedge ratio analysis is a little more difficult here than in other situations. Because there is no client at hand, Capital doesn't know the exact credit spread the loan will ultimately bear. Essentially, Capital is preserving a certain Treasury rate and assuming that the credit analysis for a particular client will lead to a spread over the Treasury rate. To the extent that it expects yields to fall and credit spreads to narrow, Capital may want to have a slightly different hedge ratio than if rates were expected to rise.

If Capital does nothing to hedge its exposure on the $10 million available and rates fall before the private placements are made, the bottom line is clear: inertia speculation will have replaced the management function.

Capital will analyze the yields on the deliverable Treasury and corresponding yields on the private placements at various levels to determine its hedge ratio. The private-placement rate can only be estimated as it will vary based on loan maturity and the effect of market level on credit spreads. Capital's rate is based on a 15-year maturity, and maturity risk exists between this rate and the longer-term deliverable Treasury bond.[1] This risk is compensated for in the hedge ratio. Using a hedge ratio and error tolerance matrix to estimate the cost of imprecision for a particular ratio (see Chapter 16), Capital can analyze the most effective prospective hedge ratio. Because private placements are highly illiquid and this type of portfolio can't easily be managed in the cash market, a less-than-perfect hedge ratio, creating a basis cost, may be relatively insignificant. Like the variable-rate-product hedges, Capital chooses to treat the effects of cash-futures relationships and variation-margin financing as items separate from the hedge ratio.

Capital's choice of contract month with which to hedge and the consequent convergence effect depends on when it expects to place the loans. At first, Capital can analyze convergence based on loans at the end of a particular contract period. If the loan is placed in the interim, the actual cash-futures spread effect will likely vary somewhat from that anticipated. Capital may have to roll into a subsequent contract month if no client becomes available prior to the expiration of the first contract. Moreover, Capital can still create a forward placement for a client and roll the hedge to the appropriate takedown period when the client will assume the loan.

To the extent that a positive yield curve exists, Capital will be the beneficiary of the futures price converging to the cash-market level. Here, convergence reduces the "cost" of not being invested in a longer-term instrument over the hedge period. With a negative yield curve, convergence would be an expense to Capital, reducing yields on short-term instruments toward the longer-term rate. In this situation, therefore, convergence effects should probably be considered adjustments to provide short-term income rather than as part of a hedge analysis.[2] The extent of after-hours delivery or other contract characteristics would also be considered.

Capital was looking to create a $10-million, 13.50 percent loan

---

[1] Capital might also consider Treasury-note contracts for the hedge if the 10-year maturity looked rich relative to the market. But bond futures are the more usual choice because of liquidity and more definable pricing.

[2] This accounting treatment, while analytically correct, may not be in accord with present generally accepted accounting treatment for hedgers. The subject of accounting for hedging is under review by the Financial Accounting Statements Board (see Chapter 24).

and is willing to assume that its loan rate will be 200 basis points above the Treasury rates of 11.50 percent. If, in fact, futures, reflecting a Treasury rate of 11.50 percent had a future equivalent value of 73-24/32, but given a positive yield curve, futures were selling at a price of 73 with a one-to-one hedge ratio, Capital would assume a gain from convergence of approximately $750 per contract. That estimate might be modified based on Capital's assessment of after hours delivery effects, if any, which would be used to adjust the return for the period of the hedge.

Capital's variation-margin financing for its futures position will be set by the average market move while the hedge is in place. A range of potential gains or losses on variation-margin financing must be calculated. Capital knows that any costs or benefits incurred on margin financing are likely to be relatively insignificant over the life of the loan. If Capital is in a futures position for three months, basis gains or losses and variation margin can be applied against the loan rate over a 15-year period. They should not have a major impact on pricing.

In the event that during a three-month period, Capital had 100 contracts which averaged three points lower than cost, the financing of an average of $300,000 of variation margin at 12 percent would approximate $9,000; the total variation margin when amortized over a period of 15 years would affect Capital's rate of return by approximately one half of a basis point per year. Similarly, a 1 percent basis differential on the hedge ($100,000) would approximate 7/10ths of a basis point per year.[3]

In this application, Capital must be aware that should rates go up not only will the company face variation-margin financing costs, but Capital could also find it more difficult to get clients on the projected dates. Capital may have to extend its hedge longer than initially anticipated. In fact, Capital can roll its contracts forward until such time as it does get a client, with the analysis both for hedge ratios and periodic income for each period being the same as that above.

Managing a floating rate

Capital realizes that it can gain a competitive edge by using futures to design flexible loan terms without excessive rate risk. Capital has funds available and a client prepared to take down the loan today. But the client expects rates to drop substantially over the next few months and wants a floating rate for a specified period of time. Capital goes long futures to protect a rate based on its fixed cost of

---

[3] For simplicity, we assumed that these costs would be paid or received when the futures contracts were offset and a client loan extended. In this example, we have not analyzed the present-value effects—cost or benefits of timing differences. This is analyzed in examples in Chapter 20. However, it might be noted that each $100,000 of hedge variables, if financed or invested at 14 percent on a 15-year level-payment, self-liquidating basis, would adjust the return by approximately one basis point.

funds. At certain agreed-upon times, the client must have the right to fix a rate for the remainder of the 15-year period at a spread of 200 basis points over the 20-year Treasury rate. If rates decline, the client benefits from the lower interest cost: an increase in the value of Capital's futures position would make up the difference between the loan income and Capital's cost. Should rates increase, Capital will lose money on the futures, but the higher rate obtained from the client would offset those losses. Capital's problem is easier in this instance. The company will set the proper hedge ratio to the 20-year Treasury bond and, because the loan is fixed at a given spread off those securities, the company's basis risk will be minimized.

Capital will analyze any convergence and variation-margin effects, as it did above to determine in advance exactly what it is offering the client. Capital would also have to be very sure that the client does not view itself as having an option. In the event that rates rise, Capital would have to be sure that the client is prepared to pay the higher rate.

Capital has provided its clients with a substantial amount of flexibility. It can establish the loan in such a way that the client can get a rate for a short, given period—possibly until the convergence of the first futures contract. If the client pays the current long-term rate during that period (or perhaps something additional to cover for possible hedging inefficiencies) Capital may even gain a better overall rate, particularly if it has a gain on convergence. If, at the end of that first period, the client chooses to extend the floating rate for another period, Capital can quote a different rate for another three-month loan by estimating variation margin and convergence expectations, based upon rolling into the second contract. This can provide a highly attractive vehicle for the client, because he then has the flexibility to extend the time period before which a permanent rate must be set.

Because there is no effective alternative to creating this kind of a variable/fixed-rate loan for a client, the use of futures can prove highly valuable with, in this case, relatively small risk.

Forward commitment

Capital has another client who believes that rates are going to increase and would like to commit for a loan in six months but at today's rates. Capital does not have funds available now for this forward commitment but will receive funds shortly at rates based upon then-existing market conditions. To accommodate the client, Capital guarantees that it will make a loan available for 15 years at 14 percent for takedown in six months. And to protect its cost of funds, Capital sells futures.

Capital is trying to maintain its loan spread. If market rates rise and its funding costs go above the current 11.50 percent base, gains in futures will make up for the difference between 11.50 percent and the ultimate cost of funding. On the other hand, should rates decline such that Capital's short position in futures deteriorates, Capital's funding costs go down. Either way, the company's net spread should be maintained.

As in the prior case, Capital must analyze hedge ratios and related basis risk, convergence, and potential variation-margin financing gains or losses. Convergence and variation margins should have a minor impact if allocated over a 15-year period. Because Capital does not have any investable funds, convergence would not be considered a periodic cost, but like variation-margin financing, an adjustment to the 15-year rate. Hedge-ratio inefficiency, while it could prove significant if measured as a percentage of par value (e.g., 1 percent), should not prove significant if amortized over a 15-year period. These factors can be taken into account when Capital prices its loan spread.

Managing a fixed rate

The final case Capital reviewed is one in which it has floating-rate money but a client wants a long-term, fixed-rate loan.[4] If Capital provides a loan at 14 percent, it must go short futures to protect against increasing rates. The hedge ratio would be analyzed on the basis of the expected relationship between the cheapest-to-deliver long-term Treasury bond and a proxy rate that can be utilized to estimate Capital's eventual longer-term rate.

A common error made by new hedgers is to assume that, if Capital will have only a variable rate for three months, a three-month Treasury bill or similar contract should be used. Clearly, such a hedging strategy would provide protection for a three-month period based on short-term rates rather than for 15 years based on longer-term rates. The contract chosen for the hedge should reflect the volatility of the rate to be hedged.

GIC CONTRACTS

Guaranteed Interest Contracts (GICs) have become an important part of insurance product lines. These contracts guarantee an interest rate, typically compounded, usually for a period of five years. GICs are attractive to pension funds and other clients looking for secure investments with relatively high rates of interest. Not surprisingly, as with variable-rate products, this product area has become very competitive with the evolution of a myriad of different rates and structures.

---

[4] If Capital and the client want to fix a rate for a period of approximately two years, the analysis in Chapter 17 would be relevant.

To generate a rate of return on a five-year basis—one that is both actuarially sound and attractive to clients—insurance companies are forced to be innovative and to take a certain degree of market risk. There are very few public investments available with five-year maturities other than Treasury notes. GICs are priced so competitively that the five-year Treasury notes will rarely provide sufficient return. To achieve the desired effects, insurance companies in a positive yield-curve environment either must go out further on the yield curve, purchasing longer-term bonds at a higher yield and accepting principal risk or go to lower-credit private placements or available public debt, in either case accepting a degree of market risk.

GICs are an important source of funds for Capital, and the company has developed reasonable investment strategies for these proceeds. Capital can use futures to manage two problems unique to this product: (1) timing gaps between "extending a rate" and receiving funds to invest, or (2) reinvestment rate guarantees.

Capital began selling GICs in a relatively stable interest-rate environment. Following industry practice, Capital offered a GIC rate for a period of time before the client would commit to accept the rate. More time would elapse before the funds were actually available for investment. These timing gaps have contracted as rate volatility increased, but are still a risk to the company. Capital is now looking to hedge its exposure in the time from when a client accepts a GIC rate to the receipt of investment funds.[5]

Capital plans to buy futures to protect against a decline in rates subsequent to the client's commitment, but prior to making its investments.[6] In this case, a long position is desired because any increase in rates will result in a loss in futures to be offset by higher investment rates. To the extent that rates decline—and with them the rate one will receive on an investment—this will be offset by gains in the futures.

In this type of hedge, the yield-curve aspect of the cash-futures spread is typically not too significant because the duration of the hedge is relatively short. Yet it is precisely because the duration is so short that any inefficiencies in pricing between the cash and futures market bear close scrutiny, although such inefficiencies can, in effect, be amortized over the five-year period of the contract.

---

[5] New types of GIC offerings include a forward-rate feature; a company may extend a five-year rate to be taken down in one year. If these proceeds are allocated to private-placement commitments, also with a deferred takedown, the company has established its profit spread. If these investments are not available, the company's investment alternatives would include futures.

[6] Futures cannot be used prior to the client's actual commitment because in the event that the client chooses not to commit, a futures positon would be at Capital's risk. In effect, the client is being granted a free option. The new market in options on Treasury futures presents an opportunity to gauge just how valuable this "free option" is in comparison to the time (extrinsic) value of the market option's price.

Basis risk, the relationship between the Treasury market and the item one anticipates buying, can be an important factor over a short period of time. Here, again, because Capital can amortize this over the five-year period of the contract, the significance is mitigated. Like the case with the anticipatory hedge, the hedge ratio is based on the relationship between a current investment-grade security and the cheapest-to-deliver Treasury bond. To the extent that other securities become available at more attractive relative yields, the hedger may actually do better than anticipated because the gain or loss on the contract position will be applied against the cheaper bonds purchased.

Reinvestment risk

Once companies invest in GIC contracts, they often face the problem of reinvestment. A 13 percent, five-year instrument involves an implicit assumption that coupons can be invested at 13 percent. If interest coupons can, in fact, be reinvested only at an average of 10 percent, the rate of return over five years would not be 13 percent compounded but closer to 12.3 percent.

Many GIC products sold in 1982 would face this problem if rates remain at levels significantly lower than those in the year of sale. To protect against this, Capital can go long a few contracts to compensate for a difference in rates over a declining period. The reinvestment time for the first year's coupons is for four years, the second year's coupon is for three years, etc. On a $1-million GIC program, an initial position approximating no more than two to three futures would be anticipated, and this would be reduced as interest payments are received and reinvested. On average, only one to two futures would be required over the five-year period.

20

Managing debt issuance

DEFERRED DEBT ISSUANCE

Northwest Corporation needs to fund the construction of a $10-million automated manufacturing facility which is scheduled for completion in a year. The company has determined that today's general rate level would lead to an acceptable interest cost on the project. Yet, for a variety of reasons, Northwest would rather defer permanent funding for the project.

Completion of the project itself can be expected to result in an improvement in the company's credit, helping issuance costs and indenture restrictions. But an increase in rates over the year could jeopardize the profitability of the project.

Doing nothing in this instance would be a clear case of inertia speculation. Instead, Northwest Corporation sells Treasury-bond futures to protect itself against the possibility of rising rate levels between now and the time it issues bonds.

Northwest evaluated a hedge strategy to determine the effective interest cost it can expect. Like all hedgers, Northwest will focus on a hedge ratio and basis analysis, convergence—including contract characteristic considerations—and variation-margin financing effects. The company can compare the effect of the hedge on its total interest cost both as to what it would cost to issue bonds today and as to the cost and risk of waiting the year. Any deviation from today's interest cost can be amortized over the 40-year life of the bonds to be issued.

Northwest will seek to maintain its net interest cost by offering a variable amount of par-value bonds. Northwest could issue bonds today at a 13-3/4 percent coupon rate to borrow the $10 million needed for its project. By selling bond futures and deferring the actual issuance, Northwest can sell bonds in a year at the then-current market rate while maintaining a net cost reflecting today's levels.

An increase in rates would allow Northwest to issue fewer par-value bonds at the higher coupon rate and fund the cash shortfall with the gain on its bond futures position.[1] A decline in rates, creating a loss in futures, would force Northwest to issue a greater number of par value bonds but at a lower coupon in line with the market rate when the bonds are issued. The company must consider the cash-flow implications of each directional move, although its net interest cost will remain near the current 13-3/4 percent level. In either case, by looking at the present value of the total cash flow, Northwest will have a net interest cost approximating the hedge rate.

Northwest's first step is to calculate a hedge ratio. Because, due to factors unique to the corporation, Northwest expects its credit spread to improve, the hedge ratio can be set relative to the level of the long-term Treasury market adjusted for the potential coupon and maturity of the bond to be sold. Northwest is then set up to benefit from anticipated positive changes in the basis.

Convergence and anticipated variation-margin financing effects can be compared to the cost of issuing bonds today at 13-3/4 percent and investing the proceeds in a money-market instrument for the year until they will be needed to fund the project. This permits an accurate assessment of the potential interest cost over the life of the project.

Table 20-1 outlines the effect of the hedge on cash flow and the net cost if market levels change by 200 basis points. Northwest sets a hedge ratio assuming that it will issue bonds 175 basis points above the long-term Treasury rate.

Northwest's hedge activated a decision to issue debt at 13-3/4 percent without entering the current market. If rates increase by 200 basis points, Northwest will actually issue bonds with a 15-3/4 percent coupon. As rates move up, the gain from Northwest's short futures position amounts to $1,266,900. Instead of having to sell $10

---

[1] In theory, Northwest could offer 13-3/4 percent bonds at a premium (if rates decline) or a discount (if rates increase). Practically speaking, however, this would create additional costs for underwriting and marketing the issue.

TABLE 20-1 Debt issuance hedge for $10 million
40-year bond issue (hedge ratio 1.33)

Coupon sold	15.75%	11.75%
Principal value	$8,733,100	$11,684,400
Variation margin balance	1,266,900	(1,684,400.)
Annual interest cost*	1,375,463	1,372,917
Convergence cost†	343,406	343,406
Variation-margin financing‡	69,680	(75,598.)
Net cost of hedge	(273,726)	(419,204.)
Realized rate on long-term bonds**	14.19	14.22

Rate to be protected = 13.75 based upon 175-basis-point spread to Treasury.
*Calculated as principal value issued times coupon sold.
†Based upon the spread between the fourth contract and the cash market, adjusted by the hedge ratio.
‡Based upon a perfectly hedged, 100-basis-point average move financed at average short-term rates of 11 percent and 9 percent, respectively.
**A comparable rate would result from the effective cost of issuing long-term bonds a year earlier instead of financing the project with lower cost short term debt.

million of par bonds, Northwest now needs to sell only $8,733,100. The bond issuance, plus the gain on the hedge, will provide the amount needed to fund the manufacturing plant. By the same token, if rates decrease, Northwest will issue extra bonds to fund its variation-margin deficit. A perfectly hedged, 200-basis-point decrease in Treasury yields would create a variation-margin deficit of $1,684,400, and Northwest will have to issue $11,684,400 par-value bonds at 11.75 percent.

The amount of bonds to be issued as well as Northwest's annual interest cost will vary depending upon the market level when the hedge is reversed. As rates increase, Northwest will issue fewer bonds, making up the difference from the gain in futures; but it will incur higher annual interest charges. If Northwest issues the 15-3/4 percent coupon, annual interest costs will be $463 more than if the corporation issues $10 million 13-3/4 percent bonds. This difference in interest expense is the annuity value of the $1,266,900 margin balance at 15-3/4 percent.[2]

As rates decrease, Northwest issues a greater number of par-value bonds to fund its variation-margin deficit, but at a lower annual interest charge. With an 11-3/4 percent issuance, Northwest's interest expense equals $1,372,917, $2,083 less than if $10 million of 13-3/4 percent bonds had been issued. This annual saving must be accumu-

[2] In other words, the payment of $463 a year is made in lieu of the obligation to repay $1,266,900 at the end of 40 years, assuming each payment of $463 could have been invested at a compounded rate of 15-3/4 percent.

lated to pay back the additional $1,684,400 par amount of bonds issued—assuming an 11-3/4 percent reinvestment rate.[3]

By hedging its issuance, Northwest is protecting the basic cost of debt without weakening its balance sheet. The company can also benefit from any improvement in its credit standing over the year. An improvement in Northwest's borrowing rate relative to Treasuries would result in issuing a lower-than-expected coupon for a given market move. If Treasury rates increase 200 basis points, but Northwest's spread to Treasuries improves by 25 basis points, the company could issue a 15-1/2 percent bond. Northwest still would have a $1,266,900 variation-margin balance, based on the 200-basis-point increase in 30-year-Treasury-bond rates. Their annual interest expense is $1,353,630, given the 15-1/2 percent coupon sold. This is a yearly savings of $21,833 due to the spread improvement.

Northwest's convergence estimate is based on full convergence through the anticipated hedge reversal period.[4] The effect actually realized might vary somewhat to Northwest's advantage, depending on a change in the cheapest to deliver or an after-hours price adjustment. In Northwest's case, the hedge contract is one year out, with a full convergence cost of $2,582 per contract—$343,406 for the total position. Variation-margin financing is estimated for a perfect hedge, based on the expected average market move and short-term financing rates for the period. The net cost of the hedge would equal $273,726 if rates increase, and $419,204 if rates decline. This outflow can be funded with additional long-term debt, which, after accounting for interest expense and principal repayment,[5] would add 44 or 47 basis points to Northwest's ultimate rate.

Convergence cost adjusted for variation-margin financing is comparable to the cost that Northwest would incur in floating its bond now at 13-3/4 percent and investing the proceeds in a short-term instrument for an equivalent period. The cost would also need to be funded eventually, adding to Northwest's ultimate issuance cost. This would suggest that these factors should be charged to periodic income or to the project, as would be done with all financing costs during construction, and not considered in comparing hedge results with a cash-market alternative.[6]

---

[3] Some risk exists depending on whether the company can earn a rate better than a compound 11-3/4 percent on its annual interest savings.

[4] Northwest can always roll the hedge forward if its bond issuance is delayed, and the convergence effect will be adjusted for the additional period.

[5] This cost estimate is based on the amount of money set aside semi-annually to compound and repay principal in 40 years, as well as the interest expense on the additional bonds issued.

[6] Current accounting theory may or may not permit this treatment. It may require amortizing convergence and reflecting variation-margin financing as a current cost (see Chapter 24).

HEDGING CURRENT ISSUANCE

The treasurer of Warren Corporation is faced with a dilemma. He knows that he will soon need $10 million to fund out short-term debt. Warren does not have a high-quality credit rating, but the treasurer believes that although general market rates are still high, he can successfully negotiate a bond issuance. Warren's economic forecast calls for a continual decline in rates, and the treasurer would like to defer the bond issuance if he can. By doing nothing, he faces a double threat—if rates increase, not only would Warren's costs increase, but the company could find itself blocked from the market altogether as its credit standing relative to Treasuries deteriorates. The treasurer takes advantage of the opportunity the market provides now and issues long-term debt to protect the corporation's capital position. By going long bond contracts, he gains the advantage of waiting for lower rates. Using futures allows Warren Corporation to maintain its desired level of rate exposure, but hedges its ability to get into the market.

Warren Corporation structures its hedge in line with general hedge considerations to capture the benefit of an overall market improvement. The hedge ratio is set in line with the maturity and coupon of the bonds issued. Basis risk is a less dominant concern because the company has already issued its debt. Warren has taken advantage of its credit standing today so that, if rates increase, the hedge ratio will reflect only the deterioration in the general market.

The convergence effect can be measured relative to Warren Corporation's short-term funding alternatives. With a positive yield curve, the convergence gain on the long futures position will tend to offset the cost of borrowing at the higher long-term rate. Variation margin must be considered relative to Warren's cash flow, because, if rates increase, funds to meet margin calls need to be immediately available.

This transaction should be carefully reviewed by the corporate treasurer. If he is wrong on rates, variation margin must be met and some definable source of longer-term cash to fund the margin must be available.

RATE PROTECTION THROUGH CALL DATE[7]

Advanced Telephone issued a bond with a 15-1/2 percent coupon, 40 years to maturity, and callable after 5 years at a price of 112. Now, two years prior to the call date, market rates have dropped

---

[7] Bond indentures typically include the right to call an issue at some time prior to maturity. Bonds are usually callable at a price greater than the initial offering price. The purpose of the call is to lower total interest cost over an issue's remaining life. The decision to call, as rates decline, depends upon the saving from a lower coupon relative to the cost of the call.

sharply and Advanced needs to consider refinancing its debt. Because the call is not yet active, Advanced must decide whether or not to wait out the time until the call, hoping that rates don't rebound, or to tender for the issue with bonds now or with cash to be funded at a later date. Futures can play an important role in formulating such strategies.

Advanced discards the "wait and see" option, but realizes that even with a tender, there is some market risk as long as outstanding bonds are being acquired in the cash tender but before it can issue new bonds at the lower rate. By going short futures, Advanced is protected from increases in market yields while managing its tender offer until a new issue is marketed. An added benefit of this hedge strategy is that Advanced does not have to bid as aggressively as it otherwise might to buy back its bonds.

This strategy is similar to that of a company using bond futures to stabilize its interest cost prior to a public debt issue. One difference is that in this case, the company knows that it has an alternative. It can tender for the bonds in cash or with other bonds to be issued now. A tender with bonds may not be desirable for many reasons, including not wanting to add another debt issue before the callable one can be completely retired. A company can always compare the choice of using futures to those alternatives.

Advanced decides to make a cash tender offer for its outstanding 15-1/2 percent bonds. At some future date, it will issue bonds to repay any short-term debt incurred. To repurchase the bonds, Advanced needs to determine a tender price that will be attractive to its bondholders, given their investment alternatives through the call date. To insure that today's level will be its basic issuance cost on new bonds, Advanced hedges with futures. With the flexibility remaining to manage the tender until the call date, it can buy bonds when they are attractive. The hedge is left in place until new bonds are issued.

This hedge strategy is set up along the same lines as the bond issuance hedge discussed earlier in this chapter. The hedge ratio is established, given the estimated yield relationship between the bonds to be issued and the cheapest-to-deliver Treasury bond, (see Chapter 16) to capture changes in the general market level while taking advantage of any improvement in the company's (or sector's) relative credit standing. Basis risk can be evaluated in terms of the risk of doing nothing until the call date or the cost of tendering with bonds now, if feasible.

Advanced must also contend with the effect of convergence. This hedge can be put on by selling the contract month that is closest to the issue's call date. Thus, the cost of the convergence can be easily approximated, if the hedge is kept on through the end of the period.

The net convergence cost should be amortized over the life of the new bond issue.

To the extent that the tendered bonds are initially financed with short-term borrowing, in a positive yield-curve environment, Advanced Telephone will have a lower interest cost for the period than it would with the issuance of a new, long-term bond with a higher coupon.[8] Evaluating the convergence effect will also help the company to determine a reasonable price to pay for its tender, relative to its net interest saving.

Variation margin can be only anticipated when the hedge is initiated. The ultimate margin-financing gain or loss from the hedged position can also be amortized over the life of the bond and will affect Advanced Telephone's ultimate issuance cost. Because the hedge is kept in place until the issuance is refinanced in the long-term debt market, Advanced must conservatively estimate the variation-margin effect over the two-year period until the call. When this potential cost is amortized over 40 years, it should not have a significant effect on the realized rate.

Using futures effectively to call its bond issue before the eligible date provides Advanced Telephone with substantial flexibility. By shorting enough futures to cover the entire issue, Advanced eliminates the risk of a rate increase and can proceed to acquire its outstanding bonds in the most efficient way. If the entire issue is repurchased before the call date, Advanced Telephone can pick the time to fund its short-term borrowing based on its credit relative to the Treasury market or to other internal considerations. If the hedge is reversed earlier than anticipated, Advanced's ultimate cost will diverge from expectation due to a difference between the realized convergence effect and that anticipated. In a positive yield-curve environment, this should be beneficial. In any event, the net interest cost will still approximate the general market level from the time that the hedge was put on.

Advanced Telephone's hedge strategy has one special feature that will apply to those hedged bonds which are not repurchased in the market. If yields rise through the outstanding coupon level—from 15-1/2 percent to 16-1/2 percent—Advanced will not call the remaining bonds. Instead, the company will close out its short position at a profit, capturing the change in yield from the hedged level but leaving the lower coupon (15-1/2 percent) bonds outstanding. In this case, the company earns an "extra" profit of 1 percent.

---

[8] In this case, because Advanced intends to issue bonds, convergence should be amortized over the life of the bonds to be issued. To the extent that Advanced temporarily borrows at a lower short-term rate to purchase outstanding bonds, periodic interest cost will be lower until new bonds are issued, offsetting part of the convergence cost.

LEVEL DEBT AND SELF-LIQUIDATING LOANS

Level debt payments and self-liquidating loans provide a slightly different problem for the interest-rate hedger. Understanding this hedge is particularly important for certain types of mortgage commitments and provides additional flexibility with private placements and other types of loan applications. In this type of loan agreement, payments are comprised of both principal and interest, with each payment a constant amount for each period, although the proportion representing principal and interest will vary. This is different from a bond which involves set interest payments per period and a balloon repayment of all principal at maturity.

The Waycroft Construction Company is in the process of constructing a $5-million industrial property. It has an agreement with the Ridgewood Corporation, a tenant of the highest quality, for Ridgewood to lease the property for 20 years upon completion of construction. Ridgewood accepts a net lease and will pay a fixed semi-annual amount of $73,923, representing the financial obligations; in addition, it will pay other amounts including, as escalation, any increase in costs relating to the property.

Waycroft has sounded out many potential long-term lenders and found that, although it can secure a mortgage commitment today to be taken down in roughly one year, after construction is completed, the price of that advanced commitment is fairly high. Waycroft believes that loan terms will improve when the project is complete and Ridgewood's occupancy is assured. Holding off on the loan commitment, though, leaves Waycroft exposed to a rate increase at the end of the year. Waycroft considers hedging with futures as an alternative to the costly advance commitment. If a futures hedge results in a better cost due to Waycroft's improved situation next year, but is unlikely to cost more than an advance commitment, Waycroft will short futures to secure its basic borrowing rate.

Waycroft is confident that, based upon Ridgewood's credit standing, it will be able to commit for a fixed-rate mortgage at 175 basis points over the existing 30-year Treasury bond rate. Its mortgage, like Ridgewood's lease agreement, will call for level debt service for interest and principal amortization. This is a more complex hedge problem due to the effect of an interest-rate change on a level payment loan as opposed to a bond and, therefore, the bond future.

Bonds operate on the assumption of a balloon payment—interest payments made over time and all principal paid back in one lump sum, or balloon, at the end. In such an obligation, any change in the interest rate will affect the bond price in line with the present value of the income stream and principal sum to be repaid. In contrast, a change in rate on an outstanding mortgage will shift the allocation of interest and principal in the level payment. With level payments, any change in interest must have a more substantial effect on the present value of the principal. The payments in each period are fixed, and the obligation is self-liquidating. Therefore, the higher interest rate leaves less money to be repaid out of principal in each period. An equal change in rate will have a different dollar effect on the value of a mortgage and bond of the same maturity. Because futures are based on bonds, the mortgage hedger will have to account for these differences in setting a hedge ratio.

The theory of the hedge remains the same—to offset the change in value of the mortgage with gains or losses in futures. Waycroft knows that, based on Ridgewood's lease agreement, to maintain its profit it can afford a 20-year, self-liquidating mortgage at 13-3/4 percent, calling for semi-annual payments of $73,923. Waycroft wants to sell futures to protect against an increase in Treasury rates. Because Waycroft feels confident of its rates relative to Treasury rates, the company doesn't have to adjust a hedge ratio for basis risk.

Waycroft concentrates on the effect of a rate change on its semi-annual mortgage payment in comparison to the level payments from Ridgewood's lease. Waycroft puts together a sensitivity analysis much like that done by a bond hedger. The anticipated gain or loss on futures can be calculated, based on the price of the cheapest-to-deliver bond at different rate levels. The amount Waycroft can afford to pay in each of the 40 semi-annual periods is known, and the present value of that income stream leads to the size of mortgage that Waycroft can afford. Any difference between that mortgage principal and the required funding must be accounted for in variation margin. Waycroft calculates its hedge ratio based upon changes in the 30-year Treasury bond from the current level of 12 percent. At each level, the amount that the company can afford to borrow to match a total $73,292 semi-annual payment is determined. At a 15-3/4 percent borrowing rate with 40 semi-annual payments, a self-liquidating mortgage of $89,345 can be assumed per $100,000 of originally anticipated mortgage takedown requiring additional upfront cash of $10,655 per $100,000 of the original mortgage. Because the future equivalent price of the contract will move in line with the increase or decrease in the price of the Treasury bond, at any yield level, the hedge ratio will be equal to the change in the principal of mortgages which can be carried per $100,000 of hedged mortgage divided by the anticipated price changes per contract.[9] This is illustrated as follows:

---

[9] The change per contract is equal to the price change in the cheapest-to-deliver bond divided by a factor for the bond and contract month. An error tolerance matrix similar to Table 16-2 could be useful in assessing hedge ratio risk.

Treasury rate	Mortgage rate	Mortgage amount	Funds required	Change per future	Hedge ratio
14%	15-3/4%	$ 89,345	$10,655	$ 9,570	1.11
13	14-3/4	94,415	5,585	5,092	1.10
11	12-3/4	106,619	(6,619)	(5,820)	1.06
10	11-3/4	113,002	(13,002)	(12,504)	1.04

By allocating the gain or loss in futures directly to the mortgage loan, Waycroft avoids the reinvestment rate risk associated with timing imbalances.

Like all hedgers, Waycroft considers the potential effect of convergence and variation-margin financing over the year it intends to stay in the hedge. The convergence effect can be estimated, given the mortgage takedown date. Waycroft retains the flexibility to roll its hedge position if construction completion is delayed, an option it may not have (without some penalty) with the negotiated advance commitment mortgage. Variation-margin financing can be estimated only at the outset based on rate direction over the year.

The financial impact of convergence, variation-margin financing, or hedge ratio error can be treated as an adjustment to Waycroft's debt-service expense. As such, it will have an impact on the ultimate profit spread realized on the agreement. Waycroft can calculate the cost of funding this net expense (or the savings, if convergence and variation-margin financing create a credit) and view it as a rate adjustment. Waycroft can compare this adjustment to the rate it could have obtained on an advanced commitment to see whether futures can create a lower rate (with a manageable hedge risk) than the one currently available.

In addition, the futures give Waycroft another alternative. To the extent that the completed building and the credit of the tenant will encourage a mortgage lender to grant a mortgage somewhat in excess of what could have been borrowed previously, Waycroft may be able to generate additional and reasonably inexpensive long-term refinancing. This could provide an opportunity for Waycroft to use that money as equity for other transactions. Futures will have provided this possible alternative in addition to the flexibility needed to vary the timing of the mortgage takedown in line with market conditions.

21

Stock index contracts

Stock-index contracts can be used as investment alternatives by money managers. In Chapter 13, we reviewed the analysis of a break-even stock-contract price and concluded that futures tend to sell at a price exceeding the cash-market index level as long as the alternative use of money is superior to dividend yields. In fact, contract prices do often deviate from these theoretical levels, occasionally even selling at prices below those of the cash index. Any price level below the calculated break-even price creates an attractive investment alternative to owning the cash index. These contracts may also be used to hedge the market-related volatility of a stock portfolio. Also, when contract prices are high relative to the cash index levels, synthetic money-market instruments, based on an equity market return, can be created.

BUYING THE INDEX

A balanced fund manager has decided to increase the portfolio's equity allocation by investing in a group of stocks reflecting the market's overall performance. As an alternative to investing in the actual stocks, the fund manager plans to consider purchasing S&P 500 contracts and investing in CDs which mature on or around the contract expiration date. The combined index contract—short-term investment strategy is selected when the position's yield exceeds the index's dividend yield. The fund manager may evaluate overall performance, given the change in the cash index value over the period, the cash-futures convergence, short-term investment rates, and variation-margin financing. Because the spread between the front contract price and cash index level tends to reflect investor sentiment in a highly volatile market, the spread may not close until actual contract settlement.[1] The fund manager may also evaluate the impact on return if the contract position is reversed at some spread to the cash index.

Table 21-1 shows a matrix approach to analyzing potential returns, given a starting S&P cash-index level (172.65) and the cash-future's spread (a 1.40 premium). If contracts are bought on October 10, 1983 at a spread of 140 are held for 66 days, until contract expiration at the cash level, the position will outperform the S&P 500 by 64 basis points on an annual basis.[2]

The matrix is designed to adjust for variation margin based on changing market levels and, as noted below, to allow the simulation of rates of return if the position is terminated prior to the contract expiration.

Inasmuch as this application is an alternative to "owning the market," the money manager is making a decision on market direction. For the period in question, the market should be either flat or up. If the manager is wrong in assessing the market, the long position will decline in value—just as the cash-market position would also decline.

At the end of the period, the fund manager may choose to reverse the contract position and invest in stocks or maintain the index contract position by rolling to the next contract month. Return, relative to market performance, for subsequent periods is primarily determined by the first to second contract spread and the rate on the short-term investment. As with the relationship between the cash index level and contract price, theoretically the cost of the roll (spread) should equate the short-term rate with the dividend yield.

VOLATILITY REDUCTION

A short hedge against an existing portfolio of stocks can be designed to reduce market-related volatility. Rocky Mountain Holding Cor-

---

[1] Because highly disproportionate percentages of stocks go exdividend in the middle of a quarter, arbitrage, i.e., buying cash stocks to replicate the index and going short the contract, or switching from the contract to a cash position should occur in a predictable pattern. While some of this is being done, at present, the amount of such activity usually has not been sufficient to overcome other market forces.

[2] The method for calculating anticipated returns is fully described in Chapter 13.

TABLE 21-1

```
*****************************************************************************
         ANALYSIS OF ADJUSTED RETURNS WHEN YOU PURCHASE S + P FUTURES AND MONEY MARKET INSTRUMENTS
            AS THE INVESTMENT ALTERNATIVE TO AN EQUITY PORTFOLIO WITH A DIVIDEND YIELD   -2-
*****************************************************************************
```

ANALYSIS FROM 10/10/83 TO 12/15/83   SCENARIO: 1   DONE ON 10-10-83
S+P FUTURES BOUGHT AT: 174.05 WITH CASH INDEX AT 172.65   (DISC/PREM OF: 1.40)
DIVIDEND YIELD ONE IS GIVING UP: 4.100 PERCENT, OR 639.99 DOLLARS DURING THE PERIOD
C.D'S PURCHASED: 75325.00 YIELD OF: 9.300 GIVES INTEREST DURING PERIOD OF: 1264.83
T-BILLS PURCHASED: 6000.00 YIELD OF: 8.600 GIVES INTEREST DURING PERIOD OF: 93.17
REPO AMOUNT OF: 5000.00 SET ASIDE FOR VARIATION MARGIN PURPOSES.
AT AVERAGE REPO RATE OF: 9.000 GIVES INCOME OVER THE PERIOD OF: 81.25

AT 9.000% CONSTANT INTEREST RATE, EACH 1 POINT CHANGE IN THE FUTURES PRICE WILL MEAN VARIATION
MARGIN FINANCING OF $ 8.13 OR A .005% CHANGE IN THE RETURN FOR THE PERIOD. LOOK AT THE TABLE BELOW
AND IDENTIFY BOTH MARKET LEVEL AND FUTURES PREMIUM OR DISCOUNT TO CASH WHEN YOU CLOSE OUT THE POSITION
TO FIND RATE OF RETURN AND ADJUST BY VARIATION MARGIN ASSUMPTION.

ADJUSTED PERCENT RETURN FOR THE PERIOD UPON CLOSING OUT POSITION

				<— MARKET LEVEL —>												
S+P CASH INDEX->	166.61	167.47	168.33	169.20	170.06	170.92	171.79	172.65	173.51	174.38	175.24	176.10	176.97	177.83	178.69
PERCENT CHANGE->	-3.50	-3.00	-2.50	-2.00	-1.50	-1.00	-.50	0.00	.50	1.00	1.50	2.00	2.50	3.00	3.50
PORTFOLIO RETURN WITH DIVIDENDS->	-2.76	-2.26	-1.76	-1.26	-.76	-.26	.24	.74	1.24	1.74	2.24	2.74	3.24	3.74	4.24

INCREMENTAL RETURN			ACTUAL RETURN FOR THE PERIOD USING FUTURES														
ANNUAL	PERIOD	SPREAD ON EXIT															
4.48	.81	1.20	-1.95	-1.45	-.95	-.45	.05	.55	1.05	1.55	2.05	2.55	3.05	3.55	4.05	4.55	5.05
4.16	.75	1.10	-2.01	-1.51	-1.01	-.51	-.01	.49	.99	1.49	1.99	2.49	2.99	3.49	3.99	4.49	4.99
3.84	.69	1.00	-2.06	-1.56	-1.06	-.56	-.06	.44	.94	1.44	1.94	2.44	2.94	3.44	3.94	4.44	4.94
3.52	.64	.90	-2.12	-1.62	-1.12	-.62	-.12	.38	.88	1.38	1.88	2.38	2.88	3.38	3.88	4.38	4.88
3.20	.58	.80	-2.18	-1.68	-1.18	-.68	-.18	.32	.82	1.32	1.82	2.32	2.82	3.32	3.82	4.32	4.82
2.88	.52	.70	-2.24	-1.74	-1.24	-.74	-.24	.25	.76	1.26	1.76	2.26	2.75	3.26	3.76	4.25	4.76
2.56	.46	.60	-2.30	-1.80	-1.30	-.80	-.30	.20	.70	1.20	1.70	2.20	2.70	3.20	3.70	4.20	4.70
2.24	.40	.50	-2.35	-1.85	-1.35	-.85	-.35	.15	.65	1.15	1.65	2.15	2.65	3.15	3.65	4.15	4.65
1.92	.35	.40	-2.41	-1.91	-1.41	-.91	-.41	.09	.59	1.09	1.59	2.09	2.59	3.09	3.59	4.09	4.59
1.60	.29	.30	-2.47	-1.97	-1.47	-.97	-.47	.03	.53	1.03	1.53	2.03	2.53	3.03	3.53	4.03	4.53
1.28	.23	.20	-2.53	-2.03	-1.53	-1.03	-.53	-.03	.47	.97	1.47	1.97	2.47	2.97	3.47	3.97	4.47
.96	.17	.10	-2.59	-2.09	-1.59	-1.09	-.59	-.09	.41	.91	1.41	1.91	2.41	2.91	3.41	3.91	4.41
.64	.11	0.00	-2.64	-2.14	-1.64	-1.14	-.64	-.14	.36	.86	1.36	1.86	2.36	2.86	3.36	3.86	4.36
.32	.06	-.10	-2.70	-2.20	-1.70	-1.20	-.70	-.20	.30	.80	1.30	1.80	2.30	2.80	3.30	3.80	4.30
-.00	-.00	-.20	-2.76	-2.26	-1.76	-1.26	-.76	-.26	.24	.74	1.24	1.74	2.24	2.74	3.24	3.74	4.24
-.33	-.06	-.30	-2.82	-2.32	-1.82	-1.32	-.82	-.32	.18	.68	1.18	1.68	2.18	2.68	3.18	3.68	4.18
-.65	-.12	-.40	-2.88	-2.38	-1.88	-1.38	-.88	-.38	.12	.62	1.12	1.62	2.12	2.62	3.12	3.62	4.12
-.97	-.17	-.50	-2.93	-2.43	-1.93	-1.43	-.93	-.43	.07	.57	1.07	1.57	2.07	2.57	3.07	3.57	4.07
-1.29	-.23	-.60	-2.99	-2.49	-1.99	-1.49	-.99	-.49	.01	.51	1.01	1.51	2.01	2.51	3.01	3.51	4.01
-1.61	-.29	-.70	-3.05	-2.55	-2.05	-1.55	-1.05	-.55	-.05	.45	.95	1.45	1.95	2.45	2.95	3.45	3.95
-1.93	-.35	-.80	-3.11	-2.61	-2.11	-1.61	-1.11	-.61	-.11	.39	.89	1.39	1.89	2.39	2.89	3.39	3.89
-2.25	-.41	-.90	-3.16	-2.66	-2.16	-1.66	-1.16	-.66	-.16	.34	.84	1.34	1.84	2.34	2.84	3.34	3.84
-2.57	-.46	-1.00	-3.22	-2.72	-2.22	-1.72	-1.22	-.72	-.22	.28	.78	1.28	1.78	2.28	2.78	3.28	3.78
-2.89	-.52	-1.10	-3.28	-2.78	-2.28	-1.78	-1.28	-.78	-.28	.22	.72	1.22	1.72	2.22	2.72	3.22	3.72
-3.21	-.58	-1.20	-3.34	-2.84	-2.34	-1.84	-1.34	-.84	-.34	.16	.66	1.16	1.66	2.16	2.66	3.16	3.66

poration owned stocks with a value of $863,250. On October 10, 1983, it established a short hedge using the S&P 500 contract, which was selling at a price of 174.05. The cash index was then selling at 172.65. By selling 10 contracts with a value of $863,250, Rocky Mountain was attempting to eliminate market risk, as measured by the S&P 500. The company might do this in lieu of selling stock either because of transaction costs, liquidity, or the desire to maintain its present portfolio composition, if it felt its stocks would outperform the general index.[3]

Rocky Mountain calculated the hedge ratio on the cash-index price rather than on the futures price; furthermore, no adjustment for the performance of its portfolio relative to the index was considered. The use of the cash-index level as a base for the hedge allows more precise measurement of the risk/benefit of the cash-futures spread. If, over a short period of time, the cash-futures spread changed by one point or $500 per contract, the effect on the hedger while not dramatic, would be noticeable. The volatility hedger is less concerned with the short-term rate of return implications of the cash-futures spread, since he is less likely to hold a position for a set time, or specifically until the contract has converged. However, even for volatility hedges, the cash-futures spread and the amplitude of potential changes should not be ignored.

Rocky Mountain chose not to adjust its hedge ratio for portfolio performance relative to the S&P index because it assumes that its portfolio will outperform the index. If that were not the case and futures were being used more because of a lack of liquidity in the stocks owned, a beta weighting might be considered (see Chapter 13).

MONEY-MARKET SURROGATE

While Rocky Mountain is not primarily interested in the short-term rate of return created by the future hedge, Jersey fund is seeking to improve yields for its short-term investment funds. Jersey believes that it can create a portfolio which will outperform the index, but these funds are not to be exposed to systematic market risk. On October 10, Jersey also shorts futures at 174.05 when the cash index was 172.65, but with a rate-of-return orientation. Table 21-2 outlines Jersey's return assessments based on holding the futures until the last day of trading and assuming the portfolio outperforms the S&P index at an annual rate of 2 percent.

Regardless of the direction of a market move, the hedged position

---

[3] Pro rata dividend returns were used. In fact, dividends which would actually be paid on a specific portfolio or for the S&P 500, for the actual time period would be utilized.

TABLE 21-2

```
****************************************************************************************************
ANALYSIS OF ADJUSTED RETURNS WHEN YOU SELL S + P FUTURES AS A PORTFOLIO HEDGE AND RATE OF RETURN VEHICLE   -3A
****************************************************************************************************
```

YOUR ADJUSTED RETURN WILL RESULT FROM: DIVIDENDS, RELATIVE PERFORMANCE OF YOUR STOCK PORTFOLIO
TO THE S+P 500, PREMIUM OR DISCOUNT OF THE FUTURES TO THE S+P INDEX WHEN STARTING AND WHEN
ENDING THE FUTURES POSITION, AND THE VARIATION MARGIN EFFECT.

ANALYSIS FROM 10/10/83 TO 12/15/83   SCENARIO: 1   DONE ON 10/10/83
S+P FUTURES SHORTED AT: 174.05 WITH CASH INDEX AT 172.65   (DISC/PREM OF: 1.40)
AND COVERED AT: 172.65   (DISC/PREM OF: 0.00)
DIVIDEND YIELD ONE IS RECEIVING: 4.100 PERCENT, OR $ 639.99 INCOME DURING THE PERIOD OR .741% BASE CASE
OPPORTUNITY COST OF HOLDING INITIAL MARGIN OF $6000. IN T-BILLS FOR THE PERIOD (AT 2% ANNUALLY): $ 21.67
RETURN FROM DIVIDENDS, CONVERGENCE, AND OPPORTUNITY COST OF HOLDING T-BILLS:
FOR THE PERIOD: 1.53%   ANNUALIZED: 8.45%
BASE CASE YIELD, INCLUDING   .35% RELATIVE PERFORMANCE FOR THE PERIOD OF YOUR PORTFOLIO RELATIVE TO THE S+P 500:
FOR THE PERIOD: 1.88%   ANNUALIZED: 10.38%
AT 9.00% CONSTANT INTEREST RATE, EACH 1% CHANGE IN THE S+P 500 INDEX AT THIS MARKET LEVEL WILL MEAN VARIATION
MARGIN FINANCING OF $ 14.03 FOR THE PERIOD, WHICH MEANS A   .02% ADJUSTMENT TO THE YIELD FOR THE PERIOD AND
A   .09% ADJUSTMENT TO THE ANNUALIZED YIELD

ANNUALIZED ADJUSTED PERCENT RETURN UPON CLOSING OUT POSITION

<— SPREAD AT END —>

SPREAD ON SHORTING	-.70	-.60	-.50	-.40	-.30	-.20	-.10	0.00	.10	.20	.30	.40	.50	.60	.70
.20	8.78	8.46	8.14	7.82	7.50	7.18	6.86	6.54	6.22	5.90	5.58	5.26	4.94	4.62	4.30
.30	9.10	8.78	8.46	8.14	7.82	7.50	7.18	6.86	6.54	6.22	5.90	5.58	5.26	4.94	4.62
.40	9.42	9.10	8.78	8.46	8.14	7.82	7.50	7.18	6.86	6.54	6.22	5.90	5.58	5.26	4.94
.50	9.74	9.42	9.10	8.78	8.46	8.14	7.82	7.50	7.18	6.86	6.54	6.22	5.90	5.58	5.26
.60	10.06	9.74	9.42	9.10	8.78	8.46	8.14	7.82	7.50	7.18	6.86	6.54	6.22	5.90	5.58
.70	10.38	10.06	9.74	9.42	9.10	8.78	8.46	8.14	7.82	7.50	7.18	6.86	6.54	6.22	5.90
.80	10.70	10.38	10.06	9.74	9.42	9.10	8.78	8.46	8.14	7.82	7.50	7.18	6.86	6.54	6.22
.90	11.02	10.70	10.38	10.06	9.74	9.42	9.10	8.78	8.46	8.14	7.82	7.50	7.18	6.86	6.54
1.00	11.34	11.02	10.70	10.38	10.06	9.74	9.42	9.10	8.78	8.46	8.14	7.82	7.50	7.18	6.86
1.10	11.66	11.34	11.02	10.70	10.38	10.06	9.74	9.42	9.10	8.78	8.46	8.14	7.82	7.50	7.18
1.20	11.98	11.66	11.34	11.02	10.70	10.38	10.06	9.74	9.42	9.10	8.78	8.46	8.14	7.82	7.50
1.30	12.30	11.98	11.66	11.34	11.02	10.70	10.38	10.06	9.74	9.42	9.10	8.78	8.46	8.14	7.82
1.40	12.62	12.30	11.98	11.66	11.34	11.02	10.70	10.38	10.06	9.74	9.42	9.10	8.78	8.46	8.14
1.50	12.94	12.62	12.30	11.98	11.66	11.34	11.02	10.70	10.38	10.06	9.74	9.42	9.10	8.78	8.46
1.60	13.26	12.94	12.62	12.30	11.98	11.66	11.34	11.02	10.70	10.38	10.06	9.74	9.42	9.10	8.78
1.70	13.58	13.26	12.94	12.62	12.30	11.98	11.66	11.34	11.02	10.70	10.38	10.06	9.74	9.42	9.10
1.80	13.90	13.58	13.26	12.94	12.62	12.30	11.98	11.66	11.34	11.02	10.70	10.38	10.06	9.74	9.42
1.90	14.23	13.90	13.58	13.26	12.94	12.62	12.30	11.98	11.66	11.34	11.02	10.70	10.38	10.06	9.74
2.00	14.55	14.23	13.90	13.58	13.26	12.94	12.62	12.30	11.98	11.66	11.34	11.02	10.70	10.38	10.06
2.10	14.87	14.55	14.23	13.90	13.58	13.26	12.94	12.62	12.30	11.98	11.66	11.34	11.02	10.70	10.38
2.20	15.19	14.87	14.55	14.23	13.90	13.58	13.26	12.94	12.62	12.30	11.98	11.66	11.34	11.02	10.70
2.30	15.51	15.19	14.87	14.55	14.23	13.90	13.58	13.26	12.94	12.62	12.30	11.98	11.66	11.34	11.02
2.40	15.83	15.51	15.19	14.87	14.55	14.23	13.90	13.58	13.26	12.94	12.62	12.30	11.98	11.66	11.34
2.50	16.15	15.83	15.51	15.19	14.87	14.55	14.23	13.90	13.58	13.26	12.94	12.62	12.30	11.98	11.66
2.60	16.47	16.15	15.83	15.51	15.19	14.87	14.55	14.23	13.90	13.58	13.26	12.94	12.62	12.30	11.98

NOTE: THE RETURN COLUMNS HAVE BEEN ANNUALIZED AND INCLUDE RELATIVE PERFORMANCE.

TABLE 21-3

```
**************************************************************************************
ANALYSIS OF ADJUSTED RETURNS WHEN YOU SELL S + P FUTURES AS A PORTFOLIO HEDGE AND RATE OF RETURN VEHICLE   -3A
**************************************************************************************
```

YOUR ADJUSTED RETURN WILL RESULT FROM: DIVIDENDS, RELATIVE PERFORMANCE OF YOUR STOCK PORTFOLIO
TO THE S+P 500, PREMIUM OR DISCOUNT OF THE FUTURES TO THE S+P INDEX WHEN STARTING AND WHEN
ENDING THE FUTURES POSITION, AND THE VARIATION MARGIN EFFECT.

ANALYSIS FROM 10/10/83 TO 11/15/83   SCENARIO: 1   DONE ON 10/10/83
S+P FUTURES SHORTED AT: 174.05 WITH CASH INDEX AT 172.65 (DISC/PREM OF: 1.40)
AND COVERED AT: 172.65   (DISC/PREM OF: 0.00)
DIVIDEND YIELD ONE IS RECEIVING: 4.100 PERCENT, OR $ 349.08 INCOME DURING THE PERIOD OR .404% BASE CASE
OPPORTUNITY COST OF HOLDING INITIAL MARGIN OF $6000. IN T-BILLS FOR THE PERIOD (AT 2% ANNUALLY): $ 11.67
RETURN FROM DIVIDENDS, CONVERGENCE, AND OPPORTUNITY COST OF HOLDING T-BILLS:
FOR THE PERIOD: 1.20%   ANNUALIZED: 12.18%
BASE CASE YIELD, INCLUDING   .35% RELATIVE PERFORMANCE FOR THE PERIOD OF YOUR PORTFOLIO RELATIVE TO THE S+P 500:
FOR THE PERIOD: 1.55%   ANNUALIZED: 15.73%
AT   9.00% CONSTANT INTEREST RATE, EACH 1% CHANGE IN THE S+P 500 INDEX AT THIS MARKET LEVEL WILL MEAN VARIATION
MARGIN FINANCING OF $ 7.55 FOR THE PERIOD, WHICH MEANS A   .01% ADJUSTMENT TO THE YIELD FOR THE PERIOD AND
A   .05% ADJUSTMENT TO THE ANNUALIZED YIELD

ANNUALIZED ADJUSTED PERCENT RETURN UPON CLOSING OUT POSITION

| SPREAD ON SHORTING | <— SPREAD AT END —> | | | | | | | | | | | | | | |
	-1.40	-1.20	-1.00	-.80	-.60	-.40	-.20	0.00	.20	.40	.60	.80	1.00	1.20	1.40
.20	16.91	15.73	14.56	13.38	12.21	11.04	9.86	8.69	7.51	6.34	5.16	3.99	2.81	1.64	.46
.30	17.49	16.32	15.15	13.97	12.80	11.62	10.45	9.27	8.10	6.92	5.75	4.58	3.40	2.23	1.05
.40	18.08	16.91	15.73	14.56	13.38	12.21	11.04	9.86	8.69	7.51	6.34	5.16	3.99	2.81	1.64
.50	18.67	17.49	16.32	15.15	13.97	12.80	11.62	10.45	9.27	8.10	6.92	5.75	4.58	3.40	2.23
.60	19.26	18.08	16.91	15.73	14.56	13.38	12.21	11.04	9.86	8.69	7.51	6.34	5.16	3.99	2.81
.70	19.84	18.67	17.49	16.32	15.15	13.97	12.80	11.62	10.45	9.27	8.10	6.92	5.75	4.58	3.40
.80	20.43	19.26	18.08	16.91	15.73	14.56	13.38	12.21	11.04	9.86	8.69	7.51	6.34	5.16	3.99
.90	21.02	19.84	18.67	17.49	16.32	15.15	13.97	12.80	11.62	10.45	9.27	8.10	6.92	5.75	4.58
1.00	21.61	20.43	19.26	18.08	16.91	15.73	14.56	13.38	12.21	11.04	9.86	8.69	7.51	6.34	5.16
1.10	22.19	21.02	19.84	18.67	17.49	16.32	15.15	13.97	12.80	11.62	10.45	9.27	8.10	6.92	5.75
1.20	22.78	21.61	20.43	19.26	18.08	16.91	15.73	14.56	13.38	12.21	11.04	9.86	8.69	7.51	6.34
1.30	23.37	22.19	21.02	19.84	18.67	17.49	16.32	15.15	13.97	12.80	11.62	10.45	9.27	8.10	6.92
1.40	23.95	22.78	21.61	20.43	19.26	18.08	16.91	15.73	14.56	13.38	12.21	11.04	9.86	8.69	7.51
1.50	24.54	23.37	22.19	21.02	19.84	18.67	17.49	16.32	15.15	13.97	12.80	11.62	10.45	9.27	8.10
1.60	25.13	23.95	22.78	21.61	20.43	19.26	18.08	16.91	15.73	14.56	13.38	12.21	11.04	9.86	8.69
1.70	25.72	24.54	23.37	22.19	21.02	19.84	18.67	17.49	16.32	15.15	13.97	12.80	11.62	10.45	9.27
1.80	26.30	25.13	23.95	22.78	21.61	20.43	19.26	18.08	16.91	15.73	14.56	13.38	12.21	11.04	9.86
1.90	26.89	25.72	24.54	23.37	22.19	21.02	19.84	18.67	17.49	16.32	15.15	13.97	12.80	11.62	10.45
2.00	27.48	26.30	25.13	23.95	22.78	21.61	20.43	19.26	18.08	16.91	15.73	14.56	13.38	12.21	11.04
2.10	28.07	26.89	25.72	24.54	23.37	22.19	21.02	19.84	18.67	17.49	16.32	15.15	13.97	12.80	11.62
2.20	28.65	27.48	26.30	25.13	23.95	22.78	21.61	20.43	19.26	18.08	16.91	15.73	14.56	13.38	12.21
2.30	29.24	28.07	26.89	25.72	24.54	23.37	22.19	21.02	19.84	18.67	17.49	16.32	15.15	13.97	12.80
2.40	29.83	28.65	27.48	26.30	25.13	23.95	22.78	21.61	20.43	19.26	18.08	16.91	15.73	14.56	13.38
2.50	30.41	29.24	28.07	26.89	25.72	24.54	23.37	22.19	21.02	19.84	18.67	17.49	16.32	15.15	13.97
2.60	31.00	29.83	28.65	27.48	26.30	25.13	23.95	22.78	21.61	20.43	19.26	18.08	16.91	15.73	14.56

NOTE: THE RETURN COLUMNS HAVE BEEN ANNUALIZED AND INCLUDE RELATIVE PERFORMANCE.

will return 10.38 percent, subject to a minor variation margin financing effect, which compares favorably with CDs which have a yield of close to 9 percent.

Jersey wants to examine the effect of interim spread or related market changes on its rate of return. This program provides flexibility if spread or market performance changes rapidly. Table 21-3 assumes Jersey closes its position on November 15, 1983. At that point, assuming the same level of relative stock performance, the return for the period will vary with the spread. If Jersey could close out the position at a spread of +20, a rate of return of 14.56 percent for the period through November 15 would have been earned.

FUTURES SHORT HEDGE VERSUS COVERED-WRITE PROGRAMS

An alternative to the short-term income instrument described above is an option's covered-write program. This entails writing call options against a long stock position. Each strategy, given certain market conditions, may be advantageous to an investor. However, option writing involves a different set of risk/reward characteristics than a futures hedge[2] and the investor must be well aware of these.[4]

Exeter Fund owns IBM stock and chooses to write IBM call options against it (a covered write). If the IBM price rises, Exeter may not benefit; the stock is called away. If IBM's market price falls, Exeter has a degree of protection, thanks to premium income, but, beyond that, downside risk is unlimited. As it turns out, Exeter Fund is very dependent on the magnitude of any market move. It benefits most in a fairly stable market environment, but only in a minor way from the stock's relative performance.

Dover Fund, on the other hand, owns some stock it feels should outperform the market. It sells stock-index contracts to hedge the systematic market risk (a short hedge). Regardless of market direction, Dover can anticipate receiving dividends—any gains due to convergence plus the relative performance in the price of its stocks.

Both the short hedge and the covered-write programs tend to be rate-of-return oriented. The investor seeks to generate a return on the funds invested. In analyzing covered-write programs, the difference in risk/return between at-the-money, in-the-money, and out-of-the-money programs are compared. The futures hedge provides another alternative.

Weighing the return from each program against the associated risk will help in choosing the most appropriate strategy for given market environments. As an example, Exeter Fund and Dover Fund each

---

[4] Covered write-strategies are discussed in Chapter 23.

considered strategies which would protect them from a degree of market risk and add a new source of return to their portfolios. Exeter's covered-write program can be specific to a stock held in a portfolio or it can be more broad based, using the CBOE's S&P 100 option. In either instance, Exeter must decide between option strike prices— as the call option is increasingly out of the money (strike exceeds current market level), the anticipated rate of return increases while downside protection is diminished. Exeter must judge where the market will be over the course of its write program to select the optimal call option position. Dover Fund's short hedge is equivalent to selling off the total market risk of its position. Dover's rate of return is now dependent upon the performance of the stocks held and the convergence between the contract price and cash index.

22

Options on debt futures

CONTROLLED MARKET TIMING

As the manager of an endowment fund, you must meet certain requirements related to rate of return. Options on Treasury-bond futures, can provide a means of enhancing your returns with minimal risk. This is a timing strategy, based on market outlook. Funds are taken out of short-term investments to buy options when you anticipate significant market moves over a defined period. These funds taken represent a known cost, should the market not move as anticipated within the period of the option. If the market does move, the gain resulting from the option can enhance overall returns. Being able to act on a negative market outlook by buying puts is a distinctive advantage because pension managers are typically not structured to short cash bonds.

To initiate this strategy, some investment in short-term instruments is necessary. Houston Endowment has $10 million invested in 10 percent six-month Eurodollars. It has determined that 9-1/2 percent is an acceptable minimum return for this portion of its portfolio; it thus has $250,000 which, during six months, can be used for the purchase of puts and/or calls. Expecting a market decline, Houston buys puts and is comfortable with this strategy, because its risk is limited.

If its options are worthless when they expire Houston will have lost only the premiums paid. Such an outcome would result in a 9-1/2 percent return—an acceptable level. Of course, if market levels do actually decline, Houston's return for the period would be improved.

The goal of this strategy is to take advantage of a leveraged market but maintain an acceptable return. Its real success is contingent on successful market timing. A program of continuous option purchases would often not be efficient. Unless Houston is particularly adept at purchasing undervalued options, the premiums paid would make Houston's performance less competitive over time.

The key is for Houston to know its required return and, thus, how many premium dollars can be spent—with no return accruing from the associated options—to maintain an acceptable return. A profitable options position, given these constraints, can help a manager maximize returns. The possibility of earning no gain at all from this options position is, therefore, a conservative and well-defined risk.

BUY-WRITE PROGRAMS[1]

Options on bond futures can also be used to structure buy/write positions against the cheapest-to-deliver Treasury bond.[2] This type of program, similar to stock-option writing programs used by institutions, involves buying a cash bond and selling (writing) call options. The writer receives income from the cash bond as well as premiums from the calls.

The risk/reward analysis of this type of program differs from the analysis of a basis trade, which creates a reasonably predictable short-term return regardless of market direction. The return on a buy-write is evaluated in terms of the tradeoff between a defined yield pickup over a short-term investment alternative, and the potentially unlimited downside price risk. Again, the investor must be sensitive to market timing and valuation because returns on a continuous writing program, over time, should not exceed the risk-free short-term rate.

Three types of buy-writes can be structured, depending on the option strike price. An in-the-money option—when the strike price is below current contract price levels—entails the least risk and the least incremental return. This may be attractive to property and casualty insurers, for example, who might want to improve short-term yield whenever possible, with limited capital risk. A deep out-of-the-money

---

[1] Buy/write and covered write are often used interchangeably. The former is used to describe an options position taken against an instrument other than the one on which the option is written. In our example, a Treasury bond rather than the future.

[2] Writing options on a bond that is *not* deliverable against the futures contract can also be done, often with a higher basic rate of return. The hedge will need to assess the price relationship between the nondeliverable bonds owned and the cheapest-to-deliver bonds.

option—where the strike price is above current market levels—would be written when the highest potential return was desired; such a strategy carries with it the greatest risk and might be undertaken by an aggressive bond manager. Finally, options can be written at the money, when the option strike price approximates current market levels. In some cases, the option strike chosen would depend on the investor's short-term market projection.

The cheapest-to-deliver Treasury bond will create the highest return potential for the Treasury buy-write position; just as the appropriate delivery factor was used to determine the number of contracts to position for a basis trade, the number of calls to be sold against a bond position for optimal premium income will be a function of this delivery factor, as well. Any greater number sold will increase premium income but will subject the writer to excess losses should bond prices rise. Any lesser number will reduce premium income in return for potential capital gains should rates decline.

The Bayle Bond Fund designed a buy-write on October 2, 1983, to create a position against the 14 percent of 11-15-11/06, then the cheapest-to-deliver bond against the December 1983 bond contract. Table 22-1 summarizes the fund's alternatives.

Based on the delivery factor, the buy-write position will be taken by writing 16.238 December calls against each $1 million par value of 14 percent. The components of the position's return are the holding period; the average amount of capital employed (based on the purchase price of the 14 percent, including accrued interest, the timing of coupons received and the holding period); interest to be earned on the bond position; premium income from the option sale, income from investing premium income; and net proceeds from the bond sale and option assignment or repurchase. Net proceeds are determined by market level when the options expire. In addition, any adjustment for cash-futures convergence will be known at option expiration:

$$\text{Annualized return} = \frac{\text{Interest} + \text{Premium income} - \text{Gain/loss on assignment and bond sale}}{\text{Average amount of capital employed}} \times \frac{360 \text{ days}}{\text{Holding period}}$$

Evaluating the buy-write as a short-term investment alternative involves calculating a break-even cash bond price and weighing the downside protection against the incremental income which can be gained by the program. The fund initially evaluates the write strategies based on the maximum return to be earned—when the option is assigned.

On October 3, 1983, one could have invested in Eurodollar CDs at 9-1/2 percent. Virtually all the sources of income for the at-the-

TABLE 22-1 Buy-write against cheapest-to-deliver Treasury bond

14% 11/15/11: 119-06/32 Dec factor: 1.6238
USZ 72-23/32 USZ adjusted for convergence 73-05/32
Holding period (10/3-11/18): 46 days
Average amount of capital employed: $1,240,951.08
Interest earned on 14% bond: 17,518.92

	In-the-money Dec 70: 3-08/64	At-the-money Dec 72: 1-48/64	Out-of-the-money Dec 74: 53/64
Premium income from sale of 16.238 calls	$50,743.75	$28,416.50	$13,447.09
Interest earned on premium at 8.50%	551.13	308.63	146.05
Gain (loss) on assignment with USZ at 73-05/32	(51,251.19)	(18,775.19)	no assignment*
Net income	17,562.61	27,468.86	31,112.06
Periodic return	1.42%	2.21%	2.51%
Annual return	11.07%	17.32%	19.62%
Assignment level bond price	114-02/32	117 10/32	120-18/32
Breakeven bond price to compare with 9.50% Eurodollars	113-26/32	116-02/32	117-19/32

*The maximum return is earned on a buy-write position when the options are assigned. For example, if the price of the 14% bond increased by five points, the Dec. bond contract should sell at 76-08/32 and the Dec. 74 call would be assigned. The return, in this case, would be as follows:

Gain on sale of bond @ 124-06/32	$50,000.00
Loss on assignment @ 76-08/32	(36,535.50)
Net income	44,576.56
Period return	3.59%
Annual return	28.11%

money write, except the cash-futures relationship on November 18, the option expiration date, are known when the options strategy is initiated. The contract price can be estimated to reflect the convergence process. For example, when the call was sold on October 3, the December contract was priced at 72-23/32, but with the price of the bond unchanged at 119-06/32, the December contract will have risen to about 73-05/32 by the option's expiration date. This is 8/32nds lower than the futures equivalent value, 73-13/32, for the 14 percents. This adjustment is especially important for the at-the-money write when contract price convergence to cash could determine the chance of being assigned. The assignment of the 72 call will result in a short position being created at 72, a loss of $18,775.19 (1-5/32 loss times 16.238 calls).

Except for this convergence, changes in the price of the 14 percent will exactly mirror the change in value of 1.6238 futures.[3] The fund

[3] To be conservative, we have not assumed a reduced value for after-hours delivery or a change in the cheapest-to-deliver; either will increase the rate of return.

will earn the 17.32 percent return if it is assigned on its option's position. This will occur as long as the price of the 14 percent remains above 117-10/32 since any change in the bond price will be offset by a reduced loss on assignment. Each point decline in the price of the cash bonds would reduce the annualized rate of return by 6.3 percent. And a decline to 116-02/32 would bring the return equal to the Eurodollar rate.[4]

If the bond fund is assigned on its options, a short December contract position will be booked to its margin account at a price of 72 and marked to the current market level. A cash variation-margin payment is required rather than Treasury bills, which, until assignment, sufficed.

If assigned, Bayle can either hold the bonds and short futures position until delivery can be made, or would reverse the position.[5] Holding the position even a few days will entail additional risk which must be assessed. Essentially, the risk/reward is now that of a basis trade; if this is attractive, the position should be held.

In comparing the in-the-money and at the money alternatives, Bayle accepts a lower rate of return with the former in the money if the market is unchanged, 11.07 percent versus 17.32 percent. However, the level to which the 14 percent can fall without affecting the yield is now 114-02/32 and the level before return is reduced to the Eurodollar rate is 113-26/32. Thus, greater downside protection exists.

The more aggressive strategy Bayle can examine is the out-of-the-money program. If market levels remain unchanged and the call is not assigned, Bayle's return would equal 19.62 percent. Any change in bond price immediately affects the return. A decline to approximately 117-19/32 reduces return to the Eurodollar investment level. However, with the higher strike price, any gain in the cash bond will be to Bayle's benefit until the bonds reach a price at which the futures sell at 74. At this level, Bayle's return would equal 28.11 percent, and higher price will not result in further gains because cash gains and options losses will offset each other.

Managing the buy-write

In evaluating its buy-write program, Bayle would consider the possibility for more active management. For example, if Bayle had, in fact, created an at-the-money call and bond prices declined rapidly from 119-6/32 to 115-30/32, it could (a) do nothing, (b) liquidate the entire position, or (c) roll down its calls to a lower strike price.

---

[4] The break-even point is based upon holding until November 18. The rate of return for any reversal of position prior to that would be adjusted by any cost incurred in repurchasing the short calls as well as reduced income.

[5] The returns noted in the table assume position reversal.

Bayle might be able to buy back its 72 calls for 51/64 and sell 70 calls at 1-46/64.

If Bayle waits and the cash market remains at this new level, its end-of-period return would be analyzed as follows:

Income from premium and interest	$46,244.05
Loss on bonds	(32,500.00)
Net income	13,744.05
Rate of return	8.67%

However, if the 14's price rebounds prior to expiration, the return will improve, and if the price exceeds 117-10/32, the maximum return will be earned. If bond prices continue to fall, the return will go down accordingly. For example, a reduction in the bond price to 114-25/32 would create an additional loss of $11,562.50, reducing position yield to approximately 1.38 percent.

If Bayle chooses to liquidate its position, it would buy in its short options for 51/64, a total cost of $12,939.66. Combined with the capital loss on the bond position, $32,500, or a total cost of $45,439.66, it is likely that Bayle would lose money.

If Bayle felt the market was now stable and it did not want to close out a position, it could roll down its options. The future will sell at about 70-23/32. Bayle would sell a 70-72 December call spread for a credit of 59/64, and take in an additional $14,969.41 in income. At this point, if the market remains unchanged or goes up, Bayle will earn a rate of return of approximately 6.3 percent, which must be weighed against its other alternatives.

Income from original premium and interest	$46,244.05
Additional premium income	14,969.41
Loss on sale of bonds	(32,500.00)
Loss on assignment of future at 71-05/32	(18,775.19)
Net income	$ 9,938.27
Rate of return	6.3%

Bayle's maximum return is now 6.3 percent, and should the market decline below 114-25/32, this return will be reduced further. Until the 114-25/32 level is reached, the loss on the cash bond will be offset by a lesser loss on assignment. By rolling down, Bayle has reduced its potential return but gains some downside protection.

A similar analysis can be done to roll up if prices have increased. In addition, Bayle could, from time to time, purchase puts to protect itself from further downside risk, recognizing that any put purchase will reduce its rate of return.

Thus, the possibilities for managing buy-write programs are numerous; the key element is always the measurement of the market risk versus the incremental rate of return.

23

Short-term rate hedges

CYCLICAL INVENTORY FINANCING[1]

Companies often have predictable seasonal needs for short-term money and can usually estimate long in advance the level their seasonal borrowings will reach. While companies work to manage their variable cost structures, attempting to fix such items as their cost of goods sold, they may remain vulnerable to short-term financing costs. Over the past few years, swings in interest costs have proved to be a major variable expense.

Hedging with CD or bill futures to cover the financing risk can avoid inertia speculation and protect against an unexpected cost increase. This type of a hedge is reasonably easy to construct, and the analysis is similar to that for the fixed-rate loan.

Design Sportswear is a medium-sized manufacturer of casual wear for men and boys. As a result of Christmas sales, its inventory financing needs expand dramatically late in the summer. In fact, Design knows by March that it will have to borrow approximately $12 million through December 15. It currently anticipates borrowing half on

---

[1] Synthetic short-term instruments can also be created. Examples are illustrated in Appendixes III, IV, and V and Chapters 21 and 22.

August 15 and half on September 15. Design has agreed with its bank that the rate established for each of the two loans at takedown would hold for the duration of the loan. The current rate level is acceptable to Design, and the company would like to be able to borrow at these levels in five-six months. Design can avoid the effect of a major increase in rates by selling futures.

In setting up its hedge, the company must evaluate basis risk, convergence, timing mismatches, and variation margin. Inventory loans are typically based on the prime rate. This rate, in turn, is based on the bank's cost of funds; thus, the CD contract, when practical, would be the appropriate contract to sell. The prime, being an administered rate, is more difficult to hedge. For a hedge against the prime, Design bears the risk of changes in the basis between CDs and the prime, and it might use a hedge ratio to manage this exposure (see Chapters 6 and 17). The basis problem can be avoided, making the hedge easier to manage and evaluate, if the company can negotiate a credit line based on a set spread to CD rates. Design opted for a one-to-one hedge ratio relative to the prime rate, expecting each contract to offset the company's rate exposure for each $1 million of loans to be taken down.

As with fixed-rate loans, convergence is accepted as a cost of the hedge (see Chapter 16). In mid-March, Design could sell September CD contracts at a rate of 9.35 percent. This CD contract hedge would protect its interest cost for the three-month period beginning in mid-September. The 9.35 percent CD rate on the September contract is 65 basis points higher than the current three-month CD rate of 8.70 percent. By setting up the hedge, Design started with a base borrowing rate somewhat higher than the three-month rate that existed in March.

Design must also contend with hedging the $6 million, 120-day loan taken down on August 15, creating a rate variance. Because a longer time period than that of the 90-day contract, is involved and contracts will be closed out prior to convergence, in mid-September, the rate realized may differ from that expected. The company will have to make some spread judgments to determine its expected borrowing cost (see Chapter 10). The differential due to convergence and spreads did not seem significant compared to the risk involved in rising rates.

Design first determines how many contracts it needs to sell to protect the 120-day inventory loan. This period is 30 days longer than the contract period; an equal increase in rates would have a greater dollar effect on the loan than on the price of the contract. Based on the ratio of maturities (120/90) and the resulting dollar effect of a rate change, Design needs to sell 1.33 contracts to cover each $1 million loan, or a total of eight September contracts for the $6-million loan during the period from August 15 to December 15.

Design will cover its short September position, booked at a 9.35 percent rate, on August 15, a month prior to contract convergence. The expected rate on the hedge will be adjusted to reflect this. Design might assume an even pace for convergence and conclude that the contract price will increase 55 basis points relative to the cash CD rate by August, rather than the 65 basis points assumed for the September 15 loan hedge. This creates an expected rate of 9-1/4 percent on the 120-day loan.

Because the loan segment is off cycle vis-à-vis the contract market, Design could realize some variance from the expected rate. This would most likely be due to the effect of the yield curve on the rate of convergence between the cash and futures market. The realized rate for the hedge will also be affected by differences between the 90-day rate and the 120-day rate at which the loan will be taken down.

The second $6 million portion of the loan would be taken down on September 15, and the portion between September 15 and December 15 can be hedged with a short position involving six contracts. That portion of the loan can be set, based on the 9.35 percent rate, because on September 15, the future will have converged fully. Combining the two loans, a weighted average base rate of 9.29 percent would be expected.

If Design's loan is to extend beyond December 15, additional contracts would be sold and the hedge again adjusted for maturity differences. If the loan rate were going to change after it was established, a contract position would be maintained with periodic reductions to match the changes in the loans—the rate of contract offsets being dependent on the timing of changes in the loan rate. If the rate can be changed every 30 days, one fourth of the first eight contracts would be covered on August 15, another fourth on September 15, and so on. Variation-margin financing would be considered, but it is unlikely to have any impact.

PERIODIC INVESTMENT PLAN

Insurance companies and other financial intermediaries often guarantee a return for a set period of time on funds received periodically from employee-deduction or IRA plans. A long futures hedge can help protect the intermediary in this type of investment program by maintaining the rate at which the funds received can be invested.

The Standard Management Company offered an IRA program in early 1982 that guaranteed a rate for a two-year period on all funds invested by IRA participants. Program participants deposited $500 per quarter, and Standard Management Company specified deposit dates to match the futures expirations, i.e., the middle of March,

June, September, and December.[2] Standard set the rate for the two years, based on the prices at which it could purchase futures contracts adjusted for hedge risk. This long hedge would allow for gains on futures if market rates declined and the program funds were invested in the market at lower rates.

A long hedge was put on, using CD contracts when this was possible, and Treasury-bill contracts when it was not. The current 90-day CD rate was 12.90 percent. Standard was able to purchase the front three CD contracts for an average yield of 14.00 percent. To protect its deferred period investment rates, Standard also purchased a string of five Treasury-bill contracts, beginning with December '82, at an average discount rate of 13.01 percent.

	Bills	CDs
March '82		86.21
June '82		85.92
September '82		85.87
December '82	87.08	
March '83	87.01	
June, '83	86.95	
September '83	86.95	
December '83	86.98	
Average	86.99	86.00

Standard Management was concerned about the effect of the CD-bill spread on its deferred month hedge results. The cash spread was at a historically narrow level (170 basis points) when the hedge was initiated. If the spread widened as rates rose, Standard would do well; as the long, it would lose less on its bill contracts than it would gain by investing in relatively higher-yielding CDs. However, further narrowing of the spread would work to the company's disadvantage, as it paid up for relatively rich CDs. Standard could decide to accept the inherent spread risk or could create a hedge ratio based on the expected bill-CD relationship.

Standard accepted the risk, but compensated for it in the product offering rate. If it could earn a 170 spread from bills, its investment rate would average 14.45 percent. If it assumed as a worst case an average spread of 80, it could also assume investment earnings on average of 13.88 percent. This would still be above the current 90-day CD rate of 12.90 percent.

Standard also has the flexibility to spread from bill contracts to deferred-month CDs as they begin to trade. This would establish a CD-based cost reflective of when the intermarket spread was done. Because the spread is most likely to narrow as rates decline, financ-

---

[2] To the extent that contract expiration dates do not match the contribution dates, convergence analysis would be similar to that of Design Sportswear's in the previous example.

ing gains on the variation-margin balance can partly offset this move. An average 200-basis-point rate improvement, financed at an average rate of 9 percent, would create an 18-basis-point annual financing gain.

Standard Management Company has some yield-curve advantage in offering this type of program. When rates are low and the yield curve positive, the futures hedge will permit the company to offer a higher rate than the current three-month rate. Because the customer's funds are available only quarterly, this may prove attractive. An inverted yield curve, at high rate levels, will create a futures market rate somewhat lower than the then current three-month cash rate. However, customers may well be interested in preserving the high rate level for two years, giving up some yield for the longer-term guarantee.

A penalty for missed contributions will have to be included in product design because the company stands at risk on unfunded hedge positions.

This hedge program permits substantial flexibility in offering terms. The company can extend its rate guarantee period at any time, in line with futures market levels. At the end of one year, for example, Standard can adjust its initial two-year rate by the rate available in the futures market for the next yearly period (four contracts). This allows Standard to extend forward its rate guarantee and ensure its cash flow for another period. This procedure could be done quarterly, semi-annually, or annually, thereby giving considerable latitude to clients with no additional risk for the company.

ASSET/LIABILITY GAP MANAGEMENT

Bank asset and liability gap management is a natural application for Treasury-bill or CD futures. Gap management allows banks the flexibility to meet customers' needs without compromising rate requirements. Once the gap is measured (or estimated) the bank can use futures to manage its duration, going long to increase maturity or going short to minimize the gap. Treasury-bill and CD contracts can be used to set up this strategy, the choice depending on the bank's source of funds.

Of course, cash-market alternatives exist, particularly for the larger banks. Forward forwards, for example, create positions that cover future time periods.[3] This is similar to futures; but in some cases it is particularly attractive because the bank is able to tailor the time period covered to its needs, avoiding the timing mismatches that can

---

[3] A forward forward is an arrangement that creates a forward rate. A bank issuing a 90-day CD and simultaneously buying a 60-day Eurodollar deposit has, for example, established a short 30-day forward.

occur with futures. However, in terms of flexibility, and especially for smaller banks, futures alternatives can be attractive.

The Federated Bank has $300 million in assets and liabilities, respectively. The average maturity of Federated's asset base is 90 days, while the average liability maturity is 60 days. The degree of interest sensitivity is contingent on this 30-day gap. Federated believes that rates are going to decline; it is happy to leave that gap to take advantage of the fact that its liabilities can be rolled over at lower rates. The bank is comfortable with its current level of sensitivity and would not like to see the gap widen any further. However, it faces substantial demand for six-month CDs and, for marketing reasons, would like to quote an attractive rate. Because Federated does not want to lengthen its liability maturity, it buys CD contracts. The long futures position acts as an asset to offset the new liabilities, leaving the gap intact.

Federated manages the hedge position relative to its cash transactions and the desired gap. To offset a six-month CD, Federated would require two CD contracts, each covering 90 days. As with most short-term rate hedges, timing mismatch can cause a variation in hedge results. The hedged rate is determined, as in prior examples, by the level of the contract purchased and changes in its basis to cash. Contract markets and months are selected with an eye toward minimizing any mismatch. At times, rate risk is more limited by stacking contracts to cover the discrete period (see Chapter 10).

Federated can use hedging techniques to deal with a mismatch between the asset or liability gap and the period covered by futures. By taking the ratio of the number of days in the gap to the number of days covered by the contract, Federated could determine position size. Federated might manage a 30-day gap with a 90-day contract by positioning 100 contracts to cover $300 million.

Federated must recognize the fact that, although the duration has been controlled, the time periods and the rates involved are somewhat different; the 30-day gap period is not the same as one third of the 90-day periods covered by the contract.

Gap management with futures brings about an interesting reporting problem. An asset/liability gap changes daily as instruments mature, but contract maturity stays constant.[4] As Federated's liabilities are rolled over, the average maturity and therefore, the duration of the gap, might change, causing the bank to adjust its futures position. Alternatively, assets and liabilities maturing simultaneously would also lead to a hedge adjustment. For example, a 30-day gap on $297

---

[4] Often, computer programs set up to manage asset/liability gaps have to be adjusted for that portion of the liability or asset mix accounted for by futures because the programs automatically assume a winding down of all assets and liabilities over a period of time.

million would require only 99 contracts. If Federated's program is large enough, it would be able to reduce its futures position every day. Otherwise, it will have to reduce its net futures position from time to time, thereby facing the risk of being slightly short, depending on where it stands. This, of course, would be taken into account with respect to the firm's overall position in asset/liability management.

24

Accounting for financial futures and options

Accounting treatment for futures has been evolving to meet expanding needs of hedgers. Substantial progress has been made in most areas. As users become more sophisticated, accounting theory will no doubt accommodate them.[1]

One remaining area of concern is that accounting theory has not yet addressed the problem of separating component parts of a hedge to reduce yield-curve speculation (see Chapters 6 and 16). As has been emphasized throughout this book, the cash-futures spread and variation-margin financing effects must often be distinguished from the principal hedge ratio. Current accounting theory does not easily reflect these differentiations—perhaps reflecting a lack of precision by hedgers. Even when futures are used to create periodic returns, as in variable-rate products (see Chapter 18), most accountants will not allow the cash-futures aspect to be treated differently from the principal hedge, either with respect to the timing or character of income-statement recognition.

The accounting treatment of variation-margin financing has also not been well documented. Arguably, such financing effects should

---

[1] One notable exception is the Federal Banking Regulatory Agencies, who still do not permit the use of hedge accounting for regulatory reporting.

have different treatment for hedges creating periodic returns as opposed to those hedging long-term assets or private placements. Most observers today, however, feel that in all cases, current accounting literature requires variable financing effects to be shown in the period in which they are incurred.

Accounting theory is in flux and probably will continue to be as usage becomes more sophisticated. This chapter is meant to reflect the July 1983 Exposure Draft issued by the Financial Accounting Standards Board (FASB).[2]

MARK-TO-MARKET VERSUS HEDGE ACCOUNTING

Generally speaking, unrealized gains and losses resulting from changes in quoted market values of futures contracts, as well as realized gains and losses, should be recognized currently in the income statement. This basis of accounting, commonly referred to as "mark to market," should be followed when futures contracts represent hedges of asset positions, contemplated asset purchases, or short positions—all of which are, or will be, carried at market value. However, the FASB Exposure Draft provides for different accounting treatment of certain futures contracts that are hedges.

A futures contract may be a hedge of an existing asset or liability, or a firm commitment to buy or sell a financial instrument at a fixed price. Or it may be a hedge of purchases or sales of financial instruments that a company expects, but is not legally obligated to make (commonly referred to as "anticipatory hedges"). Hedge accounting treatment applies only if the criteria discussed in this section are met and if the related asset or liability is or will be carried at cost, amortized cost, or the lower of cost or market.

Hedge accounting is based on a concept of symmetry between accounting for the futures contract and the asset or liability being hedged, with gain or loss on the hedge being deferred rather than being recognized currently in the income statement. Hedge accounting requires the identification of a specific asset or liability to determine the right time to recognize deferred gains and losses and/or the right amortization period of such gains and losses.

Three conditions must be met for a futures contract to qualify as a hedge of existing assets or liabilities, or a firm commitment for accounting purposes:

1. The company is exposed to the risk of price or interest-rate changes because it owns the asset, owes the liability, or has the firm commitment. The nature of the company's business and its other assets, liabilities, and commitments need to be con-

[2] *Accounting for Futures Contracts* (Financial Accounting Standards Board, July 1983).

sidered to decide whether there is exposure. A company that owns fixed-rate, interest-bearing financial instruments, for example, would not be exposed to price and interest-rate risk if the investment were funded by fixed-rate debt of similar maturity.

2. The futures contract reduces exposure to the risk of price or interest-rate changes. There must be a high degree of correlation between changes in the market value of the futures contract and the fair value of the asset, liability, or firm commitment.

3. The futures contract is designated as a hedge. At the time the futures contract is entered into, its purpose should be specifically identified and documented as part of the company's accounting records. The dollar amount should be specified, as should a description of the asset, liability, or firm commitment for which the hedge is intended.

A futures contract qualifies as a hedge of an anticipated purchase or sale of financial instruments if all of the following conditions are met:

1. The significant terms of the anticipated transaction are identified. These terms include the expected date, the type of financial instrument, and the quantity to be bought or sold.

2. The expected transaction is likely to occur because the company has little flexibility to do otherwise. (If it is likely that failure to make the expected transaction would result in little cost or disruption of operations, this condition generally would not be met.)

3. Closing the expected transaction at a price substantially different from the current price will have a direct impact on the company's profitability. This condition relates to the relationship of a company's buying and selling prices. For example, a manufacturer planning to roll over floating-rate bank debt probably cannot change the selling prices of its products immediately if interest rates change. The profitability of a bank rolling over a loan, however, may not be affected if the loan is funded with floating-rate deposits of similar maturity.

4. The futures contract reduces exposure to the risk of price or interest-rate changes. There must be a high degree of correlation between changes in the market value of the futures contract and the fair value of the asset or liability to be bought, sold, or incurred.

5. The futures contract is designated as a hedge.

PRINCIPLES OF HEDGE ACCOUNTING

The gain or loss on a futures contract that meets all of the conditions described above is deferred and reported as an adjustment of the carrying amount of the hedged item. If the futures contract hedges an existing asset or liability, the deferred gain or loss is reported as an adjustment of the carrying amount of the asset or liability. If the futures contract hedges a firm commitment, the deferred gain or loss adjusts the reported amount of the purchase or sale. Similarly, if the futures contract hedges an expected transaction, the deferred gain or loss adjusts the reported amount of the purchase or sale when it occurs.

In the case of hedges of existing assets, liabilities, or firm commitments, the gain or loss on a futures contract may be deferred only to the extent that the contract has been effective as a hedge. In other words, if the futures gain or loss is larger than the unrecognized loss or gain on the hedged item, the excess is recognized currently in income.

Let's say the item being hedged is not identical to the item that underlies the futures contract. Even though their price movements are highly correlated, they are not perfectly correlated. Or let's say that the basis (the relationship between the cash-market price and the futures market price; see Chapter 6) changes over time; the cash and futures prices tend to fluctuate together, but not necessarily by identical amounts. In either case, the hedge is not perfectly effective. This effectiveness test is one-sided—if the unrecognized loss or gain of the hedged item is larger than the futures gain or loss, the excess is not recognized currently in income.

There is no effectiveness test for anticipatory hedges; however, if it becomes known that the amount of the actual purchase or sale is likely to be less than the size of the anticipated transaction that was hedged, a pro rata portion of the gain or loss on the futures contract is recognized currently in the income statement. In the case of anticipatory hedges that are closed out before the date of the anticipated transaction, the gain or loss on the futures contract continues to be deferred until the purchase or sale occurs.

Deferred gains or losses on a futures contract are either applied to adjust the carrying amount of an existing asset or liability, or will be applied to adjust the carrying amount of a future asset or liability. Those adjustments become an integral part of the carrying amount of the asset or liability and are accounted for as such. Thus, deferred gains or losses that adjust the carrying amounts of interest-bearing assets and liabilities are like discounts or premiums and are amortized to interest income or expense.

If deferred gains or losses become part of the carrying amount of an asset carried at the lower of cost or market, they also become part of cost (in the cost versus market comparison).

Short hedge of an asset carried at cost

Futures contracts might be sold to hedge against a market-value decline of an existing fixed-rate asset. One example of such a hedge might involve selling interest-rate futures contracts against an existing investment security. Or these futures might be sold by a financial institution against existing fixed-rate loans. Gains and losses resulting from such hedges should be deferred to the extent that the contracts have been effective as hedges.

The deferred gains and losses should be recognized in income when the asset is sold—or recorded as an adjustment to the carrying amount of the asset if the futures contract is closed out before the asset is sold. Resulting premiums or discounts should be amortized to income over the remaining life of the asset as an adjustment to interest income.

On August 15, Franklin Funding Corporation buys at par a 14 percent bond maturing in 25 years. Interest is payable semiannually. One year later, interest rates have decreased, and the bonds are now yielding 13.05 percent at a price of 107. That's an increase to $1.07 million from the original purchase price of $1 million. Franklin Funding does not have any long-term, fixed-interest liabilities and is, therefore, exposed to interest-rate risk.

The treasurer of Franklin Funding does not want to sell the bond; yet, he fears an increase in interest rates. He decides to protect the value of the bond by selling December Treasury-bond contracts at a price of 70. Having studied the price correlation between the bond position and the Treasury-bond futures market, the treasurer believes that the yield correlation is very high. In constructing the appropriate hedge ratio, therefore, he evaluates the effect of interest-rate changes on his bond position versus the futures market.

The treasurer thus determines that 15 or 16 contracts should be used to hedge the $1-million bond position (see Chapter 16). He decides to use 15 contracts.

In fact, by August 15, interest rates have increased to 14.15 percent, and the bonds are now selling at 97—$100,000 lower than when the future position was established. The December bond contract price has decreased to $64.

Accounting for this is illustrated here:

Accounting journal entries

August 15—First year

```
Investment in bonds . . . . . . . . . . . . . . . . . . . . . . .$1,000,000
    Cash                                                  $1,000,000
    (To record purchase of bonds)
```

August 15—Second year

Margin deposit with broker . . . .$	30,000	
Cash		$ 30,000
(To record initial margin deposit with broker of $2,000 per contract)		

August 16—(second year) to August 15—(third year) (cumulative)

Cash . . . .$	90,000	
Unamortized discount on investment in bonds (Deferred gain on futures hedge)		$ 90,000
(To record gain on open futures position)		

Had the gain on the futures contract been larger than the loss on the bonds, the excess gain would not have been deferred.

August 15—Third year

Cash . . . .$	30,000	
Margin deposit with broker		$ 30,000
(To record return of margin from broker on closeout of futures position)		
Cash	$ 970,000	
Unamortized discount on investment in bonds	$ 90,000	
Gain on sale of investment		$ 60,000
Investment in bonds		$1,000,000
(To record sale of bonds and recognize gain on futures position)		

Had the bond not been sold and only the futures position closed out, the journal entry would be as follows:

August 15—(Third year)

Deferred gain on futures hedge . . . .$	90,000	
Unamortized discount on investment in bonds		$ 90,000

Anticipatory long hedge of an asset to be carried at cost

Futures contracts might be bought to protect against the risk of falling interest rates on expected purchases of fixed-interest-rate assets. One example of long anticipatory hedges would be the purchase of futures contracts to protect against the risk of falling interest rates on the anticipated purchase of a fixed-rate investment security (see Chapter 19). Or these contracts might be purchased to protect against the anticipated repricing of an existing asset, such as a loan held by a financial institution on which interest rates are adjusted every three months (see Chapter 23). In the case of a long anticipatory hedge, gains and losses on futures contracts should be deferred and should be included in the measurement of the dollar basis of the asset for which the hedge was intended. The gains and losses would then be amortized to income over the holding period of the asset as an adjustment of interest income.

On May 1, the treasurer of United Broadcasting Corporation expects that on September 15 he will have $5 million for a sinking-fund payment due on December 15. He plans to invest in 90-day CDs. The current market yield is 12.03 percent. However, fearing that, by September 15, interest rates will have declined sharply, the corporate treasurer seeks protection from the risk of falling interest rates by buying five September CD futures contracts at a price of 88.12 (a rate of 11.88 percent). Because he needs $5,145,000 for the sinking-fund payment, a rate of 11.6 percent, the 11.88 percent rate is acceptable.[3] The company has no short-term debt and is, therefore, exposed to interest-rate risk.

By September 15, when the $5 million becomes available for investment, the 90-day CD rate has fallen by 190 basis points to 10.13 percent. And the September bill futures contract price has increased by 175 basis points to 89.87, reflecting the 10.13 percent yield.

Because United did hedge, the reduction of income is mitigated by a gain on the futures position of $21,875, and the anticipated 11.88 percent yield is achieved.

Accounting journal entries

June 1

Margin deposit with broker . . . .$	10,000	
Cash		$ 10,000

(To record initial margin deposit put
up with broker of $2,000 per contract)

June 2-September 15 (cumulative)

Cash . . . .$	21,875	
Deferred gain on futures hedge		$ 21,875

(To record gain in open futures positions)

September 15

Cash	$ 10,000	
Margin deposit with broker		$ 10,000

(To record return of margin
deposit from broker when
futures position is closed out)

Investment in CD	$4,978,125	
Deferred gain on futures hedge	$ 21,875	
Cash		$5,000,000

(To record purchase of 90-day CD and to
include the gain on the futures hedge
position in the measurement of the CDS
purchased)

---

[3] United knows that a conservatively constructed hedge must be based upon the yield levels available in the futures market rather than those in the cash market. Constructing those hedges is discussed primarily in Chapters 10, 11, and 17.

At the end of the 90-day period, the 10.13 percent CD will be redeemed for $5,126,625. Because the CD will be carried at a cost of $4,978,125, the total interest income recorded will be $148,500, resulting in an effective 11.88 percent yield.

The following entries complete the transaction.

December 15

Cash $5,126,625		
Investment		$4,978,125
Interest income		$ 148,500

(To record redemption of CD
and accrual of periodic interest)

Short anticipatory hedge of a liability to be carried at cost

Futures contracts might be sold to protect against the risk of rising interest rates on the anticipated incurrence of a fixed interest-rate liability, such as the anticipated rollover of fixed-rate deposits by financial institutions or the periodic repricing of existing liabilities (see Chapters 16 and 17).

Gains and losses on futures contracts sold as an anticipatory hedge of a liability to be carried at cost should be deferred and should be included in the measurement of the dollar basis of the incurred liability for which the hedge was intended. The gains and losses would then be amortized to income over the holding period of the liability as an adjustment to interest expense.

Haversham-Dudley Bank is currently funding some long-term, fixed-rate loans yielding 14 percent, with 90-day deposits bearing interest at a rate of 11.25 percent. On May 1, the financial institution's asset/liability manager notes that $10 million of the 90-day deposits will mature on September 15, and anticipates that they will be "rolled over" into new 90-day deposits. Meanwhile, interest rates have been creeping up, and 90-day deposits are now selling at an interest rate of 12.03 percent. Fearing interest rates may increase, the manager seeks protection against the risk of rising interest rates on the rollover of the deposits. He sells 10 September 90-day CD contracts at the current price of 88.17 (a yield of 11.83 percent), attempting to secure a 2.17 percent spread between the interest income on the long-term, fixed-rate assets and a funding cost of 11.83 percent.[4]

By September 15, when the 90-day deposits roll over, interest rates, in fact, have fallen, and new deposits are being issued at a rate of 10.13. The September 90-day CD contract price has increased to 89.87, reflecting the yield of 10.13 percent.

---

[4] This assumes that the bank is able to issue CDs at the rate of the top-10 CD issuers (see Chapter 11).

By hedging, the manager sought to ensure a quarterly profit of $54,250. Had the asset/liability manager not hedged, he would have had income over the three-month period starting September 15 of $96,750 (14 percent return on assets less 10.13 percent funding cost on $10 million for three months). However, because he hedged, his actual gain of $96,750 was mitigated by a $42,500 loss on the futures position, but his spread income over the three-month period starting September 15 would be the anticipated $54,250.

Accounting journal entries

May 1

Margin deposit with broker . . . .$	20,000	
Cash		$ 20,000
(To record initial margin deposit made to broker of $2,000 per contract)		

May 2-September 15 (cumulative)

Deferred loss on futures hedge . . . .$	42,500	
Cash		$ 42,500
(To record loss on open futures position)		

September 15

Cash . . . .$	20,000	
Margin deposit with broker		$ 20,000
(To record return of margin deposit when futures position is closed out)		

Deposits—old	$10,000,000	
Discount on deposits issued	$ 42,500	
Deferred loss on futures hedges		$ 42,500
Deposits—new		$10,000,000

(To record issuance—rollover—of new deposits and to include the loss on futures hedge position in the measurement of the dollar basis of the new deposits)

Actual interest of 10.13 percent on the deposit will be $253,250 for the period, which when added to the $42,500 loss in futures, will result in a recognized $295,750 of interest expense for the period, at rate of 11.83 percent.

The subsequent actions to complete the periodic income would be

December 15

Cash . . . .$	350,000	
Interest income		$ 350,000
(To record quarterly income on $10,000,000 loan)		

Interest expense	$ 295,750	
Cash		$ 253,250
Discount on deposit		$ 42,500
(To record current periodic interest expense including amortization of deferred futures loss)		

DISCLOSURE REQUIREMENTS

The FASB Exposure Draft requires disclosure of (a) the nature of the items that are hedged with futures contracts, and (b) the method of accounting for the futures contracts (including a description of the events that result in recognizing the changes in value of futures contracts in income). Following are illustrations of how the Franklin Funding Corporation might disclose its hedge of its investment in bonds and how United Broadcasting Corporation might disclose its anticipatory hedge of its expected investment in CDs.

Franklin funding. During 1982 and 1983, the institution used financial futures to hedge the value of investments in fixed-interest-rate bonds. Gains and losses on futures contracts are accounted for as discount or premium on the investments in bonds up to the amount of unrecognized loss or gain on the investments. Amortization of the discount or premium begins when the futures contracts are closed. Gains and losses on futures contracts in excess of unrecognized loss or gain on the investments are recorded in income currently.

United Broadcasting. During 1982, the company entered into futures contracts to "lock in" high interest rates on anticipated temporary cash investments. Gains and losses on those futures contracts were deferred and accounted for as discount or premium on the investments. The discount or premium was amortized to income over the period the investments were held.

ACCOUNTING FOR OPTIONS

Certain aspects of accounting theory for the treatment of positions hedged with options have yet to be definitively established. Nevertheless, certain guidelines with respect to transactions qualifying as hedges can be set forth.

Purchased put/call options

If puts are purchased to hedge an existing asset carried at cost, any premium paid would be deferred.

1. If interest rates increase, making the value of the put increase, and the put is offset, any resulting gain (net of the premium paid) would be reflected as a reduction in the carrying value of the hedged asset. Therefore, the gain would be amortized over the remaining life of the asset.

2. If the hedged asset is delivered against the put option, the premium paid would be reflected as a reduction in the proceeds received, thus reducing the gain (increasing the loss) on the asset sold.

3. If interest rates decline, making the value of the put decline, and the put is offset or expires, the premium paid (net of any proceeds received) would be reflected as an increase in the carrying value of the hedged asset.

4. *However*, any gain or loss on a hedged position that exceeds the offsetting loss or gain on the hedged position should be recognized currently.

If puts are purchased to hedge anticipated rollover of deposits or acquisitions of new funding sources, any premium paid would be deferred.

1. If interest rates increase, the resulting gain (net of the premium paid) would be included in the measurement of the dollar basis of the new liability incurred.

2. If interest rates decline, the premium paid (net of the proceeds received on the closeout) would be included in the measurement of the dollar basis of the liability incurred.

If call options are purchased to hedge the anticipated purchase of an asset any premium paid would be deferred.

1. If the call option is exercised, the premium paid would be included in the measurement of the dollar basis of the asset acquired.

2. If interest rates decline, the gain (net of the premium paid) would be included in the measurement of the dollar basis of the asset acquired.

3. If interest rates increase, the premium paid (net of proceeds received on any offset) would be included in the measurement of the dollar basis of the asset acquired.

Written put/call options

Short put options and naked call options. The 1980 American Institute of Certified Public Accountants (AICPA) accounting issues paper, "Accounting for Forward Placement and Standby Commitments and Interest Rate Futures Contracts," suggests that short put options and naked call options written against noncovered securities be accounted for on a market-value basis.

Covered calls. The AICPA paper does not specifically address covered call options; however, the paper's position on short covered put options was based on the fact that there is substantial risk involved in a short put option. The maximum one can gain is the premium received, while the loss can be significant. The paper concluded that because of the speculative nature of writing options, they should be accounted for on a market-value basis.

The market risks for covered options are virtually identical to those for naked short put options (see Chapter 22). Based on the intent of the AICPA issues paper, one can conclude that the accounting for written covered call options would be the same as for written put options, i.e., market-value accounting. Presumably, this would apply to options written on futures as part of a buy/write program involving cash bonds.

A possible compromise approach for covered call options would be to defer option gains or losses to the extent that a hedge is effective and report gains or losses as adjustments to the carrying amount of the asset, but limit the amount of deferred losses on the option to an amount which offsets unrecognized changes in the fair value of the hedged item from the date the option is sold.

25

Federal income tax treatment

Federal income tax treatment[1] of financial futures transactions is completely different from accounting treatment. Unfortunately, the use of futures as a hedge vehicle has not been generally reflected by tax policy.

The major issues for tax purposes are timing: when to recognize gains and losses on futures contracts and character of income; and whether gains and losses are ordinary or capital. Such decisions are affected not only by the purpose of the futures contract and the type of related item being hedged, but also by the classification of contract users. Furthermore, the definition of a hedge for income tax purposes differs from its purely economic or financial accounting meanings.

Understanding federal income tax treatment of futures contracts is essential for calculating the return on a proposed transaction. It is also essential for financial accounting purposes, because the differences between accounting and tax treatment are timing differences requiring deferred taxes; and the amount of deferred tax required

---

[1] The chapter is intended as a guide only; users should review specific situations with tax advisers. It also is designed not only to cover hedge transactions but to provide some background for cash-futures positions, such as repurchase agreements.

depends on whether the results are ordinary or capital gains and losses.

While a hedge ratio can be managed to compensate for differences in both the character and timing of financial and tax accounting, such amendments make hedging more complicated. As is true for financial accounting, an expansion of the use and sophistication of hedging could lead to modification of existing provisions.

CLASSIFICATION OF USERS

For tax purposes, users of financial instruments and related futures contracts generally fall into three broad categories:

Dealer: a taxpayer who profits from a markup or commission on the goods sold.

Trader: a taxpayer engaged in a trade or business who profits from price fluctuation.

Speculator/investor: a taxpayer who profits solely from price fluctuation and income earned on property held.

As discussed below, a hedger is classified in one of the above categories for tax purposes, depending on the motivation for the hedge.

These distinctions are important because different users are subject to different tax rules: dealers generally are subject to ordinary tax treatment, while traders and speculators/investors usually receive capital tax treatment.

Unfortunately, the distinctions between users are not always clear, and the rules may be imprecise for specific situations. And a user can fall into different categories, depending on the transaction. (A dealer, for example, may make investment transactions.) However, existing regulatory and judicial authority provides some guidance in determining the appropriate tax status.

Dealer

Like a dealer in securities, a dealer in cash-market financial instruments is a merchant who sells to customers with a view toward making a profit from a markup in price and/or commission—which makes the dealer just like other types of merchants who sell their products to customers with a markup to produce a profit. Anyone who maintains an inventory of cash instruments with the hope of making a profit by reselling to customers at a markup (principal transactions) and not intending to hold the contract for investment or speculation, is a dealer for tax purposes. And dealer transactions are generally afforded ordinary income or loss treatment for tax purposes.

A dealer can also act in an agency capacity, earning commission income from buying and selling for customers. Transactions with customers in financial futures contracts are performed in an agency capacity and generate commission income.[2]

The taxpayer bears the burden of establishing dealer status. Although court cases have held that no single factor is controlling, the following characteristics will be weighed to determine whether the taxpayer qualifies as a dealer:

Maintenance of an inventory of the physical commodity.

Maintenance of a customer list.

Profit from a markup on inventory or a commission;

Earnings on a purchase or sale rather than a profit from market changes.

Maintenance of at least one regular place of business.

License as a dealer.

Advertisement to the public as a dealer.

Subscription to various services commonly used by dealers.

Execution of a large number of transactions.

Maintenance of customer accounts and sales personnel.

The critical factor is the manner of dealing with the "public."[3] None of the authorities suggests that all of the characteristics listed above must be present for the taxpayer to be a dealer. On the other hand, the fewer characteristics exhibited by the taxpayer, the more the taxpayer approaches the status of trader or speculator/investor, with consequent capital gain/loss tax treatment.

In general, a dealer in commodities or financial instruments reports gains and losses generated from his business as ordinary income, just as any other merchant does on the sale of products. Consequently, dealer income generally does not qualify for capital-gain treatment. However, it is possible for dealers to maintain a separate investment account and derive capital-gain tax treatment from specific investment-account transactions. Internal Revenue Code Section 1236 provides for these tax consequences for dealers in securities. There is no

---

[2] Treasury Regulation Section 1.471-5 describes a securities dealer as: "a merchant of securities, whether an individual, partnership or corporation, with an established place of business, regularly engaged in the purchase of securities and their resale to customers; that is, one who as a merchant buys securities and sells them to customers with a view to the gains and profits that may be derived therefrom. If such business is simply a branch of the activities carried on by such a person, the securities inventoried as provided in this section may include only those held for purposes of resale and not for investment. Taxpayers who buy and sell or hold securities for investment or speculation, irrespective of whether such buying or selling constitutes the carrying on of a trade or business, and officers of corporations and members of partnerships who in their individual capacities buy and sell securities, are not dealers in securities within the meaning of this section."

[3] When the courts speak of transactions with the "public," that public need not be the general public but can be a more specific public, such as financial institutions or other dealers.

similar provision for dealers in commodities. Section 1236 can, however, be used for guidance with these types of transactions.

This section provides that gains by dealers on the sale or exchange of securities will not be considered capital in nature unless the security was clearly identified as a security held for investment by the end of the day of its acquisition and was not held thereafter primarily for sale to customers in the ordinary course of the taxpayer's trade or business. A loss by a dealer on securities transactions is not an ordinary loss if the security was at any time clearly identified in the dealer's records as a security held for investment. A special rule also gives registered stock-exchange floor specialists seven days to identify acquisitions of their specialty stocks as being held for investment purposes.

Certain government instruments, such as Treasury notes or bonds, may be classified as securities for tax purposes and thus fall within the statutory rules of Section 1236. However, many other government instruments, as well as precious metals, currencies, and agricultural commodities, would not be considered securities. Therefore, common law definitions could determine what constitutes dealer status.

Case law suggests that if a commodities dealer adequately identifies, segregates, and consistently treats certain commodities and commodity contracts as investments rather than inventory, such classification will be recognized for tax purposes. However, this classification should be made immediately upon purchase. Because of the lack of clear statutory authority, the dealer's classification of certain commodity contracts as investments for tax purposes should be approached with caution and meticulously documented.

A dealer might also maintain a trading account in commodities that have not been identified in an investment account. Such commodities, not having been identified as investments by the dealer, are not accorded capital tax treatment. Consequently, there may be some question as to whether or not they should be treated as inventory for tax purposes. Dealers typically treat such goods as inventory, and the normal year-end inventory valuation rules (cost, market, or lower of cost or market) would thus be applicable, and various theories have been advanced in support of this treatment. However, there is no clear legal opinion concerning this matter.

Trader

A trader's transactions are generally afforded capital-gain or capital-loss treatment for income tax purposes. The U.S. Tax Court has defined a trader as a seller of securities who performs no merchandising function and whose status as to the source of supply of the securities is not significantly different from that of those to whom he sells. A trader performs no services that need be compensated for by a price markup on the securities he sells; the trader's access to securities is no better than that of anyone else, and he or she intends to make a profit through changes in value.

Numerous judicial decisions have held that a trader in securities or commodity futures does not hold them for sale to customers and, therefore, receives capital-gain or capital-loss treatment. Trader gains are thus capital gains and qualify for beneficial tax treatment if they are long term. Trader losses are treated as capital losses subject to capital-loss limitations.

A trader may benefit from certain tax advantages not available to a speculator/investor. For example, the individual trader may be entitled to deduct against adjusted gross income certain business expenses, such as interest paid, that a speculator/investor may claim only as itemized deductions. However, the distinction between a trader and a speculator/investor is not well defined. The question ultimately may be determined by the volume of activity and the ability of the trader to establish that these activities constitute the active conduct of a trade or business as opposed to investment activities engaged in for profit.

Most statutory authority, however, refers only to dealers or investors. Hence, if a user is classified as a trader for tax purposes, his gains and losses generally are treated in the same manner as those of a speculator/investor.

Speculator/investor

The trading activities of a speculator/investor generally are afforded capital-gain or capital-loss treatment for income tax purposes. A speculator/investor trades for his own account and performs no services or merchandising functions compensated for by a price markup. Instead, the speculator intends to profit solely from a market increase in the value of the assets purchased and from any income (such as interest) earned on those assets. The motive is purely speculative. Therefore, any users engaged in purely speculative transactions will be treated as speculators/investors with respect to those transactions.

TAX RULES PERTAINING TO
INTEREST-RATE FUTURES

For tax purposes, transactions in futures contracts are not viewed as dealings in the underlying instrument. Instead, they are viewed as transactions in the rights to the specific commodity. A commodity future is an executory contract, and the holder thus has no tax basis until the contract is executed or sold.

While the underlying commodity may be tangible property, the future rights to the commodity are clearly intangible. Transactions in tangibles generally give rise to capital-gain or capital-loss treatment—unless the transaction, viewed as a whole, constitutes a hedge for tax purposes (see below). Therefore, futures contracts will generally be viewed as capital assets unless the specifics of the transaction (for example, dealer or hedging activities) require treatment as ordinary income.

Prior to changes in futures contract taxation introduced by the Economic Recovery Tax Act of 1981 (ERTA), one needed a complete understanding of the statutory rules governing long-term capital tax treatment, short sales, and "wash sales" (described below) to determine the proper taxation of transactions involving both the cash and futures markets. Although still significant in this context, this understanding is no longer relevant for the taxation of transactions solely involving futures contracts.

Long-term capital tax treatment: Pre-ERTA '81

The sale or exchange of a capital asset (as defined) held more than one year will give rise to long-term capital-gain/loss tax treatment; if held for one year or less, short-term capital treatment will result. A statutory exception to this general rule provides that "futures transactions in any commodity subject to the rules of a board of trade or commodity exchange" are subject only to an "over six months" holding period requirement for long-term capital treatment.

There is no statutory definition of what constitutes a commodity futures contract subject to the shorter holding period. A great deal of controversy centered on the question of whether the statutory exception includes only futures contracts on agricultural commodities. The Treasury Department subsequently indicated that, regardless of legislative intent, the exception was stated broadly enough to include all commodity futures contracts (including interest-rate futures) traded on a commodity exchange or board of trade. The IRS ultimately published a Revenue Ruling indicating that futures contracts on U.S. Treasury bills were entitled to the over-six-months holding period provision for long-term capital tax treatment. Questions regarding the required holding period also arose in situations where the underlying cash commodity was acquired by taking delivery pursuant to the futures contract.

Under ERTA '81, the issue of a holding period for long-term capital tax treatment is now irrelevant for regulated futures contracts (RFCs). As will be discussed, RFC transaction net gains and losses are deemed long-term and short-term capital on a pro rata basis, without regard to the holding period. Holding period rules continue to be relevant, however, for other futures contracts.

Applicability of the wash-sale rule: Pre-ERTA '81

The wash-sale provisions of the Internal Revenue Code provide that no deduction for a loss on the sale of stock or securities is allowed if substantially identical property is acquired (directly or by option or contract to purchase) within 30 days prior to or 30 days subsequent to the initial sale or exchange. The tax benefit of the loss is not lost forever; it is merely deferred by becoming an adjustment to the basis of the property acquired. Contrary older case law notwithstanding, the IRS has ruled that commodity futures contracts are not stock or securities for this purpose and that the statutory wash-sale rule does not apply to transactions solely in futures contracts. However, care is needed to ensure that there is a business purpose, apart from tax considerations, for effecting such a transaction.

Certain cash financial instruments may be considered securities for wash-sale purposes. Therefore, when the cash instrument is sold at a loss and, within 30 days before or after such sale, a long futures position in such a financial instrument is acquired, the statutory wash-sale rule could apply to disallow the realized loss.

ERTA '81 provided for an expansion of the wash-sale concept. For RFC transactions, the abuses contemplated by the wash-sale rule are avoided through application of the mark-to-market concept. In addition, for solely non-RFC market or RFC/non-RFC market trades, the IRS is empowered to issue regulations that will produce the same result as the statutory wash-sale rule through introduction of a "balanced and offsetting position" theory in addition to the existing "substantially identical" rule.

Applicability of the short-sale rule: Pre-ERTA '81

A short sale is a contract for the future sale and delivery of property that may or may not currently be owned. The sale can be completed by a purchase of the underlying property in the marketplace or by delivery of property already owned but yet not delivered to the buyer at the time of the sale. The taxable event does not occur until the short sale is completed (covered or closed) by delivery.

Under the statutory short-sale rules, the holding period of the property delivered to close the short sale determines whether a short- or long-term capital gain or loss results. If, on the date of a short sale of a capital asset, substantially identical property has not been held for the requisite long-term holding period or is acquired after the short sale but before the closing date, then the gain on the closing of the short sale is short term, regardless of the holding period of the property actually used to close the short sale. The holding period of the substantially identical property acquired begins on the date the short sale is closed.

If, at the time of the short sale, substantially identical property has been held for more than the requisite long-term holding period, any loss on closing the short sale is long term, even if the property actually used to close the short sale was not held for more than the requisite long-term holding period.

The statutory short-sale rules apply only if substantially identical property is held or acquired. In the case of commodity futures contracts traded subject to the rules of a commodity exchange or board of trade, the Internal Revenue Code provides that "a commodity future requiring delivery in one calendar month shall not be considered as property substantially identical to another commodity future requiring delivery in a different calendar month." The practical effect of this definition is that a futures contract would be substantially identical only to another contract for the same commodity requiring delivery in the same month.

The statutory short-sale rules apply to commodity futures contracts but not to cash commodities, other than those considered securities. Therefore, concomitant purchase of a cash commodity and sale of a commodity futures contract are generally not covered by this rule. It might be argued that, if an interest-rate futures contract is sold short at a time when an underlying deliverable financial instrument is owned but has not been held for more than one year, the short sale rule could operate to cut off the holding period of the underlying instrument. Long-term capital-gain treatment may not be obtained unless the underlying financial instrument is sold more than one year after the close of the short sale of the future. However, there is no statutory or case law guidance in this area.

Under ERTA '81, the IRS has authority to issue regulations expanding the scope of the statutory short-sale rule to cover "balanced and offsetting positions," even if not substantially identical. However, the statutory provisions of the short-sale rule specifically do not apply to qualified hedging transactions.

ERTA '81

As indicated previously, in recent years some taxpayers engaged in commodity and commodity-related transactions not only for speculative purposes and to guard against the risk of economic loss, but also to create tax benefits to shelter other income, as technically permissible under the tax laws. Congress, reacting to perceived abuses, opted to change these laws and establish a new set of specific tax rules for these types of transactions.

The tax law prescribes the treatment for each basic type as follows:

Transactions in regulated futures contracts (RFCs).

Hedging transactions.

Straddle transactions in non-RFC contracts (including mixed straddles).[4]

Identified straddles.

Regulated futures contracts (RFCs). RFCs are contracts for the delivery of actively traded personal property traded on or subject to the rules of a commodity exchange or board of trade and subject to the mark-to-market method for determining margin deposit requirements. In addition, the IRS may designate other exchanges as having adequate rules so that these new ERTA '81 provisions will also apply to transactions on these exchanges. Under ERTA '81, a taxpayer must mark to market (determine the fair market value of) all RFCs held at year end and include the unrealized gains or losses in income for the year.

Contracts terminated during the year (through offsetting positions or by making or taking delivery) must also be marked to market by determining their fair market value immediately before termination. All RFCs must be marked to market whether they are balanced, offset, or part of a straddle.

RFC gains and losses, whether realized or unrealized and whether resulting from short or long positions, are netted for the year. The net RFC gain or loss is, by statute, deemed to be a 40 percent short-term and 60 percent long-term capital gain or loss. This results in a net maximum effective tax rate for individuals of 32 percent.

A taxpayer other than a corporation may carry back a net RFC loss (retaining its current year's short- or long-term character) for three years to offset net commodities futures gain. But that taxpayer may not carry the loss back to a year before 1981. These rules do not apply to qualified hedging transactions.

Hedging transactions. Economically, an interest-rate hedge is a transaction that a lender, investor, or borrower of funds uses to protect against the effects of interest-rate changes by taking a position in the futures market opposite to a position taken in the cash market. For example, a corporation with borrowings tied to the prime rate could attempt to hedge its interest cost by shorting Treasury-bills contracts (see Chapter 17). If short-term interest rates increase, then presumably the price of the futures contracts will fall. If short-term rates decline, the price should increase. The hedger anticipates that the gain or loss on a short position will offset the increased or de-

---

[4] A "straddle" involves holding an offsetting position in any personal property—other than corporate stock—that is actively traded.

creased borrowing costs as interest rates fluctuate. The hedge is designed to mitigate the effect of future changes in interest rates.

The nature of the commodity underlying the futures contract used in a hedge transaction is critical in determining tax treatment. Four different situations commonly occur.

In the first, the underlying commodity is often a product sold or inventoried by the taxpayer. Income or loss from the sale of a related commodity-futures contract is treated as ordinary income, because the merchant is using the hedging technique as a tool to help market his wares; he holds neither the underlying inventory nor the futures contract with any speculative intent and profits or losses should not be accorded capital treatment.

The second situation in which the hedge transaction is commonly used occurs when a taxpayer uses a raw-material or cash-market financial instrument in his trade or business. For example, the taxpayer is a government bond dealer maintaining long and short positions in various instruments but who may also enter into forward-delivery purchase and sale contracts. In seeking to protect against loss on these transactions due to fluctuations in the market interest rate, the dealer will enter into futures contracts positions. In this situation, the futures contracts should not be treated as capital property. And any income or loss generated from the futures transactions should be treated as ordinary income or loss because both the futures contracts and the underlying financial instrument are used by the taxpayer in the production of his income and there is no speculative motive.

The third situation develops when the taxpayer, for whatever reason, is obligated to buy or sell a commodity. This could occur in a variety of contractual and noncontractual situations, whenever a taxpayer faces a future delivery or acceptance date. In such a situation, a futures contract will allow the taxpayer to "lock in" the purchase or sale price of the commodity he is required either to buy or sell, and avoid the risk of price fluctuations. The tax consequences of such a transaction vary, depending upon the nature of the underlying contractual obligation that is being hedged.

The fourth situation occurs when the speculator/investor or the trader uses a hedge to protect the market value of his investment portfolio. If a financial instrument is held in an investment portfolio, for example, the taxpayer may sell a futures contract to prevent deterioration of market value if interest rates increase. The gain or loss generated in settlement of the futures contract by delivery of the cash instrument or by other means will generally be accorded the same tax treatment as the investment—which is usually capital tax treatment. This tax consequence arises from the fact that the commodity being hedged is a capital asset in the hands of the taxpayer.

This is not the type of transaction normally considered a hedge, and therefore, does not result in ordinary income.

Hedges for tax purposes.   Under prior law, there was no clear statutory definition of what constituted a hedge for tax purposes, with consequent ordinary (rather than capital) tax treatment. The tax concept of hedging had, however, been dealt with extensively by the courts. The guidelines established have been transformed over the years, as each newly decided case introduced refinement to the developing body of case law.

Generally speaking, a hedge for tax purposes will clearly exist when there is a direct relationship between the commodity futures transaction and the risk of exposure inherent in the taxpayer's everyday trade or business, and when the price of the commodity moves in some discernible relationship with the price of the product of the business.

According to case law, the following factors will tend to indicate that a hedge for tax purposes does *not* exist:

The commodity is not used in the taxpayer's business.

The value of the futures position does not move in the same direction as the price of the commodity being protected.

The expected profit from the hedge exceeds the potential loss.

The quantity of hedging contracts exceeds the quantity of goods protected.[5]

Futures trading is undertaken when the taxpayer is not exposed to the risk of loss or continues after the risk ends.

Rapid activity in the futures market is not directly related to changes in the underlying business risk.

There is any speculative motive present.[6]

Because courts do not consistently apply these factors, no one of them will necessarily be determinative.

ERTA '81 provides, for the first time, a statutory definition of hedging. To qualify for tax purposes, a hedging transaction must be identified as such, must produce ordinary income or loss, and must be entered into by the taxpayer in the normal course of trade or business primarily (1) to reduce either the risk of price change or currency fluctuations on ordinary assets held or to be held by the taxpayer, or (2) to reduce the risk of interest-rate changes or currency fluctuations on borrowing made (or to be made), or obligations incurred (or to be incurred), by the taxpayer. A special rule for banks

---

[5] However, quantity should not be a factor if the relative values of the two result in a balanced position.

[6] Some courts have held that substituting one contract for another is proof of speculative intent.

requires the transaction only to be entered into in the normal course of the taxpayer's trade or business. However, the case law doctrine previously enumerated may still be considered to verify whether or not the definition has been met.

Once an asset has been identified for tax purposes as part of a qualifying hedging transaction, its disposition can never be treated as capital. Qualifying hedging transactions are exempted from the mark-to-market, straddle-loss deferral, cash-and-carry capitalization (purchase of a physical commodity as a capital asset accompanying sale for later delivery), and wash-sale and short-sale rules. However, if a taxpayer hedges in a tax sense, but fails to comply with the identification criteria, the transaction still generates ordinary income, but it would be subject to the mark-to-market rules.

Straddle transactions in other than RFCs. A straddle is defined as the holding of offsetting positions—including futures, forwards, or option contracts—in any type of personal property (excluding corporate stock) that is actively traded. Personal property also includes actively traded stock options that are part of a straddle, unless they are traded on a U.S. exchange and expire in less than one year.

An offsetting position is deemed to exist when there is a "substantial diminution" of risk of loss in holding one position by virtue of holding one or more other positions in personal property. ERTA '81 lists the following five rebuttable presumptions for determining when offsetting positions exist:

The positions are in the same personal property.

The positions are in the same property, though in substantially altered form.

The positions are in debt instruments of a similar maturity or other debt instruments prescribed in regulations to be issued by the IRS.

The positions are sold or marketed as offsetting positions.

The aggregate margin requirements are lower than the sum of the margin requirements of the two positions.

The statute also allows for the IRS to issue regulations that may expand upon this list. Offsetting positions between holdings of defined related parties, or between a taxpayer and flowthrough entities (such as partnerships or trusts) are also subject to these rules.

Recognized losses from straddle positions in non-RFC straddles are deductible only to the extent they exceed unrealized gains from offsetting positions acquired before the recognition of the loss. Any loss that is not allowed by reason of this rule is carried forward to the following year, when it is again subject to this limitation. The unrealized gain is determined in the same manner as under the mark-to-market rule for RFCs and must be reported in the investor's tax return for information purposes. Reporting is not required if there are no losses realized in any position (including RFCs) during the year.

A taxpayer may have a "mixed" straddle—that is, a straddle consisting of an RFC in at least one position of the straddle with the defined personal property in the other. In that case, the taxpayer may irrevocably elect to have the entire straddle taxed under the non-RFC straddle rules discussed above. The RFC must be identified as part of the mixed straddle by the close of the day on which it was acquired. However, a practical problem exists in identifying an RFC part of a mixed straddle if the RFC is the first position in the mixed straddle acquired. If the taxpayer doesn't choose to have the entire straddle taxed as one entity, the components are treated under the applicable general rules for RFCs and non-RFCs.

Finally, as previously discussed, non-RFC straddle transactions will be subject to rules similar to those governing wash sales and short sales under regulations to be issued by the IRS. It is anticipated that this will be accomplished by using a "balanced and offsetting positions" criterion rather than the "substantially identical" criterion.

Interest expense and carrying charges allocable to personal property that is part of a straddle must be capitalized. This regulates the so-called "cash-and-carry" transactions. In this type of transaction, for example, a taxpayer would purchase a physical commodity to be held as a capital asset and then sell the same commodity for delivery one year later. The taxpayer borrows to make the purchase and currently deducts the interest, storage charges, and insurance. The price differential between the current price and the future price is usually a function of these carrying costs. (Under prior law, the taxpayer had an ordinary deduction in one year and could realize gain in the next year by closing out the short-sale position.)

Identified straddles. The tax rules applicable to RFCs and non-RFC straddles do not apply to identified straddles. If a taxpayer has an identified straddle, no loss may be recognized before the day on which he disposes of all the positions of the straddle. An identified straddle must be recorded as such by the taxpayer by the close of the day on which it was acquired. To qualify, all the original positions must be acquired on the same day and all the positions disposed of on the same day. None of the positions of the straddle may be part of a larger straddle.

TAX ACCOUNTING TREATMENT

Hedgers

An investor defined as a hedger for tax purposes is not subject to mark-to-market recognition rules. However, upon the closeout of a futures position, even if that position is rolled into another contract, recognition of any gain or loss on the contract is required. This is true despite the fact that for financial accounting, deferred treatment may be available.

Dealer

A dealer in commodities, like any other merchant, is required to maintain and value inventory in accordance with the guidelines set forth by the Internal Revenue Code, Treasury regulations, and published revenue rulings. While the following discussion is based on these published IRS positions, alternative positions may be sustainable.

In valuing an ending inventory of cash commodities, a dealer may use the normal inventory valuation methods of market, or of lower cost or market.

A more difficult problem is to value the dealer's futures contract positions that constitute hedges (as previously discussed) against his underlying inventory. As a general rule, the value of long or short positions in futures contracts cannot be included as part of ending inventory because title to the goods has not yet passed. The potential gain or loss not yet realized on futures transactions cannot be included in the cost of ending inventory inasmuch as they represent unclosed transactions. However, a taxpayer is allowed to include in taxable income the unrealized gain or loss on open futures contracts that represent hedges when (a) this is a common industry practice resulting in the clearest method of identifying operating cost or profit for the period, and (b) this practice is consistently applied. Such gain or loss is treated as a period cost and not as part of ending inventory.

Trader or speculator/investor

The trader or speculator/investor is not required or entitled to maintain an inventory for tax purposes. Unrealized gain or loss is recognized on open RFC positions in conformity with the new mark-to-market rule. This rule also applies to the dealer who maintains investment or speculative futures contracts, but only for those contracts.

MISCELLANEOUS TAX RULES

Cash-market Treasury bills

Under ERTA '81, short-term government obligations—those issued at a discount with a maturity of one year or less (generally Treasury bills)—are treated as capital assets. Upon disposition at a gain, that part of the gain representing the ratable (straight-line amortization) share of "acquisition discount" (difference between purchase price and face value) is ordinary interest income, and any excess gain is short-term capital gain. Losses are wholly capital in nature. Thus, if a $1-million, 90-day U.S. Treasury bill is purchased at issuance for $962,500 and sold 30 days later for $980,000, the seller would recognize $12,500 of ordinary income and $5,000 of short-term capital gain.

Repurchase agreements

Acquisition or disposition of a cash financial instrument, typically a Treasury bill, is often accomplished through financing arrangements known as repurchase and reverse repurchase agreements (repos and reverse repos). An investor seeking to acquire a long position in a financial instrument finances the acquisition by selling a financial instrument to a creditor and simultaneously agreeing to buy back (repo) the financial instrument at a later date at the same price, plus interest (see Chapter 7). A reverse repo is just the opposite: The investor would become the creditor by advancing funds for another party's acquisition of a financial instrument in return for an interest payment.

For tax purposes, these agreements are normally treated as mere financing transactions, and a sale or exchange is normally deemed not to have occurred. Thus, interest income is generated on the reverse repo, and interest expense is generated on the repo agreement. This interest expense is subject to the investment-interest limitation rules. Previously discussed rules governing the capitalization of interest and carrying charges allocable to personal property that is part of a straddle may also have an impact on the treatment of this interest expense.

It is arguable that these financing arrangements represent sales or exchanges of the underlying financial instrument, with consequent gain or loss treatment. It is also arguable that the repo and reverse repo agreements represent separate contract rights, and that, when such rights are settled, the gain or loss that results is capital. In either case, any interest income or expense would not be considered as resulting from transactions in federal or municipal investments. Although these two positions are arguable, the ruling posture of the IRS and of the courts has historically been that such transactions are financing arrangements.

TAXATION OF OPTIONS ON FUTURES

The subject of options on commodities was not dealt with in ERTA. Consequently, the special tax rules which apply to RFCs have created some confusion. Because the unique tax aspects of RFCs apply to nonhedging transactions, it is these areas which are unclear.

Hedgers

If a taxpayer is a hedger for tax purposes, as defined in the preceding sections, the option will be treated as ordinary income (loss) with recognition either at the time the option expires or is offset. If a purchased option is exercised, any gain or loss is deferred, with the option cost being an adjustment to the acquired asset's basis.

Nonhedgers

If a taxpayer is not a hedger for tax purposes, the rules are very unclear. This could be important because for many applications, "hedgers" will not be hedgers for tax purposes. The question is whether any gains or losses will be taxed according to the general rules for options, or whether the tax treatment will take on the characteristics of the underlying RFC discussed previously—60 percent long-term, 40 percent short-term capital gain allocation, and mark-to-market recognition.

Several commodity exchanges have asked the Internal Revenue Service for guidelines, which it has chosen not to provide. The exchanges have suggested the following for an option purchaser:

1. No tax consequence when an option is bought.
2. Mark-to-market rules do not apply.
3. Gain or loss on offset or lapse is treated as an RFC.
4. No tax consequence from exercise of an option.

And for an option grantor:

1. No tax consequence when an option is sold.
2. Mark-to-market applies at year end.
3. Gain or loss on offset or lapse of 60/40.
4. Gain or loss on exercise recognized at 60/40.

Others have sought to create a distinction between option purchases and option sales based on margin rules. They reason that the sale of an option is subject to mark-to-market margin rules if the option increases in price. Thus, an option is akin to an RFC and should receive comparable tax treatment (60/40, mark to market, etc.). However, they argue that the option purchaser pays one premium and never faces further margin adjustment. Thus, the purchase of an option should not be treated pursuant to the RFC rules.

Arguments can be made on each side, but ultimately the IRS, the courts, or Congress will have to settle the issues.

26

Regulation of financial futures

Throughout this book we have tried to chronicle the transition from a perception of futures as speculative vehicles to an understanding that they represent an important tool for the management of financial assets—and the avoidance of speculation. Accounting theory, as we noted, is beginning to reflect this change in perceptions, as are legal institutions.

Not surprisingly, however, a combination of normal time lags and a lack of broad participation by hedgers has retarded progress. Accounting rules can often be changed by accounting authorities, but legislation must, in many cases be specifically enacted. Thus, a regulator must not only come to understand hedging, which, in turn, is a function of user definition, but must often then go to higher authorities to make changes. The legal profession can sometimes be slow to react to new things; it is often easier to tell clients to wait until others do something than to take the position that the avoidance of speculation by using futures may, in fact, be the prudent act.

The examples of those who have begun to hedge have not been lost. The attitude of certain federal regulatory agencies and insurance commissions has begun to change. Technical problems that some had thought to exist with Employee Retirement Income Security Act (ERISA) accounts have been cleared up. As more professionals use futures, and as the benefits and problems become better understood, more regulatory changes should evolve.

Regulation of financial instrument futures can be broadly divided into three categories: (1) regulation of the futures markets themselves; (2) regulation of market professionals such as futures commission merchants (FCMs) and introducing brokers (IBs) the functional equivalents of securities brokers, commodity trading advisors (CTAs), commodity pool operators (CPOs), the analogs of investment advisors and investment companies and floor brokers; and (3) regulation of those who use financial instrument futures to hedge or speculate.

The primary source of such regulation is the Commodity Futures Trading Commission (CFTC), a federal agency established in 1975 under the Commodity Exchange Act (CEAct). The CFTC is charged with the responsibility for administering CEAct and adopting and enforcing regulations thereunder. CEAct gives the CFTC "exclusive jurisdiction" with respect to "accounts, agreements . . . , and transactions involving contracts of sale of a commodity for future delivery, . . ."

In general terms, the regulatory system is designed to ensure the financial integrity of transactions on futures markets, prevent fraud and manipulation, and make certain that those who intend to trade futures receive sufficient information to enable them to make an informed decision to do so.

With respect to exchanges and the National Futures Association (NFA), a recently operational, self-regulatory organization, CFTC regulation is direct. With respect to market professionals, however, the CFTC has been endeavoring to limit its responsibility largely to an overseer's function and has been relying on the exchanges and NFA for direct supervision.

Although, as noted above, the CFTC has exclusive jurisdiction with respect to futures, many types of futures traders are also subject to another layer of regulation. This type of regulation exists because the basic nature of a company's activities is subject to other federal agencies or state laws and regulators. Thus, for example, pension plans, commercial banks, savings and loan associations, investment companies, and institutions that trade financial-instrument futures are likely to be subject to restrictions imposed by other regulators.

This chapter is intended to explain in broad terms the nature and extent of such regulation. Readers should consult with a knowledgeable adviser to obtain more detailed and current information.

REGULATION OF MARKETS AND
SELF-REGULATORY ORGANIZATIONS

To maintain a market for futures contracts in the United States, an exchange must be designated as a "contract market" by the CFTC. To receive such designation, an exchange must agree to and, in fact, must comply with an array of statutory and regulatory requirements, many of which impose substantial ongoing obligations. Thus, for example, virtually all contract market rules relating to terms and conditions of futures contracts traded on that exchange (a term broadly interpreted by the CFTC) must be submitted to the CFTC for prior approval. In the same vein, the CFTC has the power to require contract markets to adopt rules and to revoke contract-market rules previously adopted.

In addition, a contract market is required by CEAct to enforce all bylaws and rules which have been approved by the CFTC or which otherwise have become effective and also must enforce all bylaws and rules which provide minimum financial standards for FCMs which are members of the contract market. These statutory requirements are supplemented by voluminous regulations and guidelines spelling out, for example, what a contract market rule-enforcement program should include.

The CFTC conducts regular trade practice investigations to monitor whether a contract market is meeting its rule-enforcement responsibilities. Needless to say, every investigation to date has concluded that more can be and should be done by the contract market. The CFTC has the power to secure compliance by contract markets. The CEAct authorizes the CFTC to make "such investigations as it deems necessary" to ascertain the facts regarding the operation of exchanges and other persons subject to the provisions of the CEAct. The CEAct also authorizes the CFTC to suspend or revoke the designation of an exchange as a contract market if the commission finds that the contract market is not enforcing its rules or otherwise is violating CEAct or CFTC regulations. The same misdeeds may subject the contract market to a penalty of up to $100,000. Although the CFTC has not suspended the designation of any contract market, it has, on a number of occasions, imposed significant fines.

In futures trading, all transactions must be made on or subject to the rules of a contract market and must be executed by or through a member of the contract market on which it is traded. These strictures contrast sharply with securities trading where there is an over-the-counter market and securities can be transferred as the result of sales negotiated directly by buyers and sellers and by gift. However, even though all futures transactions must be effected on contract markets, many market professionals need not be members of a contract market. Thus, an FCM who is not a contract-market member may maintain a customer omnibus account with an FCM who is—and sometimes good business reasons exist for such an arrangement.[1] Similarly, there is no reason for a CTA or a CPO to be a contract-market member.

CEAct seeks to deal with the regulation of non-contract market members by authorizing the creation of one or more registered futures associations. The statute contemplates that such an organization (or organizations) will play a role analogous to that of the National Association of Securities Dealers in regulating broker-dealers who are not stock-exchange members. In 1982, after many years of effort, NFA was approved by the CFTC as a registered futures association. Pursuant to CFTC authority, NFA's rules provide that a member may not deal with a market professional who does business with the public unless that market professional is also a member.

CFTC authority over NFA is similar to its authority over contract markets. It may suspend or revoke NFA's registration, it must approve NFA's rules, and it has the power to abrogate any NFA rule. In addition, the CEAct suggests that CFTC may delegate registration functions to NFA; that NFA must adopt rules which require it (1) to establish training standards and proficiency standards for sales employees—known as associated persons (APs)—of FCMs, IBs, CTAs, and CPOs, as well as a program to enforce compliance with these standards; (2) to establish minimum capital and other financial requirements applicable to those of its members for which such requirements are imposed by the CFTC: these requirements must be as stringent as those imposed by CEAct or CFTC regulations; (3) to implement a program to audit and enforce compliance with those requirements; (4) to establish minimum standards governing sales practices; and (5) to develop a comprehensive program that fully implements NFA rules approved by the CFTC.

NFA's rules provide, among other things, that the violation of certain CFTC regulations shall be deemed to violate an NFA requirement.

When NFA becomes fully operational (assuming the CFTC exercises its delegation authority), it will be performing the CFTC's registration functions, enforcing the CFTC's minimum capital and other financial requirements, and enforcing certain CFTC rules. In addition, NFA will have adopted training standards and established proficiency testing and standards for sales practices.

The CFTC, of course, will continue to have direct authority over

---

[1] An omnibus account involves an FCM who is not a member of an exchange maintaining an account with a member. Transactions in this account may be for customers of the nonmember who would be undisclosed to the member. The nonmember FCM also maintain account records for the customers.

market professionals. It is expected, however, that this authority will be exercised in the form of enforcement proceedings rather than supervision and surveillance. The CEAct also gives state officials authority to bring an action in state court against any CFTC registrant (other than a floor broker) for an alleged violation of any antifraud provision of the CEAct or any antifraud rule adopted by the CFTC thereunder.

REGULATION OF MARKET PROFESSIONALS

Regulation of financial-futures market professionals is primarily the concern of the CFTC, NFA, and contract markets—although, as noted above, state authorities and other regulators may play a role. The types of regulation to which market professionals are subject include registration, minimum financial requirements, protection of customer property, record-keeping, fitness standards, risk disclosure, and antifraud. This section attempts briefly to summarize these topics.

The types of market professionals subject to CFTC regulation include:

Futures commission merchants (FCMs): entities which solicit or accept orders for futures transactions or options for execution on contract markets and which, in this connection, accept customer funds.

Introducing brokers (IBs): entities which solicit or accept such orders but do not accept or handle any customer funds.

Commodity trading advisors (CTAs): entities which advise others or write reports concerning the value of or advisability of trading futures contracts on contract markets.

Commodity pool operators (CPOs): entities engaged in a business which is of the nature of an investment trust, a syndicate, or a similar form of enterprise for the purpose of trading futures contracts on contract markets and which, in this connection, solicit or accept funds, securities, or other property from investors.

Associated persons (APs): individuals who solicit or accept customers' orders for futures contracts on contract markets and individuals who supervise those so engaged.

Floor brokers: persons who execute orders for others on the floor of a contract market.

The CEAct and CFTC regulations exempt certain persons and entities from the foregoing definitions or exempt such persons from the registration requirements of the CEAct. The details of such exclusions and exemptions are outside the scope of this chapter. It is suggested that a reader concerned about this subject seek competent, professional guidance.

Registration

Subject to limited exceptions, all FCMs, IBs, CTAs, CPOs, and APs must be registered by the CFTC or by the NFA pursuant to delegation from the CFTC. The application for registration includes detailed questions concerning civil, criminal, and administrative proceedings to which the applicant may have been subject. In the case of individual applicants, such as APs, floor brokers, and principals of entity applicants, there are also fingerprint requirements and FBI and Securities and Exchange Commission (SEC) checks.

Minimum capital requirements

FCMs and IBs are subject to minimum capital requirements. For an FCM, the stated minimum is the greater of $50,000 or 4 percent of customer funds and other properties held in segregation (see next section) by the FCM. However, because an FCM is subject to restrictions if its adjusted net capital falls below 150 percent of the minimum, the practical minimums are $75,000 and 6 percent. For an IB, the minimum requirement is $20,000. There are no CFTC prescribed minimum capital requirements for CTAs, CPOs, APs, or floor brokers. However, by definition, a floor broker must be a member of a contract market, and most contract markets have minimum capital requirements for members.

Segregation

A feature of futures regulation that is perhaps unique is the segregation requirement. Every FCM must "segregate" all money, securities, and other property received to margin a customer's futures trades or accruing to such customer as a result of favorable price movement. That is, such money, securities, and other property must be separately accounted for and not commingled with the funds of the FCM. There are detailed CFTC regulations setting forth the procedures applicable to segregated funds. Key principles include the requirements that an FCM must obtain an acknowledgment from each bank at which segregated property is deposited that the bank waives its right of offset; and that at no time may the amount held in segregation be less than the amount which would be payable to all customers if their futures contracts were liquidated at that day's closing prices. As a result of this requirement, an FCM necessarily must *oversegregate* (keep its own money in the segregated account so that if a deficit occurs in one customer's account, the FCM will not be in violation of the segregation requirements). Similarly, CPOs are required to keep funds invested in a separate entity, such as a limited partnership, and not commingled with the funds of the CPO. The segregation rules do not apply to CTAs or IBs because they are not permitted to receive customer funds.

Record-keeping

All CFTC registrants are required to make and maintain detailed records concerning trading activities. These records must be made available to the CFTC and the Justice Department on request.

The CFTC is authorized to specify by rule appropriate standards with respect to training experience and such other qualifications as the CFTC finds necessary or desirable to ensure the fitness of APs. In this connection, the CFTC may prescribe the adoption of written proficiency examinations for such persons. The CFTC has not yet exercised this authority. However, the Chicago Board of Trade and the Chicago Mercantile Exchange, the two largest contract markets (accounting for perhaps 75 percent of all U.S. futures trading and an even higher percentage of financial-instrument futures trading) require associated persons of member FCMs to pass a written proficiency examination. In addition, NFA has proposed a rule which will require APs of introducing brokers to pass such an examination.

CFTC rules require an FCM to furnish a written disclosure statement to each prospective customer and to receive, prior to the commencement of futures trading in the customer's account, an acknowledgment (signed and dated by the customer) to the effect that the customer has received and understood the disclosure statement. The disclosure statement (the exact language of which is spelled out by CFTC regulation) points out certain inherent risks in trading futures contracts on a speculative basis. These risks include the facts that the market may be subject to a "limit move," thereby locking a trader in with a substantial trading loss, and that there is a high degree of leverage in futures trading. Similarly, each FCM is required to furnish a customer who proposes to trade futures on options with an options risk disclosure document. This document is much longer than the futures risk disclosure statement and is somewhat similar to the disclosure document distributed in connection with securities options. Finally, the CFTC requires CTAs and CPOs to furnish disclosure documents to prospective customers and pool participants, and to receive in advance of trading or investment signed acknowledgments that the customer has received and understood the applicable document. These disclosure documents must set forth information about the business experience of the CTA or CPO, the manner in which it trades and, if applicable, its trading history. Indeed, because participation in a commodity futures pool (customarily in the form of a limited partnership interest) is a security, the CPO disclosure document also must meet applicable SEC and state "blue sky" filing and disclosure requirements. Although the CFTC has adopted risk disclosure requirements in connection with futures trading, there are no suitability standards similar to those applicable to securities trading. The reason for this has been that the investment choices available with respect to securities (e.g., ranging from a money-market fund to a long-term debt instrument and from a so-called blue chip equity to a high-risk new venture) do not exist in futures markets where all trading is either speculative (and therefore risky) or hedging (and therefore risk averse). In the case of options on futures contracts, however, the CFTC, although speaking in terms of risk disclosure, has indicated that a suitability standard may be applicable.

Antifraud

The CEAct and CFTC regulations contain a general antifraud provision which has a somewhat different focus than the securities antifraud regulations. The basic futures concept is that a market professional such as an FCM is prohibited from cheating or defrauding, or from attempting to cheat or defraud a customer. The same principle applies to transactions involving options on futures. However, a futures trader has no duty to disclose what may be inside information about market conditions. This is because there is no "issuer" of a futures contract as there is an issuer of a security. Although surprising to many people, this lack of duty probably exists in the field of securities regulation to the extent that such information relates to the market in general and not to a specific issuer.

Because futures regulation focuses on preserving the integrity of the market so that prices are generally reflective of supply and demand, the CEAct makes it unlawful to willfully disseminate false market information. To the same end, FCMs are required to have procedures guarding against running ahead of customer orders and contract markets are required to have rules designed to ensure that traders on the floor do not run ahead of customers' orders.

REGULATION OF MARKET PARTICIPANTS

As noted at the outset of this chapter, regulation of users of financial-instrument futures is within the domain both of the CFTC and a number of other regulators. Turning first to the CFTC, its concerns are basically position limits and record-keeping and reporting requirements. In addition, of course, the restrictions against manipulation and attempted manipulation and dissemination of false market information previously mentioned apply to all persons, not merely to market professionals.

Position limits

The CEAct authorizes the CFTC to set limits on the size of positions speculative traders may hold in futures contracts. The CFTC has not exercised this authority with respect to financial-instrument futures, but rather has adopted regulations requiring contract markets to establish these limits. Exchange-established position limits for financial futures are not applicable to bona fide hedging positions. However, they apply to "all positions in accounts for which a person by power of attorney or otherwise directly or indirectly controls trading." This means that, if one person controls trading for two separate entities, the positions of these persons will be aggregated for limit purposes. However, if separate persons in two affiliated companies direct trading, they may not be treated as a single account for position-limit purposes. The important factor is control over accounts, not control over entities.

Reporting and record-keeping

Although position limits do not apply to hedgers, all persons and entities trading financial-instrument futures are subject to CFTC reporting and record-keeping requirements. The level of positions which must be reported is 50 contracts for Treasury-bond and GNMA futures and 25 contracts for all other financial-instrument futures. FCMs are required to inform the CFTC whenever a customer's futures position reaches a reportable level, and thereafter the CFTC will instruct that trader to file a report on Form 40. Form 40 contains certain biographical information and other data about the trader which the CFTC deems relevant. A trader must file a Form 40 annually so long as he continues to hold a reportable position, and the form must be updated whenever there are material changes in the information it contains. In addition, every trader who owns, holds, or controls a reportable position must respond in one business day to requests by the CFTC for information regarding these positions.

Foreign and domestic traders are subject to these requirements; under applicable CFTC regulations, a foreign trader's FCM is that trader's agent for service of papers by the CFTC. CFTC regulations also require traders who hold a reportable position to keep books and records "showing all details concerning all positions and transactions" not only for futures contracts and futures options, but all positions and transactions in the underlying cash commodity and its products and by-products. In the case of financial instrument futures, the "underlying" cash commodity is the security itself.

OTHER REGULATORS OF USERS OF FINANCIAL-INSTRUMENT FUTURES

Private pension plans

Private (i.e., nongovernment) pension plans ("plans") are subject to the Employee Retirement Income Security Act of 1974, colloquially known as ERISA. ERISA, which was enacted before any financial-instrument futures trading existed, does not address the use of these futures or any futures at all. It was not until 1982 that the Department of Labor, which administers ERISA, issued some advisory opinions on the use of futures.

There no longer seems to be any real question about whether a plan may use financial-instrument futures to hedge against the risk of loss in an existing portfolio or against the risk of higher prices in anticipation of investing in securities. The question of whether, and to what extent, a plan may use financial instrument futures to speculate is a closer one. Department of Labor prudence regulations offer no specific guidance. The Federal Reserve Board recently issued an advisory opinion to the effect that bank trust departments administering plans subject to ERISA could only use these futures to hedge. Some authorities, however, take the position that a limited portion of plan assets could be used to speculate. A technical problem with respect to who may make futures trading decisions for a plan was partly resolved by the labor department advisory opinion referred to above. Under ERISA, the only persons permitted to control or manage plan assets are its trustees, fiduciaries named in a plan document, or "investment managers." The problem, however, is that under ERISA only banks, insurance companies, and persons registered with the SEC as investment advisers may act as investment managers. This provision precluded FCMs and CTAs from making futures trading decisions on behalf of a plan. The Labor Department, however, has now stated that an FCM or CTA registered with the SEC as an investment adviser may function as an investment manager even though advice is limited to futures trading.

There are still many technical questions relating to the use of financial-instrument futures by pension plans. For example, a plan may not use the same FCM to act as an investment manager and to effect futures transactions.

The bottom line, however, is that if a plan wishes to use financial instruments to hedge (and the time may well come when it will be considered imprudent not to do so), these mechanical problems can be readily solved.

Commercial banks

In general terms, commercial banks—national, state, or FDIC members—can engage in interest-rate futures transactions designed to reduce the bank's risks in terms of total assets and liabilities. The policy statement describing this contains certain procedural and record-keeping requirements and answers the question of whether hedging is permitted for national banks. In addition, a number of commercial banks have commenced doing business as FCMs. The Comptroller of the Currency has permitted a number of national banks to enter this business and the Federal Reserve has permitted bank holding companies to establish separate subsidiaries to act as an FCM.

However, a state bank also must consider the banking laws and banking regulations of the jurisdiction in which it is organized. It is beyond the scope of this chapter to review all relevant state legislation and regulation. However, a review undertaken in 1982 did not disclose any statutes which either expressly permit or prohibit the use of financial instrument futures by a state-chartered bank. The banking authorities of New York and California have expressed the view that commercial banks may use financial-instrument futures for hedging.

As a practical matter, a state bank should ascertain from its state banking regulator whether, and to what extent, it can use financial-instrument futures. If a regulator in a specific state has not considered the issue and state bank legislation permits banks to take action reasonably necessary to avoid losses on investments, it can be argued that the bank should be permitted to use financial instruments to hedge an existing portfolio. Similarly, if the governing statute provides that a bank may undertake further powers which are incidental to, or necessary for its banking objectives, it can be pointed out that the Comptroller of the Currency has issued an opinion that the use of financial-instrument futures is an activity incidental to banking. This view supports the conclusion that such legislation permits hedging.

Savings and loan associations and national credit unions

The Federal Home Loan Bank Board regulates savings and loan associations. Like the federal regulators of commercial banks, the board permits savings and loan associations to use financial-instrument futures for hedging. In addition, the board has pending regulations which would permit a subsidiary of a savings and loan association to act as an FCM. National credit unions, however, at this time are not permitted to use financial-instrument futures.

Insurance companies

Insurance company investments are not subject to federal legislation or regulation. This subject is governed exclusively by state law. Again, like state banking laws, state insurance laws and regulations differ with respect to permitting use of financial-instrument futures.

Insurance legislation is an area of particular interest. Insurance laws that specified what type of investments were legal were written long before there were financial-futures markets.[2] Therefore, in most cases, futures were interpreted as not being an admitted asset. Some state laws provided basket clause flexibility, and many companies have been permitted to use futures because of leeway under such provisions. Recently, there have been legislative changes. New York, Virginia, Texas, California, and Maine all passed laws in 1983 which will permit insurance companies to participate in the market. There are several regulatory methods, surprisingly, none of which differentiate between new-products hedging, management of whole-life assets, private placements, etc. Some laws, such as that in Virginia, allow broad-based participation. At the other extreme, New York takes a very limited approach, reflecting continued political opposition of the New York commission.[3] California also regulates futures by permitting them to represent only a percentage of admitted assets— although a higher percentage than that allowed by New York.

It should be clear to the reader of this book that for a hedger, the relevant thing from an administrator's point of view should be the basis risk—i.e., any gain or loss due to the fact that the hedge is not as efficient as it should be. The amount hedged is generally irrelevant. Federal banking policy and ERISA legislation seem to implicitly recognize this, so does some state legislation. For example, Illinois regulations are based on the amount of margin an account is permitted to pay. Thus, there could be substantial real (i.e., basis) losses, but no margin paid without a problem. However, in Illinois a sound economic program could become a problem if substantive margin was paid in. California, although limiting futures to a percent of admitted assets, has an interesting provision which permits a company to apply for a specific use. Thus, companies with sound programs can, over time, hope to expand in California without further legislation. Hopefully, with time and understanding, many states—including New York, which is often used as a model—will adopt more logical regulatory methods. Otherwise, as more and more companies begin to use futures, certain others could face substantial competitive disadvantages both from in-

---

[2] It might be noted that the concept of futures as an investment for a hedger is itself illogical. Futures represent risk-management tools; they are not investment vehicles.

[3] New York, however, permits insurance companies managing separate accounts to act as they would under prevailing prudent man standards.

surance companies and other financial intermediaries. There is also diversity regarding options. For example, Calfifornia permits the purchase of puts but not the sale of calls while New York permits the sale of calls but not the purchase of puts.

The legislation and regulations described above are all recent. Insurance companies located in states not discussed will have to ascertain whether, and to what extent, the use of financial-instrument futures is permitted under statutes which do not specifically address this subject.

Other dual regulations

There are instances in which the extent that an entity clearly subject to one regulatory regimen inadvertently may find its activities within the scope of another regulator. For example, a mutual fund which trades futures contracts may find that it is a commodity pool and should have registered with the CFTC. Similarly, a commodity trading advisor whose advice goes beyond futures contracts may discover that he or she is an investment adviser subject to the jurisdiction of the SEC. Because the regulatory regimens of the CFTC and the SEC are different, especially in the area of compensation, care should be taken to avoid activities which may subject one unintentionally to the authority of a regulator.

Appendix

I. MAJOR FINANCIAL FUTURES SYMBOLS

Quotron symbols

Quotes are called up by utilizing a six-unit code. The first two letters designate the abbreviation for the commodity. The third letter represents the month and year of expiration. The last three symbols of the entry are always .SP.

For example, to call up the September Treasury bill contract, input TBU.SP.

Bunker Ramo symbols

The first letter for all Bunker Ramo commodity symbols is always a Q. The second (or second and third) letter(s) represent the Bunker Ramo abbreviation for the commodity code. The last letter of the symbol represents the month and year of expiration.

For example, to call up a second-year September Treasury-bond contract, input QTRP.

	Quotron	Bunker Ramo
	Commodity codes	
T bonds	US	TR
GNMAs	GM	M
T notes	LT	TS
T bills	TB	TB
CDs	DC	DC
Eurodollars	ED	ED
S&P 500	SP	SP
Value Line	KV	KV

Months

	Quotron			Bunker Ramo		
	Year 1	Year 2	Year 3	Year 1	Year 2	Year 3
JAN	F	D	Y	F	A	F+
FEB	G	E	D	G	B	G+
MAR	H	I	E	H	C	H+
APR	J	L	I	J	D	J+
MAY	K	O	L	K	E	K+
JUN	M	P	O	M	I	M+
JUL	N	T	P	N	L	N+
AUG	Q	R	T	Q	O	Q+
SEP	U	B	R	U	P	U+
OCT	V	C	B	V	R	V+
NOV	X	W	C	X	S	X+
DEC	Z	Y	W	Z	T	Z+

Commodity Options on Treasury Bond Futures Symbols

Quotron Symbols:

An eight-letter code is utilized to call up the Treasury bond options on futures. The first letter designates put or call. The second letter stands for Treasury bonds. The third represents the month and year of expiration. The fourth symbol refers to the lead digit of the exercise price and the fifth symbol refers to the last digit of the exercise price. The last three symbols of the entry are .SP.

For example, to monitor a March 70 call input CGHGJ.SP.

Bunker Ramo Symbols:

The first letter is always a Q. The second identifies the underlying futures contract. Third symbol represents the month and year of expiration. The fourth defines the option as put or call and includes the lead digit of its exercise price. The fifth defines the last strike digit.

For example, to monitor a March 72 put enter QBHTD.

Quotron	Bunker Ramo
C G H G J . S P	Q B H T D
1 2 3 4 5 6 7 8	1 2 3 4 5

1. C = Call, P = Put	1. Q = Designates Commodities
2. G = Government Treasury Bonds	2. B = Treasury Bond Options (CBT)
3. H, M, U, Z = Months—same as underlying futures	3. H, M, U. Z = Months—same as underlying futures
4. F, G, H = 60, 70, 80	4. F, G, H = 60, 70, 80 Calls
	S, T, U = 60, 70, 80 Puts
5. J, B, D, F, H = 0, 2, 4, 6, 8	5. T, D, H, L, P = 0, 2, 4, 6, 8
6-8. .SP	

II. UNDERSTANDING MARGINS AND STATEMENTS FOR FINANCIAL-INSTRUMENT TRANSACTIONS

Financial futures are increasingly being considered as tools available for the implementation of investment strategies. Many potential users are not familiar with the mechanical aspects of futures and options on futures. This appendix is designed to provide a background for such mechanics. It tracks margin procedures and the statements applicable to financial-instrument transactions.

Margin procedures

Under the appropriate exchange rules, initial margin for each contract purchased or sold must be established. This margin is in effect a good faith deposit to ensure that the client fulfills all obligations. The primary obligation is derived from the daily cash settlement of gains or losses. Different initial margins exist for outright purchases as opposed to spreads; a spread is a situation in which, for example, one simultaneously buys a December 1983 contract and sells a March 1984 contract. Initial margins are lower for clients who are bona fide hedgers. In this case, the client signs a special hedge form which indicates that any purchase or sale in that account is offsetting a similar cash position. During the contract month initial margins are raised. All margins are subject to change and may be retroactively raised or lowered by member firms or by the relevant exchange. Initial margins may be deposited either in cash or in Treasury bills, the interest on which would accrue to the customer's account.

While initial margins may be satisfied by the deposit of an appropriate amount of Treasury bills or similar securities, variation margin may be met only in cash. Variation-margin deposits represent the gains or losses from changes in the price of a contract. Thus, if one purchased a December 1983 Treasury-bond contract at 71, and its price increased to 72, a gain of $1,000 (32/32 × $31.25) would accrue. Under the appropriate exchange rules, these balances are settled daily in cash. Consequently, a holder of a long position would be entitled to receive the $1,000 in cash. Alternatively, should one suffer a loss, one would be expected to remit $1,000.

Currently, options are actively traded on Treasury-bond futures. The buyer of an option makes an initial premium payment. If one purchased a December 68 call at 3-62/64, a payment of $3,968.75 plus any commission and fees would be required. No further cash transfer is necessary until one: (a) offsets the position, which would generate premium income into the account; or (b) exercises the option, which would subject one to the initial- and variation-margin requirements as a futures holder. One may also abandon the option on the expiration date, allowing it to expire worthless.

Option writers, however, must post initial margin and meet mark-to-market variations which may be collateralized with Treasury bills, because unlike futures, at this point there is no transfer of cash to the holder of the other side of the position.

In the prior example, the short would receive $3,968.75 in cash from the long and then be required to meet the underlying futures margin and the premium marked to the market. If the position settled at 3-57/64, then one must keep $5,390.63 in the account ($3,890.63 plus $1,500 initial margin). If the value of the option increased, additional margin must be posted; if it declines, part of the margin may be withdrawn.

Statements

Attached are the primary accounting statements utilized for a typical financial instrument transaction. Exhibits A through G apply to an example involving a futures transaction, and 1 through 4 to a second example for an option on a futures transaction. Definitions of specific terms precede the examples.

Definitions

The following terms are used in the exhibits at the end of the appendix:

1. *Account balance* (*current balance*): consists of the sum of all realized gains or losses, and cash charges or credits, except those cash receipts which are now in the account in the form of securities such as Treasury bills.

2. *Total open trade equity*: is the total unrealized profit or loss currently existing on all open futures positions.

3. *Net market value of option*: is the mark-to-market value of all option positions.

4. *Total equity*: is the cash balance or deficit; mathematically, the sum of the open trade equity and the account balance which, as noted, is the cumulative balance of all debits and credits whether from realized transactions or cash transfers, except those which have resulted in existing security positions.

5. *Securities on deposit total*: is self-explanatory.

Combined commodity statement

For our first example (Exhibits A-E), we have chosen a client, Lawrence A. Michaels (LAM), who felt bullish about the S&P futures contracts. The following pages show a chronology of his activity.

9/14/83: LAM initiates a long position of 10 December S&P contracts at 166.65. LAM wires a $60,000 Treasury bill due 3/8/84 to cover his initial margin requirements of $6,000 per contract. The customer receives a Combined Commodity Statement (Exhibit A) detailing his purchase and Treasury bills deposited. At the close of business the settlement price was 167.50, resulting in a gain of $4,250.

9/15/83: LAM receives $4,250 from his commodity account produced by the favorable variation margin move (Exhibit B). On September 15, the settlement price for the S&P contract is 166.55. Because the contract has decreased in price from 167.50 to 166.55, LAM must cover his variation-margin call of $4,750, which represents the difference between the prior day's settlement price and today's settlement price.

9/16/83: LAM's Account Balance of —$4,250 is reflective of cash previously wired from his commodity account. Today LAM pays $4,750 (Exhibit C). During the course of the day, the market rallies and the settlement price is 168.95, resulting in a credit due LAM of $12,000.

Exhibit A

DATE		ACCOUNT NUMBER
SEP 14, 1983		300 30333

TAX ID 999-99-9999

COMBINED COMMODITY STATEMENT
CONFIRMATION AND/OR PURCHASE & SALE

LAWRENCE A MICHAELS
200 PARK AVENUE
NEW YORK NY 10166

*GRAINS IN 000 S

DATE	(IN 000S)		COMMODITY/OPTION DESCRIPTION	P/ C	• EX	TRADE PRICE	AMOUNT	
	BT	SLD					DEBIT	CREDIT
	ACCOUNT BALANCE--SEGREGATED FUNDS							.00
=+=+=+=+=	=+=	CONFIRMATION =+=+=+=+=+=+=+=+=+=+=+ CONFIRMATION =+=+=+=+=+=+=+=+						
WE HAVE MADE THIS DAY THE FOLLOWING TRADES FOR YOUR ACCOUNT AND RISK.								
	10 10*		DEC 83 S&P INDEX 3		E	166.65		
+=+=+=+=	+=+=	+=+=+=+=+=+=+=+=+=+=+=+=	+=+=	+=+=+=+=	+=+=+=			=+=
RCVD T-BL DUE 3-8-84 60 000.00								.00
CURRENT ACCOUNT BALANCE -- SEGREGATED FUNDS								.00

Exhibit B

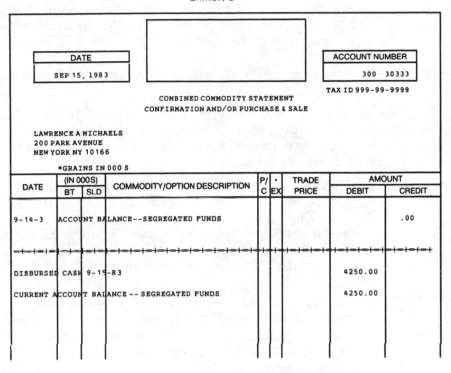

DATE		ACCOUNT NUMBER
SEP 15, 1983		300 30333

TAX ID 999-99-9999

COMBINED COMMODITY STATEMENT
CONFIRMATION AND/OR PURCHASE & SALE

LAWRENCE A MICHAELS
200 PARK AVENUE
NEW YORK NY 10166

*GRAINS IN 000 S

DATE	(IN 000S)		COMMODITY/OPTION DESCRIPTION	P/C	•EX	TRADE PRICE	AMOUNT	
	BT	SLD					DEBIT	CREDIT
9-14-3			ACCOUNT BALANCE--SEGREGATED FUNDS					.00
			DISBURSED CASH 9-15-83				4250.00	
			CURRENT ACCOUNT BALANCE -- SEGREGATED FUNDS				4250.00	

Exhibit C

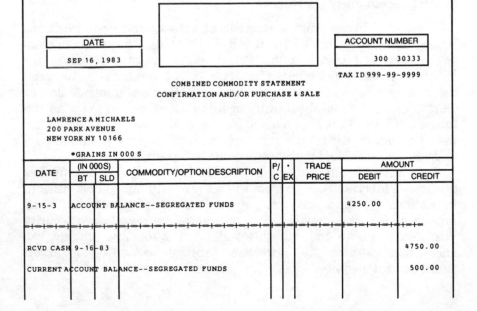

DATE		ACCOUNT NUMBER
SEP 16, 1983		300 30333

TAX ID 999-99-9999

COMBINED COMMODITY STATEMENT
CONFIRMATION AND/OR PURCHASE & SALE

LAWRENCE A MICHAELS
200 PARK AVENUE
NEW YORK NY 10166

*GRAINS IN 000 S

DATE	(IN 000S)		COMMODITY/OPTION DESCRIPTION	P/C	•EX	TRADE PRICE	AMOUNT	
	BT	SLD					DEBIT	CREDIT
9-15-3			ACCOUNT BALANCE--SEGREGATED FUNDS				4250.00	
			RCVD CASH 9-16-83					4750.00
			CURRENT ACCOUNT BALANCE--SEGREGATED FUNDS					500.00

9/19/83:   LAM receives $12,000 from his commodity account. During the course of the day, LAM sells his position at 170.35, realizing a gross profit of $18,500, or net profit after commission and exchange fees of $17,581.70 (Exhibit D).

9/20/83:   Balance of $6,081.70 is wired to LAM and his Treasury bill is returned to him (Exhibit E).

Our second example, Marc Roberts (MR) who also felt bullish about the market but did not want to take on the obligations of a futures holder, purchased an option on a Treasury bond future. Exhibits 1 through 4 describe his activity:

9/14/83:   MR initiates a long position in the December 72 Calls at 1-14/64. His commodity account is debited $1,309.95 for premium payment plus commission and fees. Unlike futures transactions, total commission is often charged on the initiation of the transaction. The final exercise date, 11/18/83, is noted on the commodity statement (Exhibit 1).

9/15/83:   MR pays $1,309.95 (Exhibit 2). No further activity is required of MR and therefore no statement is issued until:

9/19/83:   MR sells his position at 1-33/64, generating premium income of $1,515.63 into his commodity account (Exhibit 3). Please note the identical statement would be issued for an option writer.

Monthly commodity statement

A monthly commodity statement of activity and open positions is sent to LAM (Exhibit F) and MR (Exhibit 4). The difference between their statements is the notation "net option premium for month" on MR's statement. The +205.48 is the difference between the premium payment made and received. Option statements do not denote realized monthly profit and loss figures, as is done with the futures. If an option is purchased during one month and sold during the next month, the resulting statements indicate only premium payment as a negative and premium income as a positive.

Generally, the monthly statement shows all closed out futures profit and loss transactions from the prior month net of commission, indicates net option premium payment or receipt in total, lists any money or security transfers in or out, and itemizes all open security positions at month end. Monthly statements also show account balances, open positions, the unrealized profit or loss on open transactions, and total equity.

Exhibit D

DATE		ACCOUNT NUMBER
SEP 19, 1983		300 30333

TAX ID 999-99-9999

COMBINED COMMODITY STATEMENT
CONFIRMATION AND/OR PURCHASE & SALE

LAWRENCE A MICHAELS
200 PARK AVENUE
NEW YORK NY 10166

*GRAINS IN 000 S

DATE	(IN 000S)		COMMODITY/OPTION DESCRIPTION	P/ C	• EX	TRADE PRICE	AMOUNT	
	BT	SLD					DEBIT	CREDIT
9-16-3			ACCOUNT BALANCE--SEGREGATED FUNDS					500.00
—|—|—|—|—|— CONFIRMATION —|—|—|—|—|—|—|—|— CONFIRMATION —|—|—|—|—|—|—								
WE HAVE MADE THIS DAY THE FOLLOWING TRADES FOR YOUR ACCOUNT AND RISK.								
		10	DEC 83 S&P INDEX	3	E	170.35		
		10*						
—|—|—|—|—|— PURCHASE & SALE —|—|—|—|—|—|— PURCHASE & SALE —|—|—|—|—|—|—								
9-14-83	10		DEC 83 S&P INDEX	3	E	166.65		
9-19-83		10	DEC 83 S&P INDEX	3	E	170.35		
	10*	10*	COMM. (915.00)		P&S			18500.00
			FEES OR COMMISSIONS				915.00	
			NFA FEES				3.30	
			NET PROFIT OR LOSS FROM TRADES					17581.70*
—|—|—|—|—|—|—|—|—|—|—|—|—|—|—|—|—|—|—|—|—|—|—								
DISBURSED CASH 9-19							12000.00	
CURRENT ACCOUNT BALANCE -- SEGREGATED FUNDS								6081.70

Exhibit E

DATE		ACCOUNT NUMBER
SEP 20, 1983		300 30333

TAX ID 999-99-9999

COMBINED COMMODITY STATEMENT
CONFIRMATION AND/OR PURCHASE & SALE

LAWRENCE A MICHAELS
200 PARK AVENUE
NEW YORK NY 10166

*GRAINS IN 000 S

DATE	(IN 000S)		COMMODITY/OPTION DESCRIPTION	P/ C	• EX	TRADE PRICE	AMOUNT	
	BT	SLD					DEBIT	CREDIT
9-19-3			ACCOUNT BALANCE--SEGREGATED FUNDS					6081.70
—|—|—|—|—|—|—|—|—|—|—|—|—|—|—|—|—|—|—|—|—|—|—								
DISBURSED CASH 9-20							6081.70	
T-BL DUE 3-8-84 TRANSFERRED TO CUSTOMER								.00
CURRENT ACCOUNT BALANCE -- SEGREGATED FUNDS								.00

Exhibit F

MONTHLY COMMODITY STATEMENT
ACTIVITY AND OPEN POSITIONS

LAWRENCE A MICHAELS
200 PARK AVENUE
NEW YORK NY 10166

SEGREGATED ACCOUNT

DATE	BT LNG	SLD SRT	COMMODITY/OPTION DESCRIPTION	P/ C	• EX	PRICE	AMOUNT DEBIT	AMOUNT CREDIT
9-14-83	RCVD	T-BL	DUE 3-7-84 60 000.00			CASH		.00
9-15-83	DISBURSED		CASH 9-15-83			CASH	4250.00	
9-16-83	RCVD	CASH	9-16-83			CASH		4750.00
9-19-83	DISBURSED		CASH 9-19			CASH	12000.00	
9-19-83	10	10	DEC 83 S&P INDEX 3		E	P&S		17581.70
9-20-83	DISBURSED		CASH 9-20			CASH	6081.70	
9-20-83	T-BL		DUE 1-8-84 TRANSFERRED TO CUSTOMER			CASH		.00
9-30-83	ACCOUNT BALANCE -- SEGREGATED FUNDS . .				. . . .			.00*
NET FUTURES PROFIT OR LOSS (-) FOR MONTH						17,581.70		

Exhibit G

STATEMENT OF ACCOUNT—OPEN TRADES

SEP 14, 1983

LAWRENCE A MICHAELS
200 PARK AVENUE
NEW YORK NY 10166
    *GRAINS IN 000S   REGULATED COMMODITIES

DATE	POSITION* LNG	SRT	COMMODITY	TRADE PRICE	OPEN TRADE EQUITY DEBIT	OPEN TRADE EQUITY CREDIT
9-14-83	10		DEC 83 S&P INDEX 3	166.65		4,250.00
	10*	*	SETTLEMENT PRICE	167.50		4,250.00
			TOTAL OPEN TRADE EQUITY			4,250.00
			ACCOUNT BALANCE -- REGULATED COMMODITIES			.00
			TOTAL EQUITY			4,250.00

Exhibit 1

DATE	ACCOUNT NUMBER
SEP 14, 1983	300 30377

TAX ID 123-45-6789

COMBINED COMMODITY STATEMENT
CONFIRMATION AND/OR PURCHASE & SALE

MARC ROBERTS
200 PARK AVENUE
NY NY 10166

*GRAINS IN 000 S

DATE	(IN 000S) BT	(IN 000S) SLD	COMMODITY/OPTION DESCRIPTION	P/C	• EX	TRADE PRICE	AMOUNT DEBIT	AMOUNT CREDIT
			ACCOUNT BALANCE--SEGREGATED FUNDS					.00
—+—+—+—+—+—+—CONFIRMATION —+—+—+—+—+—+— CONFIRMATION —+—+—+—+—+—+—+—+—+—								
WE HAVE MADE THIS DAY THE FOLLOWING TRADES FOR YOUR ACCOUNT AND RISK.								
	1	1*	CALL DEC 83 T-BONDS 72 E COMM. (91.00) FINAL EXERCISE	C	A	1 14/64 11/18/83	1218.75	
			TOTAL FEE/COMMISSION				91.00*	
			NFA FEE				.20*	
			OPTION PREMIUM				1218.75*	
—+—								
CURRENT ACCOUNT BALANCE -- SEGREGATED FUNDS								1309.95

Exhibit 2

DATE	ACCOUNT NUMBER
SEP 15, 1983	300 30377

TAX ID 123-45-6789

COMBINED COMMODITY STATEMENT
CONFIRMATION AND/OR PURCHASE & SALE

MARC ROBERTS
200 PARK AVENUE
NY NY 10166

*GRAINS IN 000 S

DATE	(IN 000S) BT	(IN 000S) SLD	COMMODITY/OPTION DESCRIPTION	P/C	• EX	TRADE PRICE	AMOUNT DEBIT	AMOUNT CREDIT
9-14-3			ACCOUNT BALANCE--SEGREGATED FUNDS				1309.95	
—+—+—+—+—+—+—+—+—+—+—+—+—+—+—+—+—+—+—+—								
RCVD CASH 9-15-83								1309.95
CURRENT ACCOUNT BALANCE -- SEGREGATED FUNDS								.00

Exhibit 3

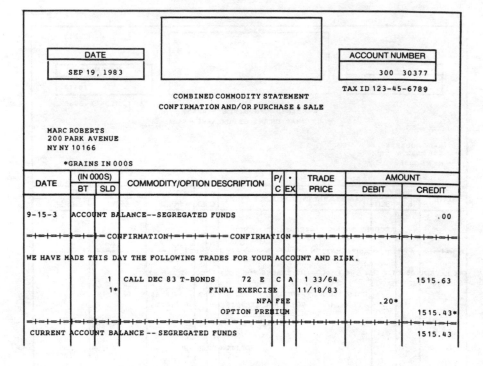

DATE	ACCOUNT NUMBER
SEP 19, 1983	300 30377

TAX ID 123-45-6789

COMBINED COMMODITY STATEMENT
CONFIRMATION AND/OR PURCHASE & SALE

MARC ROBERTS
200 PARK AVENUE
NY NY 10166

*GRAINS IN 000S

DATE	(IN 000S)		COMMODITY/OPTION DESCRIPTION	P/ C	• EX	TRADE PRICE	AMOUNT	
	BT	SLD					DEBIT	CREDIT
9-15-3			ACCOUNT BALANCE--SEGREGATED FUNDS					.00
=+=+=+=+=+=+= CONFIRMATION=+=+=+=+=+= CONFIRMATION =+=+=+=+=+=+=+=+=+=+=+=								
WE HAVE MADE THIS DAY THE FOLLOWING TRADES FOR YOUR ACCOUNT AND RISK.								
	1		CALL DEC 83 T-BONDS 72 E	C	A	1 33/64		1515.63
		1*	FINAL EXERCISE			11/18/83		
			NFA FEE				.20*	
			OPTION PREMIUM					1515.43*
=+=								
			CURRENT ACCOUNT BALANCE -- SEGREGATED FUNDS					1515.43

Exhibit 4

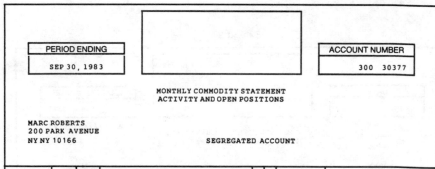

PERIOD ENDING	ACCOUNT NUMBER
SEP 30, 1983	300 30377

MONTHLY COMMODITY STATEMENT
ACTIVITY AND OPEN POSITIONS

MARC ROBERTS
200 PARK AVENUE
NY NY 10166   SEGREGATED ACCOUNT

DATE	BT LNG	SLD SHT	COMMODITY/OPTION DESCRIPTION	P/ C	• EX	PRICE	AMOUNT	
							DEBIT	CREDIT
9-14-83	1		CALL DEC 83 T-BONDS 72 E	C	A	NET PREM	1309.95	
9-15-83	RCVD CASH 9-15-83					CASH		1309.95
9-19-83		1	CALL DEC 83 T-BONDS 72 E	C	A	NET PREM		1515.43
9-20-83	DISBURSED CASH 9-20					CASH	1515.43	
9-30-83			ACCOUNT BALANCE -- SEGREGATED FUNDS					.00*
NET FUTURES PROFIT OR LOSS (-) FOR MONTH						.00		
			NET OPTION PREMIUM FOR MONTH			205.48		

Statement of account

For customers who require it, a statement of account which lists all open trades is available. This statement is mailed daily or, in some cases, sent by computer and contains open positions, settlement prices, open trade equity, net market value of option, account balance, and total equity (Exhibit G).

Margin request

Written margin notices are generated when an account falls below margin requirements and/or when new positions are entered into without sufficient equity or collateral to meet initial margin requirements. These notices are sent only in severely undermargined cases. Normally, margin notices are communicated daily by telephone.

III. IMPLIED REPO RATE CALCULATION: BONDS

The following table describes the calculation of the implied rate on the spread position between $1 million Treasury 8-3/4 percent of 11-15-08 purchased at 77-06/32 and 10.736 December 83 bond contracts sold at 71-15/32. The implied repo rate was calculated for a 74-day holding period beginning on October 16. It assumes that the position will be closed out on December 30.

Implied repo rate (74-day holding period)		
Average amount invested:		
Purchase 1,000M Treasury 8-3/4 percent		
@ 77-06/32 for settlement 10/17/83	$771,875.00	
Plus accrued interest	36,854.62	
Amount invested through 11/15/83	808,729.62	
Less coupon payment	43,750.00	
Amount invested through 12/30/83	764,979.62	
Weighted average amount invested		$782,124.89
Interest earned on 8-3/4 percent position		$ 17,772.45
Loss on redelivery:		
Principal amount received for 8-3/4 percent		
(71-15/32 × 1.0736) × 10,000	767,288.50	
Less principal paid 10/17/83	771,875.00	
Loss		$ (4,586.50)
Net income for 74 days		13,185.95
Annualized net income (360-day basis)		64,147.86
Implied repo rate (annualized net income/average		
amount invested)		8.20%

The rate *implied* in the cash-futures bond spread is only guaranteed if the market level remains static, the cheapest-to-deliver bond remains constant, and the convergence of the cash and futures market occurs by the anticipated contract closeout date (in this case, December 30). Variations from this implied rate can be evaluated with respect to the following variables to compare the position relative to the rates available in other investments of a similar maturity. The variables which will effect the return actually realized on this position include:

1. The financing cost or return on the average variation margin balance.
2. Contract characteristics.

The effect of the first item on realized return is a function of market direction and the rate at which one can finance or reinvest the variation margin balance. Contract characteristics such as after-hours delivery risk and changes in the cheapest deliverable cash bond, could cause the futures contract to sell down relative to cash, creating a realized return that is somewhat better than anticipated.

IV. SYNTHETIC SHORT-TERM SECURITY: BILLS

Short-term money-market instruments offering attractive yields relative to other short-term rates sometimes can be created through combined cash and bill futures positions. One can purchase the deliverable cash Treasury bill and simultaneously sell the appropriate futures contract on a spread basis. The deliverable bill is always the cash Treasury bill with 90/91 days remaining to maturity on the date the contract is closed out, e.g., the 91-day September 8, 1983 bill is deliverable into the June contract which closes out on June 9, 1983. The return, if the position is closed out by delivery is a function of the difference between the price paid for the cash bill and the contract delivery price. The return on this spread investment is subject only to the financing cost or return associated with variation margin which is usually not significant. With the bill contract now terminating to allow for delivery of the tail of a one-year bill, a synthetic investment of up to nine months can now be created.

Shortening maturity: Treasury bill

Cash market	
Purchase June 9 bill	
@ 7.92 for 5/6/83 settlement	$992,520.00
Repo equivalent yield	7.98%

Futures market alternative	
Purchase September 8 bill	
(@ 8.02 for 5/6/83 settlement)	972,152.78
Sell June bill contract @ 92.06	
(7.94) and deliver bill against	
contract on 6/9/83.	979,929.44
Income for 34-day holding period	7,776.66
Annualized (360-day basis)	82,341.11
Repo equivalent return	8.47%

Pick up over comparable bill = 49 basis points.
Early June CD rate = 8.40 percent.

V. SYNTHETIC SECURITY: EURODOLLAR STRIP

At times, the combined purchase of a cash instrument and a strip of futures contracts can result in a higher return than that on a cash instrument of equivalent maturity. This can occur with any of the money-market contracts. For example, the table below describes the Eurodollar strip assuming that interest is compounded for each period return at the contract rate. In the example below, the effect of variation-margin financing is not separately considered; for a short-term program, it is unlikely to be a material consideration.

Lengthening maturity: Euro strip	
Purchase 2 month Euro on 10/17/83 @ 9.50 percent	
63 days interest earned	$16,625.00
Purchase December Euro contract @ 89.91 (10.09)	
91 days interest	25,505.28
Interest on interest	424.02
Purchase March Euro contract @ 89.60 (10.40)	
91 days interest	26,288.89
Interest on interest	1,118.71
Purchase June Euro contract @ 89.33 (10.67)	
91 days interest	26,971.39
Interest on interest	1,886.97
Total interest earned: 336 days	98,820.26
Return (360-day basis)	10.588%

One-year cash Euro rate 10.0625 percent.

VI. CROSS-HEDGE RATE OF RETURN: PROGRAM OUTPUT

This section contains a series of matrixes designed to create a perspective on the sensitivity of the short-term rate created by a cross hedge. Each matrix holds some variables constant while one is varied to gauge its impact on the cross-hedge return. Thus, reasonable parameters for the relative advantage or disadvantage of the cross hedge can be established.

BOND PRICE AND YIELD INFORMATION

TIME PERIOD OF ANALYSIS FROM 12/01/82 TO 3/01/83
CASH BOND MATURITY DATE: 12/01/12   COUPON: 12.125%.   YTM AT START OF ANALYSIS: 12.170%
THIS IMPLIES CASH PRICE OF: $ 99.64   ACCRUED INTEREST AT START OF ANALYSIS : $ 2020.83
AND ACCRUED INTEREST AT END OF ANALYSIS OF: $ 32333.33
GIVES INTEREST DURING PERIOD OF: $ 30312.50 (0. COUPON(S) + END ACCRUED - BEGINNING ACCRUED

AVERAGE YTM CHANGE OF: -75.00 BASIS POINTS GIVES NEW AVG. YTM OF   11.420%
AND AVERAGE PRICE BASED ON NEW YIELD OF: $ 105.95

CONVERGENCE INFORMATION

CONVERGENCE OF:-12.(32NDS),   AND HEDGE RATIO OF: 1.300
GIVES CONVERGENCE AMOUNT OF: $ -4875.00 OR AN ANNUALIZED: -1.953%

BASIS RISK INFORMATION

END OF PERIOD BASIS RISK OF: 0.0000%
MEANS DOLLAR CHANGE OF: $ 0.00 OR AN ANNUALIZED   0.000%
AVERAGE BASIS RISK OF: 0.0000%

VARIATION MARGIN INFORMATION

AVERAGE OVERNIGHT FINANCING RATE: 8.500%
AVERAGE VARIATION MARGIN BALANCE: $ -65552.58 (BASE CASE)   STARTING BAL: 0.00

MATRIX ANALYSIS INFORMATION

MATRIX INTERVALS OF: 25.00 BASIS PTS. AVG. YTM CHANGE   AND 25.000 FOR FINANCING RATE
MATRIX INTERVALS OF: .2500% FOR AVG. BASIS RISK AND   .2500% FOR END OF PERIOD BASIS RISK
CONVERGENCE INTERVAL OF: 2.(32NDS)

OUTPUT SUMMARY

BASE CASE: 9.633

* ANALYSIS PER $1. MILLION PAR CASH BOND POSITION

EFFECT OF VARIABLES FALLING WITHIN ONE INTERVAL OF BASE CASE, IN VARYING COMBINATIONS

YIELD TO MATURITY	OVERNIGHT FIN. RATE	END OF PERIOD BASIS RISK %	AVERAGE % BASIS RISK	CONVERGENCE OVER PERIOD	ADJUSTED INCOME	ADJUSTED YIELD
11.170	8.250	-.250	-.250	-14.0	17763.50	7.117
11.170	8.250	0.000	0.000	-14.0	22796.65	9.133
11.170	8.250	.250	.250	-14.0	27829.80	11.150
11.170	8.250	-.250	-.250	-12.0	18584.38	7.446
11.170	8.250	0.000	0.000	-12.0	23617.53	9.462
11.170	8.250	.250	.250	-12.0	28650.67	11.479
11.170	8.250	-.250	-.250	-10.0	19405.26	7.775
11.170	8.250	0.000	0.000	-10.0	24438.40	9.791
11.170	8.250	.250	.250	-10.0	29471.55	11.808
11.420	8.500	-.250	-.250	-14.0	13188.67	7.287
11.420	9.500	0.000	0.000	-14.0	23223.38	9.304
11.420	9.500	.250	.250	-14.0	28253.08	11.322
11.420	9.500	-.250	-.250	-12.0	19009.81	7.616
11.420	8.500	0.000	0.000	-12.0	24044.51	9.633
11.420	8.500	.250	.250	-12.0	29079.21	11.651
11.420	8.500	-.250	-.250	-10.0	19830.94	7.945
11.420	8.500	0.000	0.000	-10.0	24865.64	9.962
11.420	9.500	.250	.250	-10.0	29900.35	11.930
11.670	9.750	-.250	-.250	-14.0	18623.58	7.462
11.670	9.750	0.000	0.000	-14.0	23659.84	9.479
11.670	8.750	.250	.250	-14.0	28596.10	11.497
11.670	8.750	-.250	-.250	-12.0	19444.97	7.791
11.670	3.750	0.000	0.000	-12.0	24481.23	9.808
11.670	9.750	.250	.250	-12.0	29517.49	11.825
11.670	8.750	-.250	-.250	-10.0	20266.35	8.120
11.670	8.750	0.000	0.000	-10.0	25302.61	10.138
11.670	8.750	.250	.250	-10.0	30338.87	12.155

* ANALYSIS PER $1. MILLION PAR CASH BOND POSITION

ADJUSTED ANNUALIZED YIELD MATRIX
VARYING YTM AND MARGIN FINANCING RATE

ANALYSIS FROM 12/07/82 TO 3/07/83
CONVERGENCE OF: -12. (32NDS), AND HEDGE RATIO OF: 1.300
AVERAGE BASIS RISK OF: 0.000 END OF PERIOD BASIS RISK OF: 0.000

MARGIN FINANCING RATE

YTM	7.750	8.000	8.250	8.500	8.750	9.000	9.250
10.420	8.935	8.894	8.854	8.813	8.773	8.732	8.692
10.670	9.133	9.099	9.065	9.031	8.997	8.962	8.928
10.920	9.323	9.295	9.267	9.239	9.211	9.183	9.155
11.170	9.507	9.484	9.462	9.440	9.418	9.396	9.374
11.420	9.683	9.666	9.650	9.633	9.617	9.601	9.584
11.670	9.852	9.841	9.830	9.819	9.808	9.797	9.787
11.920	10.015	10.010	10.004	9.998	9.993	9.987	9.931
12.170	10.173	10.172	10.171	10.171	10.170	10.170	10.159
12.420	10.324	10.328	10.333	10.337	10.341	10.346	10.350
12.670	10.470	10.479	10.488	10.497	10.506	10.515	10.524
12.920	10.611	10.625	10.638	10.652	10.655	10.679	10.693
13.170	10.747	10.765	10.783	10.801	10.819	10.837	10.355
13.420	10.879	10.901	10.923	10.945	10.967	10.939	11.012
13.670	11.006	11.032	11.058	11.084	11.111	11.137	11.163
13.920	11.128	11.158	11.189	11.219	11.249	11.279	11.309

ADJUSTED INCOME MATRIX
VARYING YTM AND MARGIN FINANCING RATE

ANALYSIS FROM 12/07/82 TO 3/07/83
CONVERGENCE OF:-12.(32NDS), AND HEDGE RATIO OF: 1.300
AVERAGE BASIS RISK OF: 0.000 END OF PERIOD BASIS RISK OF: 0.000

MARGIN FINANCING RATE

YTM	7.750	8.000	8.250	8.500	8.750	9.000	9.250
10.420	22301.07	22199.90	22098.72	21997.55	21896.37	21795.20	21694.02
10.670	22795.61	22710.38	22625.16	22539.94	22454.72	22369.50	22284.27
10.920	23270.86	23200.96	23131.07	23061.13	22991.29	22921.40	22851.50
11.170	23727.83	23672.68	23617.53	23562.37	23507.23	23452.07	23396.92
11.420	24167.42	24126.45	24085.48	24044.51	24003.54	23962.57	23921.60
11.670	24590.52	24563.19	24535.87	24508.55	24481.23	24453.90	24426.58
11.920	24997.89	24983.71	24969.53	24955.35	24941.16	24926.98	24912.30
12.170	25390.27	25388.75	25387.23	25385.70	25384.18	25382.66	25381.13
12.420	25768.54	25779.21	25789.89	25800.57	25811.25	25821.93	25832.61
12.670	26133.25	26155.70	26178.14	26200.58	26223.03	26245.47	26267.91
12.920	26485.07	26518.86	26552.65	26586.45	26620.23	26654.03	26687.82
13.170	26824.62	26869.37	26914.11	26958.86	27003.61	27048.35	27093.10
13.420	27152.46	27207.78	27263.10	27318.42	27373.75	27429.07	27484.39
13.670	27469.14	27534.67	27600.21	27665.75	27731.28	27796.82	27862.36
13.920	27775.16	27850.57	27925.98	28001.38	28076.80	28152.20	28227.61

* ANALYSIS PER $1. MILLION PAR CASH BOND POSITION

ADJUSTED ANNUALIZED YIELD MATRIX
VARYING AVERAGE AND END OF PERIOD BASIS RISK

ANALYSIS FROM 12/07/82 TO 3/07/83
CONVERGENCE OF:-12.(32NDS), AND HEDGE RATIO OF: 1.300
AVERAGE YIELD TO MATURITY OF: 11.420   AVERAGE OVERNIGHT FINANCING RATE OF: 8.500

END OF PERIOD BASIS RISK (%)

AV B.R. %	-1.000	-.750	-.500	-.250	0.000	.250	.500	.750	1.000
-1.000	1.565	2.563	3.561	4.559	5.557	6.555	7.553	8.551	9.549
-.750	2.584	3.582	4.580	5.578	6.576	7.574	8.572	9.570	10.568
-.500	3.603	4.601	5.599	6.597	7.595	8.593	9.591	10.589	11.587
-.250	4.622	5.620	6.618	7.616	8.614	9.612	10.610	11.608	12.606
0.000	5.642	6.640	7.638	8.635	9.633	10.631	11.629	12.627	13.625
.250	6.661	7.659	8.657	9.655	10.653	11.651	12.649	13.647	14.645
.500	7.630	8.678	9.676	10.674	11.672	12.670	13.668	14.666	15.664
.750	8.699	9.597	10.695	11.593	12.691	13.689	14.687	15.685	16.633
1.000	9.718	10.716	11.714	12.712	13.710	14.708	15.706	16.704	17.702

ADJUSTED INCOME MATRIX
VARYING AVERAGE AND END OF PERIOD BASIS RISK

ANALYSIS FROM 12/ 7/82 TO 3/ 7/83
CONVERGENCE OF:-12.(32NDS), AND HEDGE RATIO OF: 1.300
AVERAGE YIELD TO MATURITY OF: 11.420   AVERAGE OVERNIGHT FINANCING RATE OF: 8.500

END OF PERIOD BASIS RISK (%)

AV B.R. %	-1.000	-.750	-.500	-.250	0.000	.250	.500	.750	1.000
-1.000	3905.70	6396.59	8887.47	11378.36	13869.24	16360.13	18851.01	21341.90	23832.79
-.750	6449.52	8940.40	11431.29	13922.17	16413.06	18903.95	21394.83	23385.72	26376.61
-.500	8993.33	11484.22	13975.11	16465.99	18956.88	21447.76	23938.64	26429.54	28920.42
-.250	11537.15	14028.04	16518.92	19009.80	21500.69	23991.58	26482.46	28973.35	31464.23
0.000	14080.96	16571.85	19062.74	21553.62	24044.51	26535.39	29026.28	31517.16	34008.05
.250	16624.79	19115.67	21606.56	24097.44	26588.33	29079.22	31570.10	34060.98	36551.88
.500	19168.60	21659.48	24150.37	26641.25	29132.14	31623.03	34113.91	36604.80	39095.69
.750	21712.42	24203.30	26694.19	29185.08	31675.96	34166.85	36657.73	39148.62	41639.51
1.000	24256.24	26747.12	29238.01	31728.90	34219.78	36710.67	39201.55	41692.44	44183.33

* ANALYSIS PER $1. MILLION PAR CASH BOND POSITION

ADJUSTED ANNUALIZED YIELD MATRIX
VARYING CONVERGENCE AND MARGIN FINANCING RATE

ANALYSIS FROM 12/07/82 TO 3/07/83
AVERAGE BASIS RISK OF: 0.000   END OF PERIOD BASIS RISK OF: 0.000
AVERAGE YIELD TO MATURITY OF: 11.420%
HEDGE RATIO: 1.300

| | | | | | CONVERGENCE | | | | |
REPO	-20.0	-18.0	-16.0	-14.0	-12.0	-10.0	-8.0	-6.0	-4.0
7.7500	8.368	8.697	9.025	9.354	9.683	10.011	10.340	10.669	10.997
8.0000	8.351	8.680	9.009	9.338	9.666	9.995	10.324	10.653	10.981
8.2500	8.334	8.663	8.992	9.321	9.650	9.979	10.303	10.637	10.965
8.5000	8.318	8.646	8.975	9.304	9.633	9.962	10.291	10.620	10.949
8.7500	8.301	8.630	8.959	9.288	9.617	9.946	10.275	10.604	10.933
9.0000	8.284	8.613	8.942	9.271	9.601	9.930	10.259	10.538	10.917
9.2500	8.267	8.596	8.926	9.255	9.584	9.914	10.243	10.572	10.901

ADJUSTED INCOME MATRIX
VARYING CONVERGENCE AND MARGIN FINANCING RATE

ANALYSIS FROM 12/07/82 TO 3/07/83
AVERAGE BASIS RISK OF: 0.000 END OF PERIOD BASIS RISK OF: 0.000
AVERAGE YIELD TO MATURITY OF: 11.420%
HEDGE RATIO: 1.300

CONVERGENCE

REPO	-20.0	-18.0	-16.0	-14.0	-12.0	-10.0	-8.0	-6.0	-4.0
7.750	20885.93	21706.31	22526.68	23347.05	24167.42	24987.79	25808.16	26628.53	27448.90
9.000	20843.95	21664.57	22485.20	23305.82	24126.45	24947.07	25767.70	26588.32	27403.95
8.250	20801.96	21622.84	22443.72	23264.60	24085.48	24906.36	25727.24	26548.11	27368.99
8.500	20759.98	21581.11	22402.24	23223.38	24044.51	24865.64	25686.77	26507.91	27329.04
8.750	20717.99	21539.38	22360.76	23182.15	24003.54	24824.92	25646.31	26467.70	27289.08
9.000	20676.00	21497.65	22319.29	23140.93	23962.57	24784.21	25605.85	26427.49	27249.13
9.250	20634.02	21455.91	22277.81	23099.70	23921.60	24743.49	25565.39	26387.28	27209.17

* ANALYSIS PER $1. MILLION PAR CASH BOND POSITION

ADJUSTED INCOME MATRIX
VARYING CONVERGENCE AND YIELD TO MATURITY

ANALYSIS FROM 12/07/82 TO 3/07/83
AVERAGE BASIS RISK OF: 0.000 END OF PERIOD BASIS RISK OF: 0.000
AVERAGE OVERNIGHT FINANCING RATE= 8.500%
HEDGE RATIO: 1.300

CONVERGENCE

YTM	-20.0	-18.0	-16.0	-14.0	-12.0	-10.0	-8.0	-6.0	-4.0
10.420	18713.02	19534.15	20355.28	21176.42	21997.55	22818.68	23639.31	24460.95	25282.08
10.670	19255.41	20076.54	20897.67	21718.31	22539.94	23361.07	24182.20	25002.34	25824.47
10.920	19776.65	20597.78	21418.91	22240.05	23061.19	23882.31	24703.45	25524.53	26345.71
11.170	20277.84	21098.98	21920.11	22741.24	23562.37	24383.51	25204.64	26025.77	26346.91
11.420	20759.93	21581.11	22402.24	23223.37	24044.51	24865.64	25686.77	26507.91	27329.04
11.670	21224.02	22045.15	22866.28	23687.41	24508.55	25329.68	26150.81	26971.95	27793.08
11.920	21670.82	22491.95	23313.08	24134.21	24955.35	25776.48	26597.61	27413.74	28239.33
12.170	22101.17	22922.30	23743.44	24564.57	25385.70	26206.84	27027.97	27849.10	28670.23
12.420	22516.04	23337.18	24153.31	24979.44	25800.57	26621.71	27442.84	28263.97	29085.10
12.670	22916.05	23737.19	24558.32	25379.45	26200.58	27021.72	27842.85	28663.98	29485.11
12.920	23301.91	24123.05	24944.18	25765.31	26585.44	27407.58	28228.71	29049.34	29870.97
13.170	23674.33	24495.46	25316.59	26137.73	26953.86	27779.99	28601.13	29422.26	30243.39
13.420	24033.89	24855.02	25676.16	26497.29	27313.42	28139.56	28960.69	29781.82	30602.95
13.670	24381.21	25202.35	26023.48	26844.61	27665.75	28436.88	29308.01	30129.14	30950.28
13.920	24716.85	25537.99	26359.12	27180.25	28001.39	28822.52	29643.65	30464.78	31285.92

* ANALYSIS PER $1. MILLION PAR CASH BOND POSITION

ADJUSTED ANUALIZED YIELD MATRIX
VARYING CONVERGENCE AND YIELD TO MATURITY

ANALYSIS FROM 12/07/82 TO 3/07/83
AVERAGE BASIS RISK OF: 0.000 END OF PERIOD BASIS RISK OF: 0.000
AVERAGE OVERNIGHT FINANCING RATE= 8.500%
HEDGE RATIO: 1.300

CONVERGENCE

YTM	-20.0	-18.0	-16.0	-14.0	-12.0	-10.0	-8.0	-6.0	-4.0
10.420	7.497	7.826	8.155	8.484	8.813	9.142	9.471	9.800	10.129
10.670	7.715	8.044	8.373	8.702	9.031	9.360	9.689	10.018	10.347
10.920	7.924	8.253	8.582	8.910	9.239	9.568	9.897	10.226	10.555
11.170	8.124	8.453	8.782	9.111	9.440	9.769	10.098	10.427	10.756
11.420	8.318	8.646	8.975	9.304	9.633	9.962	10.291	10.620	10.949
11.670	8.503	8.832	9.161	9.490	9.819	10.148	10.477	10.806	11.135
11.920	8.682	9.011	9.340	9.669	9.998	10.327	10.655	10.985	11.314
12.170	8.855	9.184	9.513	9.842	10.171	10.500	10.829	11.158	11.487
12.420	9.021	9.350	9.679	10.008	10.337	10.666	10.995	11.324	11.653
12.670	9.181	9.510	9.839	10.168	10.497	10.826	11.155	11.484	11.813
12.920	9.336	9.665	9.994	10.323	10.652	10.981	11.310	11.639	11.968
13.170	9.485	9.814	10.143	10.472	10.801	11.130	11.459	11.788	12.117
13.420	9.629	9.958	10.287	10.616	10.945	11.274	11.603	11.932	12.261
13.670	9.768	10.097	10.426	10.755	11.084	11.413	11.742	12.071	12.400
13.920	9.903	10.232	10.561	10.890	11.219	11.548	11.877	12.206	12.535

Glossary

Administered rate: an interest rate, such as the prime rate, which is established periodically by a financial intermediary.

After-hours market: the period during which the cash market in bonds continues trading after the futures market is closed.

Anticipatory hedge: the use of contracts to secure a market position on funds to be employed at a later date.

Arbitrage: trading activity, usually a simultaneous purchase and sale, aimed at profiting from price dislocations within a market—or between two markets, such as futures and cash.

Asked price: the price at which securities are offered for sale.

Assignment: the process by which the seller of an option delivers or receives the underlying instrument or contract.

At the money: that point at which the strike price of an option is equal to the market price of the underlying instrument.

Auction market: a market characterized by centralized trading and access by many participants in which transactions are made through open bidding by those participants.

Back (month) contract: a contract that has a comparatively longer time to expiration. Also called a *deferred (month)* or *distant contract.*

Basis: the price difference between a contract and the cash market for a commodity.

Basis point: also referred to as an "01," the value of which is equal to 1/100 of 1 percent.

Basis risk: the possibility that changes in the value of a cash position will differ from changes in the value of an offsetting futures contract position.

Basis trade: also called "cash and carry," the assumption of offsetting positions in a deliverable cash instrument and the related futures contract to benefit from changes in the basis spread.

Bid price: the price one is willing to pay for purchase of securities.

Buy-write: the sale of call options (write) and the simultaneous purchase (buy) of a cash instrument for the purpose of generating a rate of return.

CDR: see Collateralized Depositary Receipt.

Call option: the right to buy the underlying instrument over a specified period at a given price; this right may be exercised by the purchaser of the option.

Cash and carry: see Basis trade.

Cash-equivalent value: the price of a futures contract adjusted by the relevant factor to calculate the current delivery value for the underlying instrument.

Cash market: the market in which an actual physical commodity is traded; also known as a spot market.

Cash settlement: the process by which a dollar adjustment rather than a physical instrument is used to satisfy the delivery requirement of a given contract at expiration.

Cheapest to deliver: the instrument (bonds, notes, GNMAs, or CDs) that can be used to satisfy a given contract at the least cost.

Clearing function: that aspect of an exchange's activities which serves to settle all trades.

Clearinghouse: the division of an exchange or related corporation responsible for its clearing function and for many of its financial guarantees.

Close: the price range of trades recorded at the end of a trading session.

Collateralized Depositary Receipt: a receipt confirming the deposit of appropriate GNMA securities with a depositary bank; delivered in satisfaction of a GNMA-CDR contract.

Commercial: a professional market participant.

Commission house: a brokerage firm that handles trading on behalf of clients.

Commodities exchange: a nonprofit organization set up to facilitate trading in commodity futures and options on such futures.

Commodity Futures Trading Commission (CFTC):   the federal agency responsible for regulation of futures trading.

Contract: in futures, a standardized agreement obligating two parties to a transaction involving a set amount and grade of a commodity at a price and time specified by an exchange.

Convergence: the process by which a futures contract approaches its deliverable value at expiration.

Cost of carry: the return from a cash instrument including the cost, either positive or negative, of financing that cash instrument.

Covered write: the sale of call options against an existing position in the instrument underlying the option.

Cross hedge: the use of a futures contract to protect the principal value of a market item other than one deliverable against the contract.

Day order: an order to buy or sell good only for the day on which it is entered.

Day trader: usually local traders who try to take advantage of intraday price changes.

Dealer market: a decentralized market in which each participant buys and sells for his own account and/or resale.

Deferred (month) contract: see Back (month) contract.

Deliverable instrument: an instrument that meets the requirements of a futures contract and can be tendered in satisfaction of that contract.

Delivery factor: an established numerical value that equilibrates the price of a contract to the value of a deliverable instrument.

Delivery month: the calendar month during which a given contract expires and delivery can be made; also called *expiration month*.

Discount instrument: an instrument, such as a Treasury bill, issued below its par value but redeemed at par at maturity.

Distant contract: see Back (month) contract.

Equilibrium delivery prices: for contracts subject to a delivery factor adjustment, those prices at which a short would be indifferent with regard to which available cash instrument he delivers.

Expiration month: see Delivery month.

Extrinsic value: see Time value.

Factor: see Delivery factor and Paydown factor.

Fill or kill: a limit order specifying cancellation if the order cannot be immediately filled.

Financial futures: in this book, contracts for future delivery based on debt and equity market instruments; in a broader context, financial futures also include contracts for future delivery of foreign currencies.

Floating rate: a rate on a financial product subject to periodic changes generally based on the rate of a market instrument.

Floor broker: the individual responsible for execution of trades on an exchange floor.

Forward contract: a private, nonregulated, and nonstandardized contract for future delivery.

Front (month) contract: a contract closer in time, usually the first traded contract; also referred to as a nearby contract.

Futures contract: see Contract.

Futures equivalent value: the price of a cash deliverable instrument adjusted by the relevant delivery factor.

Futures option: see Option on futures.

Good 'til canceled (GTC): an order which stands until specifically canceled.

Hedge: a position that reduces an existing risk.

Hedge ratio: the number of futures contracts required to offset a change in value of a hedged asset with a change in value of a futures position.

Hedger: a risk reducer; one who seeks to offset or manage an existing risk.

Implied repo rate: the rate of return inherent in a spread position.

Inertia speculation: literally doing nothing; managing risk through lack of action.

In the money: an option with intrinsic value; in the case of a call, the strike price is lower than the market price of the underlying instrument; for a put, the option strike price is higher than the instrument's market price.

Initial margin: see Margin.

Intrinsic value: the difference between the value of an underlying instrument and the strike price of an option.

Limit: the permitted daily maximum or minimum change in a commodity price under exchange rules; up limit refers to a rise in the daily maximum, down limit to a decline to the daily minimum.

Limit order: an order to be executed at a specified price.

Liquidity: the ease with which trading can be undertaken in a market without excessively influencing pricing.

Local: holder of an exchange seat trading primarily for his or her own account.

London Interbank Offered Rate (LIBOR): the Eurodollar time deposit rate used in a manner similar to the prime rate, as the base rate for commercial loans.

Long: the buyer of a contract position.

Margin: funds that must be deposited to maintain a futures account. Initial margin is a good faith deposit to ensure adherence to contract terms; variation margin involves maintenance funds to cover changes in the market value of a contract.

Mark to market: the process by which an item is valued at its current market price; in futures, a mark to market is settled by the transfer of variation margin into or out of commodity accounts.

National Futures Association (NFA): a nonprofit, self-regulating organization established pursuant to the Commodity Exchange Act whose primary function is to ensure that its members conduct business according to just and equitable principals of trade.

Nearby contract: see Front (month) contract.

Offered price: see Asked price.

Offset: an equal and opposite transaction made for purposes of eliminating an existing position or for minimizing the effect of price volatility of an existing position.

Open interest: the number of contracts outstanding.

Option on futures: the right or obligation, as the case may be, to assume a short or long position in a specified futures contract within a specified time period at a specified price.

Out of the money: an option with a strike price above (in the case of a call) or below (in the case of a put) the price of the underlying instrument.

Out trade: a trade recorded by one floor broker but not by the counterpart in the trade; these are settled by the exchanges.

Paydown factor: a value used to calculate the amount of outstanding principal remaining in a GNMA cash pool each month.

Pit: see Trading pit.

Point: 100 basis points, or 1 percent of the par value of a Treasury bond or note.

Position trader: a long-term holder of positions trading to take advantage of large-scale market moves.

Premium: the price of an option; also the amount over par at which a bond trades.

Put option: the right to sell the underlying instrument over a specified period at a given price; the right may be exercised by the purchaser of the option.

Repo rate: the negotiated interest rate to be paid on the cash balance for the term of a repurchase agreement.

Repurchase (Repo) agreement: the transfer of a security in exchange for cash at a given rate, with the income and price risk from the ongoing security remaining with the original owner of the securities.

Reverse repurchase agreement: the transfer of cash at an agreed rate in exchange for securities with the income and price risk remaining with the original owner of the securities.

Rolling: the process by which a futures contract position is moved into another contract month.

Runner: an employee of a member firm responsible for carrying orders and confirmations between a broker's floor booth and the trading pit.

Scale in: the accumulation of a position at various price levels to result in the desired average cost.

Settlement price: the final price determined by an exchange for a contract at the end of a trading session.

Short: the seller of a contract position.

Short squeeze: a situation in which deliverable supply is limited and exerts upward price pressure on the contract market.

Speculator: one who invests for the prospect of gain rather than to offset a risk position.

Spot market: see Cash market.

Spot month: the month in which delivery against a contract can be made.

Spread: the difference in price between two instruments.

Stacking: using a number of futures in one contract month to cover exposure in other periods.

Stop loss order: an order placed to offset a position, thereby limiting losses or protecting gains; it becomes a market order at the stop level.

Stop limit order: an order placed to offset a position, thereby limiting losses or protecting gains; it becomes a limit order at the stop level.

Strike price: the price at which the instrument underlying an option can be bought or sold.

Strip: a position in a series of contract months.

Synthetic instrument: a short-term investment created by a combined cash and futures postion.

Systematic risk: general market risk.

Tail: some portion of a trading instrument — for example, the three-month end of a six-month Treasury bill.

Tick: the minimum amount by which the value of a contract must change to record a new trade.

Time and sale: the exchange record of the time and price for each transaction. This record does not specify quantity.

Time value: the premium value of an option less its intrinsic value.

Trading pit: the area on an exchange floor designated for trading activity in a particualr commodity or future.

Unsystematic risk: price change in an investment instrument not attributable to the general market.

Unwind: closing out a position.

Variation margin: see Margin.

Wasting asset: an asset, such as an option, with value that diminishes over a period of time.

When issued: the market for an issue, such as a Treasury bill, from the time of its announcement until actual issue.

Yield curve: the relationship between the yield on securities with different maturities; an inverted or negative yield curve exists when short-term rates are higher than long-term rates; a normal or positive yield curve exists when short-term rates are lower than long-term rates.

Index*

*In this index everything is understood as being related to *Financial Futures*, even though that term and others germane to it do not *always appear*.

This book has been set in IBM, in 10 and 9 point Century, leaded 2 points. Part number and title are 24 point Caledonia Bold and Chapter number is 24 point Caledonia and Chapter title is 18 point Caledonia Bold. The size of the type page is 27 picas by 47 picas.